Brecht on Theatre

Brecht on Theatre

THE DEVELOPMENT OF AN AESTHETIC

edited and translated by
JOHN WILLETT

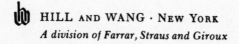

HILL AND WANG · NEW YORK
A division of Farrar, Straus and Giroux

LIBRARY OF CONGRESS CATALOG CARD NUMBER: 63-18479
Printed in the United States of America
First American edition published by Hill and Wang in 1964

Thirty-first printing, 2000

'. . . the inflexible rule that
the proof of the pudding is
in the eating'

Contents

CONTENTS

Illustrations

Cover of first issue of Das Wort, *July, 1936, appears on page 113*

The sources of the photographs that appear in this book are as follows: Ullstein—1, 3, 4, 11, 12, 15, 17, 18, 21, 22, 41; Ruth Berlau—27, 30, 32, 35; Society for Cultural Relations with the USSR—5, 26; Neher executors— 19, 31, 34; Carl Koch—7, 13; United Artists Corporation—14; Foto-Schmidt—6; *Das politische Theater*—8; *Versuche I*—9; The New York Public Library—23; Sovphoto—24; British Film Institute—28; A.C.L. Brussels—29; Hainer Hill—33; Percy Paukschta—38; Kurt Saurin-Sorani—39; Horst E. Schulze—40.

Photographs whose source is unstated come from the Brecht Archive or the Berliner Ensemble. Particular thanks are due to Peter Ihle and to Professor Mordecai Gorelik for the loan of the prints, and to Percy Paukschta and to the Ullstein archivists for various help.

Introduction

This selection from Brecht's notes and theoretical writing is meant to give English-language readers the main texts and set these in chronological order so as to show how his ideas evolved, gradually forming into a quite personal aesthetic which applied to other spheres besides the theatre. Too often the theory is treated as if it were a coherent whole which sprang from Brecht's head ready-made. The endless working and re-working which it underwent, the nagging at a particular notion until it could be fitted in, the progress from an embryo to an often very differently formulated final concept, the amendments and the after-thoughts . . .: all this is something that tends to be overlooked.

The original basis for the selection was the volume *Schriften zum Theater* compiled by Suhrkamp-Verlag, Brecht's Frankfurt publishers, in 1957, the year following his death. This was far from complete, for it omitted everything before 1930 and several other important texts, and it also included items that were not by Brecht himself. We therefore asked the Brecht Estate for copies of all the other theoretical articles listed in Mr Walter Nubel's Brecht bibliography (in *Sinn und Form*, Potsdam, nos. 1-3, 1957), and these, together with the Berliner Ensemble's collective volume *Theaterarbeit* (Dresdner Verlag, Dresden, 1952) and a number of posthumous essays in magazines, have been drawn on for additional material.

A great many unpublished articles, notes and fragments of all periods have also come to light in the Brecht Archive since 1957, and been worked on there, but Brecht's German publishers have the first right to these, and only in one case (the two essays under no. 32) were we allowed to reproduce them. They are now appearing in an entirely re-edited seven-volume *Schriften zum Theater*, which will include even the smallest scraps. In the meantime we have been able to look through most of the relevant files in the Archive and to quote from the unpublished manuscripts in the translator's notes. Besides trying to explain unfamiliar references and supply something of the background, these notes also give a provisional account (no. 37) of the most important of the unfinished theoretical works.

The plan of the book is thus ours, and it has led to one or two other innovations. Mixed collections of notes of different periods (such as *Theaterarbeit* or the notes to *Die Mutter*) have been resolved into their separate elements and the essential items fitted into the chronology; wherever possible, too, earlier texts have been detached from later revisions. There are necessarily some cuts, designed to eliminate or at least to reduce repetitions and irrelevancies, and keep the book to a manageable length. The poems on the theatre have had to go, partly because there are many more of them than appeared in *Schriften zum Theater*, partly so as not to overlap with any new selection of Brecht's poems in English versions; some of them have already been published as *Poems on the Theatre* in a translation by John Berger and Anna Bostock. Wherever cuts have been made the reader will find a note detailing them, and the original text used is always specified. (Items 1, 3–7 and 9–11, it may be noted, are not taken directly from the originals but from transcripts.)

The translation tries to convey the flavour of Brecht's style as it too evolved, from the aggressiveness of the first essays to the slightly forced formality of some of his late pronouncements. The main German editions drawn on or referred to are:

Versuche. Fifteen volumes of Brecht's writings published by Kiepenheuer, Berlin, from 1930–32, and by Suhrkamp, Frankfurt, and Aufbau, East Berlin, from 1949 on.

Gesammelte Werke. Two volumes of collected plays, published by Malik Verlag, London, 1938.

Stücke. Collected plays in twelve volumes, published by Suhrkamp and by Aufbau from 1953 on.

Gedichte. Collected poems, appearing from the same publishers and in similar format.

Schriften zum Theater. Selection of theoretical writings, published by Suhrkamp, 1957.

Schriften zum Theater 1, 2, etc. Seven volumes of theoretical writings, to be published by Suhrkamp and by Aufbau in 1963 and 1964.

Other references are given in full in the notes, the bibliography at the end of the book being restricted to a list of other English-language translations of individual theoretical texts.

Besides these the notes will be found to refer to *Hecht* (Werner Hecht: *Brechts Weg zum epischen Theater*, Henschel Verlag, East Berlin, 1962), *Esslin* (Martin Esslin: *Brecht: A Choice of Evils*, Eyre and Spottiswoode, London, 1959), and *Mittenzwei* (Werner Mittenzwei: *Bertolt Brecht. Von der 'Massnahme' zum 'Leben des Galilei'*, Aufbau Verlag, East Berlin, 1962). The first of these is a study by the editor of the revised *Schriften zum*

Theater of Brecht's theoretical writings up to 1933; some of it appeared in a shortened preliminary version in *The Tulane Drama Review* for September 1961. The only other book to have been devoted purely to the theory has been Helge Hultberg's *Die ästhetischen Anschauungen Bertolt Brechts* Munksgaard, Copenhagen, 1962. This too has been read with profit. Other references are given in full where they occur.

We would like to thank the Brecht Archive and Mr Stefan Brecht for their kind help, and Helene Weigel and Dr Unseld (of Suhrkamp Verlag) for the latitude which they have allowed us. We are also much indebted to Herr Hecht, Frau Elisabeth Hauptmann, Mr Nubel, Professor Bentley, Professor Gorelik, Herr Piscator and Dr Reinhold Grimm for providing material or settling queries directly and by correspondence.

September 1963

Brecht on Theatre

Part 1

1918-1932

(Augsburg, Munich, Berlin)

1 · Frank Wedekind

Last Saturday night we sang his songs to the guitar as we swarmed down the Lech under the star-dusted sky: the song to Franziska, the one about the blind boy, a dance song. Then very late on, as we sat on the weir with our feet almost in the river, the one about fortune's caprices and their exceeding strangeness, which suggests that the best answer is to turn a somersault every day. On Sunday morning we were horrified to read that Frank Wedekind had died the day before.

It is hard to believe it. His vitality was his finest characteristic. He had only to enter a lecture-room full of hundreds of noisy students, or a room, or a stage, with his special walk, his sharp-cut bronze skull slightly tilted and thrust forward, and there was silence. He was not a particularly good actor (he even kept forgetting the limp which he himself had prescribed, and couldn't remember his lines), but as Marquis von Keith he put the professionals in the shade. He filled every corner with his personality. There he stood, ugly, brutal, dangerous, with close-cropped red hair, his hands in his trouser pockets, and one felt that the devil himself couldn't shift him. He came before the curtain as ringmaster in a red tail coat, carrying whip and revolver, and no one could forget that hard dry metallic voice, that brazen faun's head with 'eyes like a gloomy owl' set in immobile features. A few weeks ago at the Bonbonnière he sang his songs to guitar accompaniment in a brittle voice, slightly monotonous and quite untrained. No singer ever gave me such a shock, such a thrill. It was the man's intense aliveness, the energy which allowed him to defy sniggering ridicule and proclaim his brazen hymn to humanity, that also gave him this personal magic. He seemed indestructible.

In the autumn, when a small group of us heard him give a reading of *Herakles*, his last work, I was amazed at his brazen energy. For two and a half hours without a break, without once dropping his voice (and what a strong brazen voice it was!), without taking a moment's breather between acts, bent motionless over the table, partly by heart, he read those verses wrought in brass, looking deep into the eyes of each of us in turn as we listened to him.

The last time I saw and heard him was six weeks ago at the farewell party given by the members of Kutscher's seminar. He seemed in the best of health, spoke animatedly and at our request, well after midnight, sang three of his finest songs to the lute. Without actually seeing him buried I cannot conceive that he is dead. Like Tolstoy and Strindberg he was one of the great educators of modern Europe. His greatest work was his own personality.

[From *Augsburger Neueste Nachrichten*, 12 March 1918]

NOTE: Wedekind died on the afternoon of 9 March. The Lech is the river at Augsburg, where Brecht lived with his parents. Then aged just twenty, he was reading medicine and philosophy at Munich University, where he sometimes attended the theatre seminar conducted by Professor Artur Kutscher (1878–1960), Wedekind's friend and biographer. His first play, *Baal*, was written the same year. It includes a number of songs to the guitar which, like Wedekind, he set to tunes of his own devising and was in the habit of singing himself.

Franziska and *Der Marquis von Keith* are two of Wedekind's best-known plays. The songs referred to in the opening sentence must be 'Der blinde Knabe' and 'Franziskas Abendlied'.

2 · A Reckoning

The chief difficulty for anyone wanting to make an assault on our municipal theatre, which he cannot help doing if he has spent an entire season having to go there and write about it, and has taken his job seriously at least for as long as he has been writing – his chief difficulty is that there can be no question of revealing a mystery. He cannot just point a stumpy finger at the theatre's ongoings and say, 'You may have thought this amounted to something, but let me tell you, it's a sheer scandal; what you see before you proves your absolute bankruptcy; it's your own stupidity, your mental laziness and your degeneracy that are being publicly exposed.' No, the poor man can't say that, for it's no surprise to you; you've known it all along; nothing can be done about it. It is true enough that it's bad, but that it's as bad as all that . . . that's exaggeration, sensationalism, self-importance. Liberalism is your justification; live and let live is the motto, in other words (judged morally, e.g.) go to bits and let go to bits; shut your trap and maintain the peace, H.M. Bavarian peace of blessed memory. But supposing somebody tells the more intelligent spectators: You really must try to improve your theatre, it just won't do – they calmly answer: Ach, it's good enough for Augsburg. And all the time they are treating themselves as exceptions. But let me tell you, dear readers: there is nothing to stop one from filling a theatre with the exceptions. For they'll be followed by all those who'd like to be exceptions. Of course the theatre's director can always shrug his shoulders sadly and say: But nobody comes to the plays. It's always half empty. You can't expect me to spend money under those conditions. And it never seems to strike anyone that it may be a half empty house because he doesn't spend money. If the theatre here were better, if it got the same publicity as the opera, if the same trouble were taken to build up its tradition, if a nucleus of playgoers could be formed – possibly by subscription – then more people would go to the plays and more money would come in. But as things are a whole heap of money, relatively speaking, is splashed on the opera; expensive guest singers are hired in order to draw in the snobs; the latest fashionable works are put on, and the theatre is denied the slightest new acquisition. On top of that the actors are all raw youngsters and the leading actor a mediocrity who is not bad as Valentin but unbearable as Faust. Now and then the young people may show all sorts of talent, but they will be just spoilt if everything has to depend on them. An actor of undoubted ability gets given a notoriously difficult part like Don Carlos; there are not enough rehearsals and he is continually in demand; as a result he is forced to give a more or less stereotyped performance. A promising actress, flung too soon into major plays, gets given the part of Elizabeth or Magdelena, and has to take refuge in superficialities in order to make up for lack of experience; all it can teach her is the art of getting out of a jam. These people are being over-exploited. The producer is a rarity, competent and hard-working. Filled with literary ambition, he laboriously works up the performances of beginners and old hacks alike till they reach a more or less bearable level, in front of impossible settings, extremely and obviously penurious, for the benefit of rows of utterly ill-mannered stalls. He himself is an intelligent actor of some consequence, but hardly a draw, whether for the general public or for the exceptions.

After a whole season of honest toil in this theatre, which was not without talents and ideals, it is worth considering whether the old system of inviting small guest companies was not better. You may think that is going too far, but there is something in it; maybe that's why we haven't much use for the theatre. But then only the opera succeeds in Augsburg; even a good theatre would have empty houses. Against that it can be said: all right, perhaps the public does go for the bigger noise (though a lot of noise could also be made for the theatre and in the theatre). But it's not just a matter of people's preference for music, rather for lavishness – as well as sheer habit. There are other cities where the public is hardly more intelligent than here, yet the opera attracts no more custom than the theatre. And with the money used to create such a very average opera as Augsburg's one could create a really good theatre – for the exceptions. That's why I think the Augsburgers ought sooner or later to break with their favourite habit of having a bad theatre.

['Eine Abrechnung.' From 'Augsburger Theater-kritiken' in *Sinn und Form*, Zweites Sonderheft Bertolt Brecht, Potsdam, 1957]

NOTE: Between October 1919 and January 1921 Brecht wrote some two dozen theatre criticisms for the USPD (left-wing Socialist) paper *Die Augsburger Volkswille*, of which this, originally published on 14 May 1920, is perhaps the most far-reaching. The producer mentioned was Friedrich Merz. Since 1903 the theatre had been directed by Carl Häusler (see Hecht, pp. 11–12). Three years after Brecht's attack it turned over entirely to opera, relying on visiting Munich companies to perform plays.

Brecht left the university in the summer of 1921 and settled in Munich, where three of his first four plays had their premières. He published nothing more about the theatre until after he had moved to Berlin in 1924 and established himself as a freelance writer.

3 · Emphasis on Sport

We pin our hopes to the sporting public.

Make no bones about it, we have our eye on those huge concrete pans, filled with 15,000 men and women of every variety of class and physiognomy, the fairest and shrewdest audience in the world. There you will find 15,000 persons paying high prices, and working things out on the basis of a sensible weighing of supply and demand. You cannot expect to get fair conduct on a sinking ship. The demoralization of our theatre audiences springs from the fact that neither theatre nor audience has any idea what is supposed to go on there. When people in sporting establishments buy their tickets they know exactly what is going to take place; and that is exactly what does take place once they are in their seats: viz. highly trained persons developing their peculiar powers in the way most suited to them, with the greatest sense of responsibility yet in such a way as to make one feel that they are doing it primarily for their own fun. *Against that the traditional theatre is nowadays quite lacking in character*.

There seems to be nothing to stop the theatre having its own form of 'sport'. If only someone could take those buildings designed for theatrical purposes which are now standing eating their heads off in interest, and treat them as more or less empty spaces for the successful pursuit of 'sport', then they would be used in a way that might mean something to a contemporary public that earns real contemporary money and eats real contemporary beef.

It may be objected that there is also a section of the public that wants to see something other than 'sport' in the theatre. But we have never seen a single piece of evidence to prove that the public at present filling the theatres *wants* anything at all. The public's well-padded resistance to any attempt to make it give up those two old stalls which it inherited from grandpa should not be misinterpreted as a brand-new assertion of its will.

People are always telling us that we mustn't simply produce what the public demands. But I believe that an artist, even if he sits in strictest seclusion in the traditional garret working for future generations, is unlikely to produce anything without some wind in his sails. And this wind has to be the wind prevailing in his own period, and not some future wind. There is nothing to say that this wind must be used for travel in any particular direction (once one has a wind one can naturally sail against it; the only impossibility is to sail with no wind at all or with tomorrow's wind), and no doubt an artist will fall far short of achieving his maximum effectiveness today if he sails with today's wind. It would be quite wrong to judge a play's relevance or lack of relevance by its current effectiveness. Theatres don't work that way.

A theatre which makes no contact with the public is a nonsense. Our theatre is accordingly a nonsense. The reason why the theatre has at present no contact with the public is that it has no idea what is wanted of it. It can no longer do what it once could, and if it could do it it would no longer wish to. But it stubbornly goes on doing what it no longer can do and what is no longer wanted. All those establishments with their excellent heating systems, their pretty lighting, their appetite for large sums of money, their imposing exteriors, together with the entire business that goes on inside them: all this doesn't contain five pennyworth of *fun*. There is no theatre today that could invite one or two of those persons who are alleged to find fun in writing plays to one of its performances and expect them to feel an urge to write a play for it. They can see at a glance that there is no possible way of getting any *fun* out of this. No wind will go into anyone's sails here. There is no 'sport'.

Take the actors, for instance. I wouldn't like to say that we are worse off for talent than other periods seem to have been, but I doubt if there has ever been such an overworked, misused, panic-driven, artificially whipped-up band of actors as ours. *And nobody who fails to get fun out of his activities can expect them to be fun for anybody else.*

The people at the top naturally blame the people at the bottom, and the favourite scapegoat is the harmless garret. The people's wrath is directed

7

against the garret; the plays are no good. To that it must be said that so long as they have been fun to write they are bound to be better than the theatre that puts them on and the public that goes to see them. A play is simply un-recognizable once it has passed through this sausage-machine. If we come along and say that both we and the public had imagined things differently – that we are in favour, for instance, of elegance, lightness, dryness, objectivity – then the theatre replies innocently: Those passions which you have singled out, my dear sir, do not beat beneath any dinner-jacket's manly chest. As if even a play like *Vatermord* could not be performed in a simple, elegant and, as it were, classically rounded way!

Behind a feigned intensity you are offered a naked struggle in lieu of real competence. They no longer know how to stage anything remarkable, and therefore worth seeing. In his obscure anxiety not to let the audience get away the actor is immediately so steamed up that he makes it seem the most natural thing in the world to insult one's father. At the same time it can be seen that acting takes a tremendous lot out of him. *And a man who strains himself on the stage is bound, if he is any good, to strain all the people sitting in the stalls.*

I cannot agree with those who complain of no longer being in a position to prevent the imminent decline of the west. I believe that there is such a wealth of subjects worth seeing, characters worth admiring and lessons worth learning that once a good sporting spirit sets in one would have to build theatres if they did not already exist. The most hopeful element, however, in the present-day theatre is the people who pour out of both ends of the building after the performance. They are dissatisfied.

['Mehr guten Sport.' From *Berliner Börsen-Courier*, 6 February 1926]

NOTE: This article appeared eight days before the Berlin production of Brecht's first play *Baal*, which he staged himself in collaboration with Oscar Homolka. His friend Arnolt Bronnen's *Vatermord*, referred to in the article, had been the object of his first attempt at production in 1922, but was taken over by another producer because of the actors' resistance to Brecht's conception of the play.

About the same time, Brecht was insisting on the need for what he called a 'smokers' theatre', where the audience would puff away at its cigars as if watching a boxing match, and would develop a more detached and critical outlook than was possible in the ordinary German theatre, where smoking was not allowed. 'I even think,' says a fragment (*Schriften zum Theater 1*, p. 165),

that in a Shakespearean production one man in the stalls with a cigar could bring about the downfall of Western art. He might as well light a bomb as light his cigar. I would be delighted to see our public allowed to smoke during performances. And I'd be delighted mainly for the actors' sake. In my view it is quite impossible for the actor to play unnatural, cramped and old-fashioned theatre to a man smoking in the stalls.

A notebook entry of 10 February 1922 (*Schriften zum Theater 2*, p. 31) gives a much earlier statement of the same idea:

> I hope in *Baal* and *Dickicht* I've avoided one common artistic bloomer, that of trying to carry people away. Instinctively, I've kept my distance and ensured that the realization of my (poetical and philosophical) effects remains within bounds. The spectator's 'splendid isolation' is left intact; it is not *sua res quae agitur*; he is not fobbed off with an invitation to feel sympathetically, to fuse with the hero and seem significant and indestructible as he watches himself in two simultaneous versions. A higher type of interest can be got from making comparisons, from whatever is different, amazing, impossible to take in as a whole.

Such opinions must be set against the pretentious German classical stage of that time. A brief essay, evidently dating from Brecht's first years in Berlin, and entitled 'Less Plaster' ('Weniger Gips!!!' *Schriften zum Theater 1*, p. 84ff.), begins thus:

> We Germans are uncommonly good at putting up with boredom and are thoroughly hardened to the unfunny. Naturally a specific instinct for mediocrity suits the German theatre very well. A theatre is a business that sells evening entertainment. But nobody here is really satisfied with that. All kinds of things rank higher than entertainment. So far as our theatre goes, the unpretentious entertainment supplied by it is thoroughly decent and adequate; the middle grade is most in demand; but what we take really seriously is entertainment in monumental form. Today in any town of more than 50,000 inhabitants you can buy plenty of monumentalities for five marks.

The idea of 'fun' (Spass) occurs again and again in Brecht's writings. 'If Brecht gets no fun out of what he has created,' wrote Elisabeth Hauptmann, his secretary and lifelong collaborator, in her diary a day after 'Emphasis on Sport' appeared in print, 'he immediately goes and changes it. . . . He says that Shakespeare was undoubtedly the best member of his own audience, and wrote things primarily that he and his friends got fun out of.'

The theatre section of the *Berliner Börsen-Courier* was then under the direction of Herbert Ihering, who had been responsible for awarding the Kleist Prize to Brecht's *Trommeln in der Nacht* in 1922. Many of these early essays, answers to questionnaires, etc. appeared there, and an apparently unpublished note (Brecht-Archive 331/104) shows that Brecht already saw some danger of their being interpreted as a kind of gospel:

> Bertolt Brecht has written a small series of essays for the *Berliner Börsen-Courier* which give a rough picture of his views about the present-day theatre. These remarks . . . are not intended to supply an aesthetic; they are meant rather to give a portrait of this generation and show its attitude to the stage. We will keep space for answers.

4 · Three Cheers for Shaw

I · SHAW AS TERRORIST

Shaw's experience and doctrine is that if one is to express oneself freely on any subject one has first of all to overcome a certain inborn fear: of being conceited.

Very early on he secured himself against the possibility of anybody at any time of his life burning incense to him (and he did so without fear of becoming famous. It was clear to him that any decent man's working equipment had to include that vital piece of apparatus, his own trumpet. He proudly refused to bury his pound sterling.)

Shaw has applied a great part of his talent to intimidating people to a point when it would be an impertinence for them to prostrate themselves before him.

It will have been observed that Shaw is a terrorist. Shaw's brand of terror is an extraordinary one, and he uses an extraordinary weapon, that of humour. This extraordinary man seems to be of the opinion that nothing in the world need be feared so much as the ordinary man's calm and incorruptible eye, but that this must be feared without question. This theory is for him the source of a great natural superiority, and by applying it systematically he has ensured that nobody who comes across him, in print, on the stage or in the flesh, can conceive for a moment of his undertaking an action or speaking a sentence without being afraid of that incorruptible eye. Indeed even the younger generation, whose qualifications lie largely in their aggressiveness, limit their aggressions to a strict minimum when they realize that any attack on one of Shaw's habits, even his habit of wearing peculiar underwear, is likely to end in the disastrous downfall of their own ill-considered garb. If at the same time it is realized that it is he who broke with the unthinking custom of speaking in a whisper, instead of loudly and cheerfully, in anything resembling a place of worship, and that it is he who proved that the right attitude to any really important phenomenon is a casual (contemptuous) one, because it is the only one which permits complete concentration and real alertness; then it will be understood how high a degree of personal freedom he has achieved.

Shaw's terrorism consists in this: that he claims a right for every man to act in all circumstances with decency, logic and humour, and sees it as his duty to do so even when it creates opposition. He knows just how much courage is needed to laugh at what is amusing, and how much seriousness to pick it out. And like all people who have a definite purpose he knows that there is nothing more time-wasting and distracting than a particular kind of seriousness which is popular in literature but nowhere else. (As a playwright he takes just as naïve a view of writing for the theatre as young writers do, and he shows not the least trace of wishing to behave as if he ignored the fact; he makes free use of such naïvety. He gives the theatre as much fun as it can stand. Strictly speaking what makes people go to the theatre is nothing but stuff that acts as a vast incubus to the quite real business which really interests the advanced dramatist and constitutes the true value of his plays. The logic of this is that his problems must be such good ones that he can bury them beneath the most wanton transgressions, and it is the transgressions that people will then want to have.)

2 · SHAW DEFENDED AGAINST HIS OWN GLUM FOREBODINGS

I seem to remember a short while ago that Shaw himself formulated his views about the future of the drama. He said that in future people would no longer go to the theatre in order to understand something. What he probably meant was that, odd as it may seem, the mere reproduction of reality does not give an impression of truth. If so the younger generation will not contradict him; but I must point out that the reason why Shaw's own dramatic works dwarf those of his contemporaries is that they so unhesitatingly appealed to the reason. His world is one that arises from opinions. The opinions of his characters constitute their fates. Shaw creates a play by inventing a series of complications which give his characters a chance to develop their opinions as fully as possible and to oppose them to our own. (Such complications cannot be too hoary and too well known for Shaw; he has no pretentions about this. A perfectly ordinary usurer is worth his weight in gold to him; a patriotic girl comes into the story; and all he cares is that the girl's story should be as familiar and the usurer's sticky end as natural and desirable as possible, so that he may strip us all the more thoroughly of our old-fashioned opinions about such characters and, even more, about *their* opinions.)

Probably every single feature of all Shaw's characters can be attributed to his delight in dislocating our stock associations. He knows that we have a horrible way of taking all the characteristics of a particular type and lumping them under a single head. We picture a usurer as cowardly, furtive and brutal. Not for a moment do we think of allowing him to be in any way courageous. Or wistful, or tender-hearted. Shaw does.

As for the hero, Shaw's less gifted successors have developed his refreshing view that heroes are not models of good conduct and that heroism consists of an impenetrable but exceedingly lively hotchpotch of the most contradictory qualities; they have arrived at the lamentable conclusion that there is no such thing as either heroism or heroes. Probably in Shaw's view this is unimportant. He seems to find less point in living among heroes than among ordinary men.

Shaw's approach to composing his works is completely above-board. He has no hesitation in writing under the incessant supervision of the public. To give extra weight to his judgments he helps to make that supervision easier; he keeps emphasizing his own peculiarities, his individual taste, and even his (minor) weaknesses. For this he must be thanked. Even when his opinions go very much against those of today's younger generation they will listen to him with pleasure; he is (and what more could be said of anybody?) a good man. Moreover his is a time that seems to preserve opinions better than it does moods and feelings. Of all that has been laid down in the present period it looks as if opinions will last the longest.

3 · A CATCHING INFECTION: FUN

It is significantly hard to find out anything about what other European writers think. But I take it that where literature, for instance, is concerned they all share more or less the same view, namely that writing is a melancholy business. As usual Shaw, whose views about anything under the sun are far from unknown, differs from his colleagues here. (It is not his fault, but at most an embarrassment to him, a thorn in his side, if his vast difference of opinion with all other European writers, covering almost every subject in the world, is not thrown into sufficiently clear relief because the others refrain from voicing their views even when they have any.) At any rate Shaw would at least agree with me on this point: that he *likes* writing. There is no room for a martyr's halo even outside his head. His literary activities have in no sense cut him off from life. On the contrary. I am not sure if it is the right way to measure his gifts, but I can only say that the effect of this inimitable cheerfulness and infectious good mood is quite exceptional. Shaw truly is able to give the impression that his mental and physical well-being increases with every sentence that he writes. Reading his works may not induce bacchic intoxication, but there is no doubt that it is extraordinarily healthy. And his only enemies (if they need be mentioned at all) would need to be the kind of people who don't care all that much about health.

As for Shaw's own ideas, I cannot at the moment recollect a single one that could be called typical of him, though I know of course that he has a lot; but I could name a great deal that he has found to be typical of other people. He himself may well think that his way of viewing things is necessarily more important than his actual views. That says much for a man of his sort.

I get the impression that a lot revolves for him round a particular theory of evolution which in his view differs widely and decisively from another evolutionary theory of a clearly inferior brand. At any rate his faith in mankind's infinite capacity for improvement plays an overriding part in his works. It will be understood as equivalent to giving three heartfelt cheers for Shaw if I simply admit that, although I am familiar with neither of these two theories, I blindly and unconditionally plump for Shaw's. For it seems to me that so keen-witted and fearlessly eloquent a man is wholly to be trusted. Just as it always and in all circumstances seems to me that the force of a statement is more important than its applicability, and a man of stature than the trend of his activities.

['Ovation für Shaw.' From *Berliner Börsen-Courier*, 25 July 1926]

NOTE: Shaw's *Saint Joan*, with Elisabeth Bergner and Rudolf Forster, was produced by Max Reinhardt at the Deutsches Theater, Berlin, on 14 October 1924, a fortnight before Erich Engel's production of Brecht's *Dickicht* in the same theatre. Brecht was then on the theatre's staff, and attended Reinhardt's rehearsals. According to Miss Bergner Shaw never himself saw the production, nor is it likely that Brecht ever met him.

Elisabeth Hauptmann says that the present essay was a tribute for Shaw's seventieth birthday written for the *Neue Freie Presse* of Vienna. Brecht was staying near Vienna at the time.

There are also some other essays of his on English writers dating from the 1920s: 'Glossen zu Stevenson' (*Berliner Börsen-Courier*, 19 May 1925, where he seems to imagine that Stevenson was an American), a review of *The Way of All Flesh* in *Das Tagebuch* (Berlin), 21 December 1929, and an unfinished essay on Maugham, 'Resignation eines Dramatikers' (*Schriften zum Theater 3*, pp. 136–142).

The 'younger writers' and 'younger generation' referred to in the present essay probably included such friends of that time as Arnolt Bronnen, Alfred Döblin, Jakob Geis, and Melchior Vischer, not to mention Engel himself.

5 · Conversation with Bert Brecht

Q. Am I wrong in regarding you as both a poet and a playwright?

A. My poetry is more private. It's designed for banjo or piano accompaniment, and needs to be performed dramatically. In my plays I don't just give my own private mood, but also the whole world's. In other words, an objective view of the business, the opposite of mood in the usual poetic sense.

Q. This isn't always clear from performances of your plays.

A. How could it be? They are usually performed all wrong. People perform the poet they imagine me to be – something that I hardly am outside my plays, and certainly not in them.

Q. So you reject the idea that the author participates poetically in the characters and events he portrays, and whatever may consequently come to be expressed in the play?

A. I don't let my feelings intrude in my dramatic work. It'd give a false view of the world. I aim at an extremely classical, cold, highly intellectual style of performance. I'm not writing for the scum who want to have the cockles of their hearts warmed.

Q. Who do you write for?

A. For the sort of people who just come for fun and don't hesitate to keep their hats on in the theatre.

Q. But most spectators want their hearts to flow over. . . .

A. The one tribute we can pay the audience is to treat it as thoroughly intelligent. It is utterly wrong to treat people as simpletons when they are grown up at seventeen. I appeal to the reason.

Q. But the intellectual mastery of the material is just what I sometimes feel to be lacking with you. You don't make the incidents clear.

A. I give the incidents baldly so that the audience can think for itself. That's why I need a quick-witted audience that knows how to observe, and gets its enjoyment from setting its reason to work.

Q. So you don't want to make things easy for the audience?

A. The audience has got to be a good enough psychologist to make its own sense of the material I put before it. All I can guarantee is the absolute correctness and authenticity of what happens in my plays; I'm prepared to bank on my knowledge of human beings. But I leave the maximum freedom of interpretation. The sense of my plays is immanent. You have to fish it out for yourself.

Q. There can't be any objection to an actor making the material immediately intelligible, though, as against your way of doing things?

A. There are writers who simply set down what happened. I'm one of them. My material *is* intelligible; I don't first have to make it so. There are other writers who not only put down what happened but give a theoretical explanation as a separate element. And then there is a third way of going about things, which aims at the mutual fusion of live material and conceptual analysis. To my mind only the first approach suits the dramatic form.

Q. Certainly. But sometimes it can confuse the audience. They lose the thread of the material.

A. If so then it's the fault of the modern theatre, which takes anything that would repay analysis and plays it for its mystic meaning.

Q. Do you mean that it's not only the author but the producer too who has to make the dramatic sequence of events intelligible?

A. For the period of the performance, yes. Proper plays can only be understood when performed. But we've got to get away from the prevailing muzziness – even from *monumental* muzziness. The height of muzziness is bad posters. I'm for the epic theatre! The production has got to bring out the material incidents in a perfectly sober and matter-of-fact way. Nowadays the play's meaning is usually blurred by the fact that the actor plays to the audience's hearts. The figures portrayed are foisted on the audience and are falsified in the process. Contrary to present custom they ought to be presented quite coldly, classically and objectively. For they are not matter for empathy; they are there to be understood. Feelings are private and limited. Against that the reason is fairly comprehensive and to be relied on.

Q. That's uncompromising intellectualism. It's a great thing, to my mind, not to have given in to the anti-intellectual fashions of recent years.

A. Maybe. At any rate I am not so discouragingly chaotic as people think. I may confine my plays to the raw material, but I show only what is typical. I select; that is where discipline comes in. Even when a character behaves by contradictions that's only because nobody can be identically the same at two unidentical moments. Changes in his exterior continually lead to an inner reshuffling. The continuity of the ego is a myth. A man is an atom that perpetually breaks up and forms anew. We have to show things as they are.

Q. But what this amounts to is an intellectual confirmation of the confused state of the real world, and you have reached it. . . .

A. . . . by using my head. And the confusion itself only exists because our head is an imperfect instrument. What's beyond it we call the irrational.

Q. I can't go, you know, till I've asked you what you're working on at the moment.

A. I've got two things on. The first is a biography of Samson-Körner.

Q. Why that?

A. Samson-Körner is a splendid type and a significant one. I wanted to get him down on paper for myself. The best way was to make him tell me his life story. I've a high regard for reality. Not that there are many realities like Samson-Körner; they are windfalls. The first thing that struck me about Samson was that the sporting principle underlying his boxing seemed un-German. He boxed in a matter-of-fact way. There's great plastic charm in that. It's quite impossible for instance to imitate Samson-Körner putting a bus ticket in his pocket. That's why he's also a considerable cinema actor.

Q. How do you go to work?

A. It's more a pleasure than work. I ask him to talk to me, and I've a high regard for his views. People's opinions interest me far more than their feelings. Feelings are usually the product of opinions. They follow on. But opinions are decisive. Only experience sometimes ranks higher. Though we all know that not every opinion stems from experience.

Q. That's pure intellectualism again!

A. Every act comes from a realization. There's really no such thing as acting on impulse. There again the intellect is lurking in the background.

Q. And what else are you working at?

A. A comedy called *Mann ist Mann*. It's about a man being taken to pieces and rebuilt as someone else for a particular purpose.

Q. And who does the re-building?

A. Three engineers of the feelings.

Q. Is the experiment a success?

A. Yes, and they are all of them much relieved.

Q. Does it produce the perfect human being?

A. Not specially.

[From *Die Literarische Welt*, Berlin, 30 July 1926]

NOTE: This interview is not in Brecht's own words, and Bernard Guillemin, the interviewer, prefaced it with a note saying that he had 'deliberately translated into normal language all that Brecht told me in his own manner, in Brecht-style slang'. Nonetheless it is important as containing the first expression of his doctrine of the 'epic theatre', here as later identified with the reason (*Verstand*) and opposed to *Einfühlung* or empathy, the process by which the audience is made to identify itself with the character on the stage and actually to feel his emotions.

At the same time Brecht was working on a further play, the unfinished *Joe P. Fleischhacker aus Chicago*, whose very complicated subject, the workings of the American wheat market, was another factor impelling him towards a new dramatic form. Four days before Guillemin's interview appeared Mrs Hauptmann had noted in her diary:

> Brecht said: 'Such matters aren't dramatic in our sense; and if one writes them up then they aren't true any longer, and the drama ceases to be anything of the sort; and as soon as one sees that the modern world is no longer reconcilable with the drama then the drama can no longer be reconciled with the world.' In the course of these researches Brecht developed his theory of the 'epic drama'.

The phrase itself was of course not a new one, and already on 23 March of that year Mrs Hauptmann had noted that 'Brecht has found the formula for the "epic theatre": playing from memory (quoting gestures and attitudes); and is aiming entirely in this direction in his writing'. There were in fact three threads that went to make up Brecht's own epic theory, and all three – the playing in quotation marks, the portrayal of new and complex processes and the detached, unemotional style – can be traced repeatedly in what follows.

Here, at the outset, just before Brecht began seriously to study Marxism, the epic theatre is very close to the movement known as *Neue Sachlichkeit*; 'sachlich' being the word which has above been translated twice as 'matter of fact.' This was the sober, functional aesthetic associated with the Bauhaus, with painters like Grosz, Schlichter and Beckmann, with Hindemith's early music, with reportage and documentary and (in typography) with the abolition of upper-case letters. Coining the term in 1924, G. F. Hartlaub had applied it to 'the new realism bearing a socialist flavour', and the definition was certainly just. In a fragmentary essay on the subject, however, reconstituted in *Schriften zum Theater 1*, p. 129ff., and written perhaps as late as 1928, Brecht concluded that

> of course i'm not in favour of that ghastly flabby lack of matter-of-factness that alone keeps the present-day bourgeois theatre on its legs i find these people's lack of matter-of-factness ludicrous but about your 'new matter-of-factness' i'm bitter i suppose it's bound to come it's already there in painting it'll have to come in the theatre . . . *sachlichkeit* will come and it'll be a good thing when it does* till then nothing more can be done but this quite necessary and inevitable step forward will be a reactionary affair that's what i'm getting at *neue sachlichkeit* is reactionary. . . .

The footnote reads '*i hope so by lenin'.

Mann ist Mann was first performed about two months after the interview. Brecht made no notes on it until he gave the radio talk which follows. Samson-Körner was the German middleweight champion; Brecht's biography of him, to be called *Die menschliche Kampfmaschine* ('The Human Fighting-Machine'), was never finished. Its beginning is quoted in Hans Mayer's *Brecht und die Tradition*, Neske, Pfullingen 1961, p. 33.

6 · A Radio Speech

Look: our plays embrace part of the new things that came into the world long before the world war. This means at the same time that they no longer embrace a large part of the old things to which we are accustomed. Why don't they now embrace these old things which *were* once recognized and proper? I think I can tell you exactly. They no longer embrace these old things because the people to whom these things were important are today on the decline. But whenever a broad stratum of humanity is declining its vital utterances get weaker and weaker, its imagination becomes crippled, its appetites dwindle, its entire history has nothing more of note to offer, not even to itself. What a declining stratum like this does can no longer lead to any conclusions about men's doings. In the case of the arts this means that such people can no longer create or absorb art of any sort.

This stratum of humanity had its great period. It created monuments that have remained, but even these remaining monuments can no longer arouse enthusiasm. The great buildings of the city of New York and the great discoveries of electricity are not of themselves enough to swell mankind's sense of triumph. What matters most is that a *new human type* should now be evolving, at this very moment, and that the entire interest of the world should be concentrated on his development. The guns that are to hand and the guns that are still being manufactured are turned for him or against him. The houses that exist and are being built are built to oppress him or to shelter him. All live works created or applied in our time set out to discourage him or to put courage in him. And any work that has nothing to do with him is not alive and has nothing to do with anything. This new human type will not be as the old type imagines. It is my belief that he will not let himself be changed by machines but will himself change the machine; and whatever he looks like he will above all look human.

I would now like to turn briefly to the comedy *Mann ist Mann* and explain why this introduction about the new human type was necessary. Of course not all these problems are going to arise and be elucidated in this particular play. They will be elucidated somewhere quite different. But it struck me that all sorts of things in *Mann ist Mann* will probably seem odd to you at first – especially what the central figure, the packer Galy Gay, does or does not do – and if so it's better that you shouldn't think you are listening to an old acquaintance talking about you or himself, but to a new sort of type, possibly an ancestor of just that new human type I spoke of. It may be interesting for you to look straight at him from this point of view, so as to bring out his attitude to things as precisely as possible. You will see that among other things he is a great liar and an incorrigible optimist; he can fit in with anything, almost without difficulty. He seems to be used to putting up with a great deal. It is in fact very seldom that he can allow himself an opinion of his own. For instance when (as you will hear) he is offered an utterly spurious elephant which he can resell, he will take care not to voice any opinion of it once he hears a possible purchaser is there. I imagine also that you are used to treating a man as a weakling if he can't say no, but this Galy Gay is by no means a weakling; on the contrary he is the strongest of all. That is to say he becomes the strongest once he has ceased to be a private person; he only becomes strong in the mass. And if the play finishes up with him conquering an entire fortress this is only because in doing so he is apparently carrying out the unqualified wish of a great mass of people who want to get through the narrow pass that the fortress guards. No doubt you will go on to say that it's a pity that a man should be tricked like this and simply forced to surrender his precious ego, all he possesses (as it were); but it isn't. It's a jolly business. For this Galy Gay comes to no harm; he wins. And a man who adopts such an attitude is bound to win. But possibly you will come to quite a different conclusion. To which I am the last person to object.

['Vorrede zu *Mann ist Mann.*' From *Die Szene*, Berlin, April 1927]

NOTE: This talk on Berlin radio introduced a broadcast of *Mann ist Mann* on 27 March 1927. It was reprinted in shortened and adapted form as a contribution to the opening programme of Erwin Piscator's 1927–8 season at the Theater am Nollendorfplatz, where Brecht figured as one of Piscator's collaborators. It seems to mark the first stage in Brecht's social view of the arts, and of that idea of the comparative unimportance of individual identity which underlay much of his work up till 1933, together with his collective method of working.

The word translated as 'seem odd to' is 'befremden', a cousin of the term 'verfremden' that occurs so often later and will be translated as 'alienate'. There are early symptoms of this key concept in Brecht's emphasis on what was 're-markable, and therefore worth seeing' as against 'the most natural thing in the world' (p. 8) and in his praise of Shaw for 'dislocating our stock associations' (p. 11). It emerges even more strongly in a fragment 'On the Theatre We Have in Mind' (*Schriften zum Theater 1*, pp. 168–9):

It's hard for anybody young to realize why older people go to the theatre. Personally I think it's because they've nothing else to do. (Riding a motor-bike is too difficult, and anyway it tends to be only the young who can afford it.) . . .

It's a young man's agreeable business to acquire sins (and an old man's grisly preoccupation to cling to his habits). Sin is what is new, strong, surprising, strange. The theatre must take an interest in sin if the young are to be able to go there. . . . Yes, what appealed most to us in any episode was its strangeness and incomprehensibility. Our real element was the element of chaos challenging our simple minds to sort it out.

Another fragment 'On the Purpose of the Theatre' consists just of two sentences: It strikes me that those plays of this period that are of any use spring from their authors' astonishment at the things that happen in life. Our wish to put them straight, to create precedents and found a tradition of overcoming difficulties, gives rise to the plays of a period that will be filled by the rush of humanity to the big cities.

In 1927 he prefaced the published version of his third play, *Im Dickicht der Städte*, with a note: 'You are about to observe an incomprehensible wrestling match between two humans. . . . Do not worry unduly as to the motives of this struggle, but take part in the human effort, judge the competitors' form dispassionately and concentrate your attention on the finish.' Already there seems to have been a dynamic element in this pursuit of strangeness. It implied the need for change.

7 · Shouldn't we Abolish Aesthetics?

Dear Mr X,

When I invited you to look at the drama from a sociological point of view I did so because I was hoping that sociology would be the death of our existing drama. As you immediately saw, there was a simple and radical task for sociology: to prove that there was no justification for this drama's continued existence and no future for anything based (now or in the future) on the assumptions which once made drama possible. To quote a sociologist whose vocabulary I hope we both accept, there is no sociological space for it. Yours is the only branch of knowledge that enjoys sufficient freedom of thought; all the rest are too closely involved in perpetuating our period's general level of civilization.

You were immune to the usual superstition which holds that a play has undertaken to satisfy *eternal* human urges when the only eternal urge that it sets out to satisfy is the urge to see a play. You know other urges change, and you know why. As you don't feel that the disappearance of an urge means the collapse of humanity, you, the sociologist, are alone in being prepared to admit that Shakespeare's great plays, the basis of our drama, are no longer effective. These works were followed by three centuries in which the individual developed into a capitalist, and what killed them was not capitalism's consequences but capitalism itself. There is little point in mentioning post-Shakespearean drama, as it is invariably much feebler, and in Germany has been debauched by Latin influences. It continues to be supported just out of local patriotism.

Once we adopt the sociological point of view we realize that so far as literature is concerned we are in a bog. We may possibly be able to persuade the aesthete to admit what the sociologist believes – namely that present-day drama is no good – but we shall never deprive him of his conviction that it can be improved. (The aesthete won't hesitate to admit that he can only conceive of such an 'improvement' of the drama by using the hoary old tricks of the trade: 'better' construction in the old sense, 'better' motivation for those spectators who are used to the good old motivation, and so on.) Apparently the sociologist will only support us if we say that this kind of drama is beyond repair and beg for it to be done away with. The sociologist knows that there are circumstances where improvement no longer does any good. His scale of judgment runs not from 'good' to 'bad' but from 'correct' to 'false'. If a play is 'false' then he won't praise it on the grounds that it is 'good' (or 'beautiful'); and he alone will remain deaf to the aesthetic appeal of a 'false' production. Only he knows what is false; he does not deal in relativity; he bases himself on vital interests; he gets no fun from being able to prove everything but just wants to find out the one thing worth proving; he doesn't by any means take responsibility for everything, but only for one thing. The sociologist is the man for us.

The aesthetic point of view is ill-suited to the plays being written at present, even where it leads to favourable judgments. You can see this by looking at any move in favour of the new playwrights. Even where the critics' instincts guided them right their aesthetic vocabulary gave them very few convincing arguments for their favourable attitude, and no proper means of informing the public. What is more, the theatre, while encouraging the production of new plays, gave absolutely no practical guide. Thus in the end the new plays only served the old theatre and helped to postpone the collapse on which their own future depended. It is impossible to understand what is being written today if one ignores the present generation's active hostility towards all that preceded it, and shares the general belief that it too is merely clamouring to be let in and taken notice of. This generation doesn't want to capture the theatre, audience and all, and perform good or merely contemporary plays in the same theatre and to the same audience; nor has it any chance of doing so; it has a duty and a chance to capture the theatre for a *different* audience. The works now being written are coming more and more to lead towards that great epic theatre which corresponds to the sociological situation; neither their content nor their form can be understood except by the minority that understands this. They are not going to satisfy the old aesthetics; they are going to destroy it.

With you in this hope,

Brecht

['Sollten wir nicht die Aesthetik liquidieren?' From *Berliner Börsen-Courier*, 2 June 1927]

NOTE: Mr X was the late Professor Fritz Sternberg (d. 1963) who had published a letter in the same paper on 12 May; he was also the sociologist referred to in the first paragraph. The two men were concerned with Piscator in a plan to produce *Julius Caesar* the following winter. (See *Schriften zum Theater 1*, p. 153, and Brecht's radio discussion with Sternberg and Ihering, *ibid.* p. 117ff.) Sternberg's letter and subsequent answer are appended to his *Der Dichter und die Ratio* (Sachse und Pohl, Göttingen 1963), which gives a short account of their relations. The answer comments that 'It wasn't Marx who led you to speak of the decline of the drama and to talk of the epic theatre. It was you yourself. For, to put it gently, "epic theatre" – that's you, Mr Brecht.'

Brecht himself seems first to have used the phrase in print in an article in *Der neue Weg* (Berlin) of 16 May, where he referred to 'the creation of a great epic and documentary theatre which will be suited to our period'. In July an unsigned programme note to the first version of *Mahagonny*, written presumably by Brecht, called it 'a small epic play which draws the logical conclusions from our existing class structure's inevitable collapse', adding that Kurt Weill, its composer, had 'begun to turn to an audience which goes to the theatre naïvely and for fun'.

8 · The Epic Theatre and its Difficulties

Any theatre that makes a serious attempt to stage one of the new plays risks being radically transformed. What the audience sees in fact is a battle between theatre and play, an almost academic operation where, in so far as it takes any interest in the process of renovating the theatre, all it has to do is observe whether the theatre emerges as victor or vanquished from this murderous clash. (Roughly speaking, the theatre can only emerge victorious over the play if it manages to avoid the risk of the play's transforming it completely – as at present it nearly always succeeds in doing.) It is not the play's effect on the audience but its effect on the theatre that is decisive at this moment.

This situation will continue until our theatres have worked out the style of production that our plays need and encourage. It won't be an adequate answer if theatres invent some kind of special style for them, in the same way as the so-called Munich Shakespearean stage was invented, which could only be used for Shakespeare. It has to be a style that can lend new force to a whole section of the theatrical repertoire which is still capable of life today.

It is understood that the *radical transformation of the theatre* can't be the result of some artistic whim. It has simply to correspond to the whole radical transformation of the mentality of our time. The symptoms of this transformation are familiar enough, and so far they have been seen as symptoms of disease. There is some justification for this, for of course what one sees first of all are the signs of decline in whatever is *old*. But it would be wrong to see these phenomena, so-called *Amerikanismus* for instance, as anything but unhealthy changes stimulated by the operation of really new mental influences on our culture's aged body. And it would be wrong too to treat these new ideas as if they were not ideas and not *mental* phenomena at all, and to try to build up the theatre against them as a kind of bastion of the mind. On the contrary it is precisely theatre, art and literature which have to form the 'ideological superstructure' for a solid, practical rearrangement of our age's way of life.

In its works the new school of play-writing lays down that the *epic theatre* is the theatrical style of our time. To expound the principles of the epic theatre in a few catch-phrases is not possible. They still mostly need to be worked out in detail, and include representation by the actor, stage technique, dramaturgy, stage music, use of the film, and so on. The essential point of the epic theatre is perhaps that it appeals less to the feelings than to the spectator's reason. Instead of sharing an experience the spectator must come to grips with things. At the same time it would be quite wrong to try and deny emotion to this kind of theatre. It would be much the same thing as trying to deny emotion to modern science.

['Schwierigkeiten des epischen Theaters.' From *Frankfurter Zeitung* (Literaturblatt), 27 November 1927]

NOTE: 'Ideological superstructure' is the Marxist phrase for the whole body of art, ideas, morality, etc., of any given society, which Marx saw as resting on certain basic economic relationships. Brecht had begun reading *Das Kapital* about a year before, according to Elisabeth Hauptmann. A note of his printed in *Schriften zum Theater 1* (p. 181) says:

When I read Marx's *Capital* I understood my plays. Naturally I want to see this book widely circulated. It wasn't of course that I found I had unconsciously written a whole pile of Marxist plays; but this man Marx was the only spectator for my plays I'd ever come across. For a man with interests like his must of necessity be interested in my plays, not because they are so intelligent but because he is – they are something for him to think about. This happened because I was as hard up for opinions as for money, and had the same attitude to both: that they are there not to be hoarded but to be spent.

In 1928 he listed a biography of Marx as one of the three best books of the year (*Das Tagebuch*, Berlin, 8 December). He put *Ulysses* top, however, apparently on Alfred Döblin's recommendation. The same year (24 July) a programme note for the Heidelberg production of *Im Dickicht der Städte* said that 'This is a world and a kind of drama where the philosopher can find his way about better than the psychologist.' (*Schriften zum Theater* 2, p. 67.)

9 · Last Stage: Oedipus

1. At present it's Germany, the home of philosophy, that is leading in the large-scale development of the theatre and the drama. The theatre's future is philosophical.
2. This development does not run straight. Sometimes it runs dialectically, by opposites, sometimes parallel; either way it is so swift that it goes through several stages in a single year. The last of these seems to be *Oedipus*.
3. The present season shows the strength of Piscator's influence. Seen from the theatre, it looks as if Piscator has stimulated discussion less about formal questions (theatrical technique) than about the problem of subject matter. And he has had an influence. Middle-grade theatres have turned to new subjects (*Verbrecher, Revolte, Ton in Töpfers Hand*). There were two exceptions: *The Threepenny Opera* and *Oedipus*. Both tackled the question of form.
4. As far as concern with subject matter goes, it was not brilliant. With Piscator absent from the scene, there was no productive force behind it (apart from *Revolte*, a posthumous studio production of his). The year's gains were made in the direction of mastering major forms. Last stage: *Oedipus*.
5. Concern with subject and concern with form are complementary. Seen from inside the theatre it appears that progress in theatrical technique is only progress when it helps to realize the material; and the same with progress in play writing.
6. As for major forms: the great modern subjects must be seen in the

light of mime, they must have the character of gestures. They must be arranged according to the mutual relationships of men or groups of men. But the traditional major form, dramatic form, isn't suitable for present-day subjects. To put it bluntly, for those in the business, present-day subjects cannot be expressed in the old 'major' form.

7. Major form is designed to realize material for 'eternity'. The typical element also applies on the time-scale. Whoever uses a major form is narrating his material to the future quite as well as to his own time, if not better.

8. Our dramatic form is based on the spectator's ability to be carried along, identify himself, feel empathy and understand. To put it bluntly, for those in the business: a play that is set, say, in a wheat exchange isn't suited to major, dramatic form. While it's hard for us to imagine a time and adopt an attitude in which such a situation does not seem natural, our *successors* will observe such an unnatural and incomprehensible situation with amazement. So what ought our major form to be like?

9. Epic. It must report. It must not believe that one can identify oneself with our world by empathy, nor must it want this. The subject-matter is immense; our choice of dramatic means must take account of the fact.

10. About the last stage: *Oedipus*. N.B.: 1. The major form. 2. The technique of the second half (Oedipus on Colchis) when a story is told, and very effectively. Here words that used to be shouted are theatrically effective. Here the 'experience', if it comes from anywhere, comes from the philosophical realm.

['Letzte Etappe: Oedipus.' From *Berliner Börsen-Courier*, 1 February 1929]

NOTE: This referred to an arrangement by Heinz Lipmann of *Oedipus Rex* and *Oedipus at Kolonnos*, played in one evening at the Berlin Staatstheater. Leopold Jessner produced; Georg Antheil wrote the music; Hans Poelzig designed the scenery. The actors included Fritz Kortner (Oedipus), Alexander Granach (Shepherd), Veit Harlan (Polyneikes), Lotte Lenya (Ismene), and Helene Weigel (Maid or Second Messenger). The first night was on 4 January 1929. Brecht and Helene Weigel were married the previous year.

In the meantime Brecht's and Weill's *Threepenny Opera* was running with great success at the Theater am Schiffbauerdamm, where it had opened in August.

Verbrecher is by Ferdinand Bruckner, *Revolte im Erziehungshaus* by P. M. Lampel, *Ton in Töpfers Hand* by Theodore Dreiser. Piscator had been 'absent from the scene' since his company at the Theater am Nollendorfplatz shut its doors in the summer. A number of early fragments of Brecht's are concerned with his productions there or (previously) at the Volksbühne, and it is clear that Brecht had a high regard for his work and learnt a great deal from it. Thus a note headed 'The Piscator Experiment' (and calling, incidentally, for 'a naïve theatre') speaks of Piscator as doing for production what *Baal* had first done for epic playwriting. (*Schriften zum Theater 1*, p. 188. Werner Hecht assigns this to 1926.) Another, 'The new theatre and the new drama' (*ibid.* p. 194), is rather more guarded:

> If we ignore a certain tendency on this producer's part to misuse his technical resources for cheap symbolism, the new drama is here offered the makings of a theatre that at least raises no positive obstacles in its way.

10 · A Dialogue about Acting

The actors always score great successes in your plays. Are you yourself satisfied with them?

No.

Because they act badly?

No. Because they act wrong.

How ought they to act then?

For an audience of the scientific age.

What does that mean?

Demonstrating their knowledge.

Knowledge of what?

Of human relations, of human behaviour, of human capacities.

All right; that's what they need to know. But how are they to demonstrate it?

Consciously, suggestively, descriptively.

How do they do it at present?

By means of hypnosis. They go into a trance and take the audience with them.

Give an example.

Suppose they have to act a leave-taking. They put themselves in a leave-taking mood. They want to induce a leave-taking mood in the audience. If the seance is successful it ends up with nobody seeing anything further, nobody learning any lessons, at best everyone recollecting. In short, everybody feels.

That sounds almost like some erotic process. What ought it to be like, then?

Witty. Ceremonious. Ritual. Spectator and actor ought not to approach one another but to move apart. Each ought to move away from himself. Otherwise the element of terror necessary to all recognition is lacking.

Just now you used the expression 'scientific'. You mean that when one observes an amoeba it does nothing to offer itself to the human observer. He can't get inside its skin by empathy. Yet the scientific observer does try to understand it. Do you think that in the end he succeeds?

I don't know. He tries to bring it into some relationship with the other things that he has seen.

Oughtn't the actor then to try to make the man he is representing understandable?

Not so much the man as what takes place. What I mean is: if I choose to see Richard III I don't want to feel myself to be Richard III, but to glimpse this phenomenon in all its strangeness and incomprehensibility.

Are we to see science in the theatre then?

No. Theatre.

I see: scientific man is to have his theatre like everybody else.

Yes. Only the theatre has already got scientific man for its audience, even if it doesn't do anything to acknowledge the fact. For this audience hangs its brains up in the cloakroom along with its coat.

Can't you tell the actor then how he ought to perform?

No. At present he is entirely dependent on the audience, blindly subject to it.

Haven't you ever tried?

Indeed. Again and again.

Could he do it?

Sometimes, yes; if he was gifted and still naive, and still found it fun; but then only at rehearsals and only so long as I was present and nobody else, in other words so long as he had in front of him the type of audience I was telling you about. The nearer he got to the first night, the further away he drifted; he became different as one watched, for he probably felt that the other spectators whose arrival was imminent might not like him so much.

Do you think they really wouldn't like him?

I fear so. At any rate it would be a great risk.

Couldn't it happen gradually?

No. If it happened gradually it wouldn't seem to the audience that something new was being gradually developed but that something old was gradually dying out. And the audience would gradually stay away. For if the new element were introduced gradually it would only be half introduced and as a result it would lack force and effectiveness. For this isn't a matter of qualitative improvement but of adaptation to an entirely different purpose; that is to say, the theatre would not now be fulfilling the same purpose better, but would be fulfilling a new purpose, quite possibly very badly at

27

first. What would be the effect of such an attempt to smuggle something in? The actor would simply strike people as 'jarring'. But it wouldn't be his way of acting that would jar them, but he himself. He would grate on them. And yet a jarring element is one of the hallmarks of this new way of acting. Or else the actor would be accused of being too self-conscious; self-consciousness being another hallmark of the same sort.

Have attempts of this kind been made?

Yes, one or two.

Give an example.

When an actress of this new sort was playing the servant in *Oedipus* she announced the death of her mistress by calling out her 'dead, dead' in a wholly unemotional and penetrating voice, her 'Jocasta has died' without any sorrow but so firmly and definitely that the bare fact of her mistress's death carried more weight at that precise moment than could have been generated by any grief of her own. She did not abandon her voice to horror, but perhaps her face, for she used white make-up to show the impact which a death makes on all who are present at it. Her announcement that the suicide had collapsed as if before a beater was made up less of pity for this collapse than of pride in the beater's achievement, so that it became plain to even the most emotionally punch-drunk spectator that here a decision had been carried out which called for his acquiescence. With astonishment she described in a single clear sentence the dying woman's ranting and apparent irrationality, and there was no mistaking the tone of her 'and how she ended, we do not know' with which, as a meagre but inflexible tribute, she refused to give any further information about this death. But as she descended the few steps she took such paces that this slight figure seemed to be covering an immense distance from the scene of the tragedy to the people on the lower stage. And as she held up her arms in conventional lamentation she was begging at the same time for pity for herself who had seen the disaster, and with her loud 'now you may weep' she seemed to deny the justice of any previous and less well-founded regrets.

What sort of reception did she have?

Moderate, except for a few connoisseurs. Plunged in self-identification with the protagonist's feelings, virtually the whole audience failed to take part in the moral decisions of which the plot is made up. That immense decision which she had communicated had almost no effect on those who regarded it as an opportunity for new sensations.

['Dialog über Schauspielkunst.' From *Berliner Börsen-Courier*, 17 February 1929]

NOTE: The actress here described was Helene Weigel. Virtually the same account will be found in Brecht's tribute 'Über eine grosse Schauspielerin unserer Nation' printed in the album *Die Schauspielerin Helene Weigel*, Berlin, 1959. The references are to lines 1234 ff of *Oedipus Rex*, and if they do not correspond (e.g. the analogy of the 'beater') it is no doubt due to the German adaptation.

The dialogue includes Brecht's first reference to an 'audience of the scientific age', though a note 'Der Mann am Regiepult' in *Das Theater*, Berlin, 1928, No. 1 had spoken of the producer's duty 'to raise the theatre to the level of science, and present its repertoire to an audience that in *better* surroundings is used to seeing all attempts to involve it in illusions rejected'. It should perhaps be pointed out that 'Wissenschaft' in German is a broader term than the English 'science' and that Brecht certainly regarded it as embracing the Marxist view of history as well as the natural sciences.

11 · On Form and Subject-Matter

1. Difficulties are not mastered by keeping silent about them. Practice demands that one step should follow another; theory has to embrace the entire sequence. The new subject-matter constitutes the first stage; the sequence however goes further. The difficulty is that it is hard to work on the first stage (new subjects) when one is already thinking about the second (humanity's new mutual relationships). Establishing the function of helium is not much use in helping one to establish a vast picture of the world; yet there is no hope of establishing it if one has anything other than (or more than) helium in one's mind. The proper way to explore humanity's new mutual relationships is via the exploration of the new subject-matter. (Marriage, disease, money, war, etc.)

2. The first thing therefore is to comprehend the new subject-matter; the second to shape the new relations. The reason: art follows reality. An example: the extraction and refinement of petroleum spirit represents a new complex of subjects, and when one studies these carefully one becomes struck by quite new forms of human relationship. A particular mode of behaviour can be observed both in the individual and in the mass, and it is clearly peculiar to the petroleum complex. But it wasn't the new mode of behaviour that created this particular way of refining petrol. The petroleum complex came first, and the new relationships are secondary. The new relationships represent mankind's answers to questions of 'subject-matter'; these are the solutions. The subject-matter (the situation, as it were) develops according to definite rules, plain necessi-

ties, but petroleum creates new relationships. Once again, these are secondary.

3. Simply to comprehend the new areas of subject-matter imposes a new dramatic and theatrical form. Can we speak of money in the form of iambics? 'The Mark, first quoted yesterday at 50 dollars, now beyond 100, soon may rise, etc.' – how about that? Petroleum resists the five-act form; today's catastrophes do not progress in a straight line but in cyclical crises; the 'heroes' change with the different phases, are interchangeable, etc.; the graph of people's actions is complicated by abortive actions; fate is no longer a single coherent power; rather there are fields of force which can be seen radiating in opposite directions; the power groups themselves comprise movements not only against one another but within themselves, etc., etc. Even to dramatize a simple newspaper report one needs something much more than the dramatic technique of a Hebbel or an Ibsen. This is no boast but a sad statement of fact. It is impossible to explain a present-day character by features or a present-day action by motives that would have been adequate in our fathers' time. We allowed ourselves (provisionally) not to inspect motives at all (for instance: *Im Dickicht der Städte*, *Ostpolzug*) in order at least not to impute false ones, and showed actions as pure phenomena by assuming that we would have to show characters for some time without any features at all, this again provisionally.

4. All this, i.e. all these problems, only bears on serious attempts to write *major* plays: something that is at present very far from being properly distinguished from common or garden entertainment.

5. Once we have begun to find our way about the subject-matter we can move on to the relationships, which at present are immensely complicated and can only be simplified by *formal* means. The form in question can however only be achieved by a complete change of the theatre's purpose. Only a new purpose can lead to a new art. The new purpose is called paedagogics.

['Über Stoffe und Formen.' From *Berliner Börsen-Courier*, 31 March 1929]

NOTE: The references to petroleum here probably relate to Leo Lania's play about oil interests, *Konjunktur*, which Brecht helped to adapt for Piscator's company in the spring of 1928, and to Lion Feuchtwanger's very Brecht-like play *Die Petroleuminseln* (produced at the Staatstheater on 28 November of the same year, with Lotte Lenya in the cast). Brecht's own attempts to embrace new areas of subject-matter continued with *St Joan of the Stockyards* and the fragment *Der Brotladen*, on both of which he was working about this time.

Ostpolzug by Arnolt Bronnen was produced by Jessner at the Staatstheater on 29 January 1926, with Fritz Kortner in the one and only part (Alexander the Great in modern dress). Brecht also refers to it in a fragmentary note (Brecht Archive 156/25) about Georg Kaiser, his senior by twenty years, which praises Kaiser for his intellectualism, then goes on to say:

> the first works of the younger playwrights – *Vatermord*, *Trommeln in der Nacht* – signified a reaction. Before that of course there had been a Battle of the Marne. The younger playwrights saw no chance of consolidating the positions that had been so dashingly and (alas) unthinkingly won. They tagged along. Then with *Mann ist Mann* and *Ostpolzug* there was a general counter-offensive – of two men – with a fresh weapon and a different objective.

The call for a change in the theatre's purpose was echoed in the same number of the *Berliner Börsen-Courier* by Emil Burri, one of Brecht's collaborators. In July the first two of Brecht's *Lehrstücke*, or purely didactic works, were performed at the Baden-Baden music festival: *Der Flug der Lindberghs* (for radio) and *Badener Lehrstück*.

12 · An Example of Paedagogics
(Notes to *Der Flug der Lindberghs*)

Der Flug der Lindberghs is valueless unless learned from. It has no value as

Der Flug der Lindberghs for instruction, not for pleasure

art which would justify any performance not intended for learning. It is an *object of instruction* and falls into two parts. The first part (songs of the elements, choruses, sounds of water and motors, etc.) is meant to help the exercise, i.e. introduce it and interrupt it – which is best done by an apparatus. The other, *paedagogical* part (the Flier's part) is the text for the exercise: the participant listens to the one part and speaks the other. In this way a collaboration develops between participant and apparatus, in which expression is more important than accuracy. The text is to be spoken and sung mechanically; a break must be made at the end of each line of verse; the part listened to is to be mechanically followed.

'In obedience to the principle that the State shall be rich and man shall be poor, that the State shall be obliged to have many possibilities and man shall be allowed to have few possibilities, where music is concerned the State shall furnish whatever needs special apparatus and special abilities; the individual, however, shall furnish an exercise. Free-roaming feelings aroused by music, special thoughts such as may be entertained when listening to music, physical exhaustion such as easily arises just from listening to music, are all distractions from music. To avoid these distractions the individual shares in the music, thus obeying the principle that doing is better than feeling, by following the music with his eyes as printed, and contributing the parts and places reserved for him by singing them for himself or in conjunction with others (school class).'

Der Flug der Lindberghs is not intended to be of use to the present-day *The radio not* radio but to alter it. The increasing concentration of *to be served but* mechanical means and the increasingly specialized training *to be changed* – tendencies that should be accelerated – call for a kind of resistance by the listener, and for his mobilization and redrafting as a producer.

The employment of *Der Flug der Lindberghs* and the use of radio in its *The Baden-Baden* changed form was shown by a demonstration at the Baden-*radio experiment* Baden music festival of 1929. On the left of the platform the radio orchestra was placed with its apparatus and singers, on the right the listener, who performed the Flier's part, i.e. the paedagogical part, with a score in front of him. He read the sections to be spoken without identifying his own feelings with those contained in the text, pausing at the end of each line; in other words, in the spirit of an *exercise*. At the back of the platform stood the theory being demonstrated in this way.

This exercise is an aid to discipline, which is the basis of freedom. The *Why can't Der* individual will reach spontaneously for a means to pleasure, Flug der Lind- but not for an object of instruction that offers him neither *berghs be used as* profit nor social advantages. Such exercises only serve the *an object of in-* individual in so far as they serve the State, and they only *struction and the* serve a State that wishes to serve all men equally. Thus *Der* *radio be changed?* Flug der Lindberghs* has no aesthetic and no revolutionary value independently of its application, and only the State can organize this. Its proper application, however, makes it so 'revolutionary' that the present-day State has no interest in sponsoring such exercises.

Here is an example of the effect of this application on the text: the figure of a public hero in *Der Flug der Lindberghs* might be used to induce the listener at a *concert* to identify himself with the hero and thus cut himself off from the masses. In a concert performance (consequently a false one) at least the Flier's part must be sung by a *chorus* if the sense of the entire work is not to be ruined. Only *concerted I – singing* (I am so-and-so, I am starting forth, I am not tired, etc.) can save something of the paedagogical effect.

[From *Versuche 1*, Berlin 1930. Signed 'Brecht, Suhrkamp'.]

NOTE: The music to *Der Flug der Lindberghs* was by Kurt Weill and Paul Hindemith. Brecht subsequently changed its title to *Der Ozeanflug*, as which it now figures in the reprint of the *Versuche*. Peter Suhrkamp, his collaborator on the notes, became his West German publisher after 1948.

The principle underlying the *Lehrstück* form – which began as a kind of didactic cantata, with solos, choruses and scraps of acting – was the notion that moral and political lessons could best be taught by participation in an actual performance. 'When performing a Lehrstück,' says a note (*Schriften zum Theater 2*, p. 128),

> you must act like pupils. The pupil will use a particularly clear manner of speaking in order to run over a difficult passage again and again so as to get at its meaning or fix it in the memory. His gestures too are clear and help towards clarification. Then there are other passages which have to be quickly and fleetingly delivered as if they were frequently practised ritual actions. These are the passages which correspond to sections of a speech conveying particular items of information needed for the understanding of the more important item that follows. Such passages are wholly useful to the overall process and must be delivered as performances. Then there are parts that demand acting ability of very much the old kind. E.g. when a typical way of behaving has to be shown. For there is a certain practical human way of behaving which may bring about situations that demand or facilitate new ways. To show the typical gestures and manners of speech of a man trying to convince somebody, one has to apply the art of acting.

The next few essays were published and almost certainly written subsequently to the switchover to 'paedagogics', even though the plays to which they relate were written earlier. They should be read in the light of the political and economic crisis which developed in Germany during the second half of 1929, making revolutionary change seem not only desirable but imminent. This was the period of Brecht's most sharply Communist works.

13 · The Modern Theatre is the Epic Theatre

(Notes to the opera *Aufstieg und Fall der Stadt Mahagonny*)

OPERA – WITH INNOVATIONS!

For some time past there has been a move to renovate the opera. Opera is to have its form modernized and its content brought up to date, but without its culinary character being changed. Since it is precisely for its backwardness that the opera-going public adores opera, an influx of new types of listener with new appetites has to be reckoned with; and so it is. The intention is to democratize but not to alter democracy's character, which consists in giving the people new rights, but no chance to appreciate them. Ultimately it is all the same to the waiter whom he serves, so long as he serves the food. Thus the *avant-garde* are demanding or supporting innovations which are supposedly going to lead to a renovation of opera; but nobody demands a fundamental discussion of opera (i.e. of its function), and probably such a discussion would not find much support.

The modesty of the *avant-garde*'s demands has economic grounds of whose existence they themselves are only partly aware. Great apparati like the opera, the stage, the press, etc., impose their views as it were incognito. For a long time now they have taken the handiwork (music, writing, criticism, etc.) of intellectuals who share in their profits – that is, of men who are economically committed to the prevailing system but are socially near-proletarian – and processed it to make fodder for their public entertainment machine, judging it by their own standards and guiding it into their own channels; meanwhile the intellectuals themselves have gone on supposing that the whole business is concerned only with the presentation of their work, is a secondary process which has no influence over their work but merely wins influence for it. This muddled thinking which overtakes musicians, writers and critics as soon as they consider their own situation has tremendous consequences to which far too little attention is paid. For by imagining that they have got hold of an apparatus which in fact has got hold of them they are supporting an apparatus which is out of their control, which is no longer (as they believe) a means of furthering output but has become an obstacle to output, and specifically to their own output as soon as it follows a new and original course which the apparatus finds awkward or opposed to its own aims. Their output then becomes a matter of delivering the goods. Values evolve which are based on the fodder principle. And this leads to a general habit of judging works of art by their suitability for the apparatus without ever judging the apparatus by its suitability for the work. People say, this or that is a good work; and they mean (but do not say) good for the apparatus. Yet this apparatus is conditioned by the society of the day and only accepts what can keep it going in that society. We are free to discuss any innovation which doesn't threaten its social function – that of providing an evening's entertainment. We are not free to discuss those which threaten to change its function, possibly by fusing it with the educational system or with the organs of mass communication. Society absorbs via the apparatus whatever it needs in order to reproduce itself. This means that an innovation will pass if it is calculated to rejuvenate existing society, but not if it is going to change it – irrespective whether the form of the society in question is good or bad.

The *avant-garde* don't think of changing the apparatus, because they fancy that they have at their disposal an apparatus which will serve up whatever they freely invent, transforming itself spontaneously to match their ideas. But they are not in fact free inventors; the apparatus goes on fulfilling its function with or without them; the theatres play every night; the papers come out so many times a day; and they absorb what they need; and all they need is a given amount of stuff.[1]

You might think that to show up this situation (the creative artist's utter dependence on the apparatus) would be to condemn it. Its conceal-ment is such a disgrace.

And yet to restrict the individual's freedom of invention is in itself a progressive act. The individual becomes increasingly drawn into enormous events that are going to change the world. No longer can he simply 'express himself'. He is brought up short and put into a position where he can fulfil more general tasks. The trouble, however, is that at present the apparati do not work for the general good; the means of production do not belong to the producer; and as a result his work amounts to so much merchandise, and is governed by the normal laws of mercantile trade. Art is merchandise, only to be manufactured by the means of production (apparati). An opera can only be written for the opera. (One can't just think up an opera like one of Böcklin's fantastic sea-beasts, then hope to exhibit it publicly after having seized power – let alone try to smuggle it into our dear old zoo. . . .)

OPERA –

Even if one wanted to start a discussion of the opera as such (i.e. of its function), an opera would have to be written.
Our existing opera is a culinary opera. It was a means of pleasure long before it turned into merchandise. It furthers pleasure even where it re-quires, or promotes, a certain degree of education, for the education in question is an education of taste. To every object it adopts a hedonistic approach. It 'experiences', and it ranks as an 'experience'.

Why is *Mahagonny* an opera? Because its basic attitude is that of an opera: that is to say, culinary. Does *Mahagonny* adopt a hedonistic ap-proach? It does. Is *Mahagonny* an experience? It is an experience. For . . . *Mahagonny* is a piece of fun.

The opera *Mahagonny* pays conscious tribute to the senselessness of the operatic form. The irrationality of opera lies in the fact that rational ele-ments are employed, solid reality is aimed at, but at the same time it is all washed out by the music. A dying man is real. If at the same time he sings

[1] The intellectuals, however, are completely dependent on the apparatus, both socially and economically; it is the only channel for the realization of their work. The output of writers, com-posers and critics comes more and more to resemble raw material. The finished article is produced by the apparatus.

we are translated to the sphere of the irrational. (If the audience sang at the sight of him the case would be different.) The more unreal and unclear the music can make the reality – though there is of course a third, highly complex and in itself quite real element which can have quite real effects but is utterly remote from the reality of which it treats – the more pleasurable the whole process becomes: the pleasure grows in proportion to the degree of unreality.

The term 'opera' – far be it from us to profane it – leads, in *Mahagonny*'s case, to all the rest. The intention was that a certain unreality, irrationality and lack of seriousness should be introduced at the right moment, and so strike with a double meaning.[1]

The irrationality which makes its appearance in this way only fits the occasion on which it appears.

It is a purely hedonistic approach.

As for the content of this opera, *its content is pleasure*. Fun, in other words, not only as form but as subject-matter. At least, enjoyment was meant to be the object of the inquiry even if the inquiry was intended to be an object of enjoyment. Enjoyment here appears in its current historical role: as merchandise.[2]

It is undeniable that at present this content must have a provocative effect. In the thirteenth section, for example, where the glutton stuffs himself to death; because hunger is the rule. We never even hinted that others were going hungry while he stuffed, but the effect was provocative all the same. It is not everyone who is in a position to stuff himself full that dies of it, yet many are dying of hunger because this man stuffs himself to death. His pleasure provokes, because it implies so much.[3]

In contexts like these the use of opera as a means of pleasure must have provocative effects today. Though not of course on the handful of opera-goers. Its power to provoke introduces reality once more. *Mahagonny* may not taste particularly agreeable; it may even (thanks to guilty conscience)

---

[1] This limited aim did not stop us from introducing an element of instruction, and from basing everything on the gest. The eye which looks for the gest in everything is the moral sense. In other words, a moral tableau. A subjective one, though . . .

> Jetzt trinken wir noch eins
> Dann gehen wir nicht nach Hause
> Dann trinken wir noch eins
> Dann machen wir mal eine Pause.

– The people who sing this are subjective moralists. They are describing themselves.

[2] Romanticism is merchandise here too. It appears only as content, not as form.

[3] 'A dignified gentleman with an empurpled face had fished out a bunch of keys and was making a piercing demonstration against the Epic Theatre. His wife didn't desert him in this decisive moment. She had stuck two fingers in her mouth, screwed up her eyes and blown out her cheeks. The whistle was louder than the key of the safe.' (Alfred Polgar on the first production of *Mahagonny* in Leipzig.)

make a point of not doing so. But it is culinary through and through. *Mahagonny* is nothing more or less than an opera.

– WITH INNOVATIONS!

Opera had to be brought up to the technical level of the modern theatre. The modern theatre is the epic theatre. The following table shows certain changes of emphasis as between the dramatic and the epic theatre:[1]

DRAMATIC THEATRE	EPIC THEATRE
plot	narrative
implicates the spectator in a stage situation	turns the spectator into an observer, but
wears down his capacity for action	arouses his capacity for action
provides him with sensations	forces him to take decisions
experience	picture of the world
the spectator is involved in something	he is made to face something
suggestion	argument
instinctive feelings are preserved	brought to the point of recognition
the spectator is in the thick of it, shares the experience	the spectator stands outside, studies
the human being is taken for granted	the human being is the object of the inquiry
he is unalterable	he is alterable and able to alter
eyes on the finish	eyes on the course
one scene makes another	each scene for itself
growth	montage
linear development	in curves
evolutionary determinism	jumps
man as a fixed point	man as a process
thought determines being	social being determines thought
feeling	reason

When the epic theatre's methods begin to penetrate the opera the first result is a radical *separation of the elements*. The great struggle for supremacy between words, music and production – which always brings up the question 'which is the pretext for what?': is the music the pretext for the events on the stage, or are these the pretext for the music? etc. – can simply be by-passed by radically separating the elements. So long as the expression 'Gesamtkunstwerk' (or 'integrated work of art') means that the integration is a muddle, so long as the arts are supposed to be 'fused' together, the various elements will all be equally degraded, and each will

[1] This table does not show absolute antitheses but mere shifts of accent. In a communication of fact, for instance, we may choose whether to stress the element of emotional suggestion or that of plain rational argument.

act as a mere 'feed' to the rest. The process of fusion extends to the spectator, who gets thrown into the melting pot too and becomes a passive (suffering) part of the total work of art. Witchcraft of this sort must of course be fought against. Whatever is intended to produce hypnosis, is likely to induce sordid intoxication, or creates fog, has got to be given up.

Words, music and setting must become more independent of one another.

(a) Music

For the music, the change of emphasis proved to be as follows:

DRAMATIC OPERA	EPIC OPERA
The music dishes up	The music communicates
music which heightens the text	music which sets forth the text
music which proclaims the text	music which takes the text for granted
music which illustrates	which takes up a position
music which paints the psychological situation	which gives the attitude

Music plays the chief part in our thesis[1]

(b) Text

We had to make something straightforward and instructive of our fun, if it was not to be irrational and nothing more. The form employed was that of the moral tableau. The tableau is performed by the characters in the play. The text had to be neither moralizing nor sentimental, but to put morals and sentimentality on view. Equally important was the spoken word and the written word (of the titles). Reading seems to encourage the audience to adopt the most natural attitude towards the work.[2]

(c) Setting

Showing independent works of art as part of a theatrical performance is a new departure. Neher's projections adopt an attitude towards the events on the stage; as when the real glutton sits in front of the glutton whom Neher has drawn. In the same way the stage unreels the events that are fixed on the screen. These projections of Neher's are quite as much an independent component of the opera as are Weill's music and the text. They provide its visual aids.

---

[1] The large number of craftsmen in the average opera orchestra allows of nothing but associative music (one barrage of sound breeding another); and so the orchestral apparatus needs to be cut down to thirty specialists or less. The singer becomes a reporter, whose private feelings must remain a private affair.

[2] The significance of the titles is explained in the 'Notes to the Threepenny Opera' [see page 43], and in note 1 to the 'Dreigroschenfilm' [in Brecht's *Versuche 3*].

Of course such innovations also demand a new attitude on the part of the audiences who frequent opera houses.

EFFECT OF THE INNOVATIONS: A THREAT TO OPERA?

It is true that the audience had certain desires which were easily satisfied by the old opera but are no longer taken into account by the new. What is the audience's attitude during an opera; and is there any chance that it will change?

Bursting out of the underground stations, eager to become as wax in the magicians' hands, grown-up men, their resolution proved in the struggle for existence, rush to the box office. They hand in their hat at the cloakroom, and with it they hand their normal behaviour: the attitudes of 'everyday life'. Once out of the cloakroom they take their seats with the bearing of kings. How can we blame them? You may think a grocer's bearing better than a king's and still find this ridiculous. For the attitude that these people adopt in the opera is unworthy of them. Is there any possibility that they may change it? Can we persuade them to get out their cigars?

Once the content becomes, technically speaking, an independent component, to which text, music and setting 'adopt attitudes'; once illusion is sacrificed to free discussion, and once the spectator, instead of being enabled to have an experience, is forced as it were to cast his vote; then a change has been launched which goes far beyond formal matters and begins for the first time to affect the theatre's social function.

In the old operas all discussion of the content is rigidly excluded. If a member of the audience had happened to see a particular set of circumstances portrayed and had taken up a position *vis-à-vis* them, then the old opera would have lost its battle: the 'spell would have been broken'. Of course there were elements in the old opera which were not purely culinary; one has to distinguish between the period of its development and that of its decline. *The Magic Flute*, *Fidelio*, *Figaro* all included elements that were philosophical, dynamic. And yet the element of philosophy, almost of daring, in these operas was so subordinated to the culinary principle that their *sense* was in effect tottering and was soon absorbed in sensual satisfaction. Once its original 'sense' had died away the opera was by no means left bereft of sense, but had simply acquired another one – a sense *qua* opera. The content had been smothered in the opera. Our Wagnerites are now pleased to remember that the original Wagnerites posited a sense of which they were presumably aware. Those composers who stem from Wagner still insist on posing as philosophers. A philosophy which is of no use to man or beast, and can only be disposed of as a means of sensual satisfaction.

(*Elektra, Jonny spielt auf.*) We still maintain the whole highly-developed technique which made this pose possible: the vulgarian strikes a philosophical attitude from which to conduct his hackneyed ruminations. It is only from this point, from the death of the sense (and it is understood that this sense *could* die), that we can start to understand the further innovations which are now plaguing opera: to see them as desperate attempts to supply this art with a posthumous sense, a 'new' sense, by which the sense comes ultimately to lie in the music itself, so that the sequence of musical forms acquires a sense simply *qua* sequence, and certain proportions, changes, etc. from being a means are promoted to become an end. Progress which has neither roots nor result; which does not spring from new requirements but satisfies the old ones with new titillations, thus furthering a purely conservative aim. New material is absorbed which is unfamiliar 'in this context', because at the time when 'this context' was evolved it was not known in any context at all. (Railway engines, factories, aeroplanes, bathrooms, etc. act as a diversion. Better composers choose instead to deny all content by performing – or rather smothering – it in the Latin tongue.) This sort of progress only indicates that something has been left behind. It is achieved without the overall function being changed; or rather, with a view to stopping any such change from taking place. And what about *Gebrauchsmusik*?

At the very moment when neo-classicism, in other words stark Art for Art's sake, took the field (it came as a reaction against the emotional element in musical impressionism) the idea of utilitarian music, or Gebrauchsmusik, emerged like Venus from the waves: music was to make use of the amateur. The amateur was used as a woman is 'used'. Innovation upon innovation. The punch-drunk listener suddenly wants to play. The struggle against idle listening turned into a struggle for keen listening, then for keen playing. The cellist in the orchestra, father of a numerous family, now began to play not from philosophical conviction but for pleasure. The culinary principle was saved.[1]

What is the point, we wonder, of chasing one's own tail like this? Why this obstinate clinging to the pleasure element? This addiction to drugs?

---

[1] Innovations of this sort must be criticized so long as they are helping to renovate institutions that have outlived their usefulness. They represent progress as soon as we set out to effect radical changes in the institutions' function. Then they become quantitative improvements, purges, cleansing operations which are given meaning only by the functional change which has been or is to be made.

True progress consists not in being progressive but in progressing. True progress is what enables or compels us to progress. And on a broad front, at that, so that neighbouring spheres are set in motion too. True progress has its cause in the impossibility of an actual situation, and its result is that situation's change.

Why so little concern with one's own interests as soon as one steps outside one's own home? Why this refusal to discuss? Answer: nothing can come of discussion. To discuss the present form of our society, or even of one of its least important parts, would lead inevitably and at once to an outright threat to our society's form as such.

We have seen that opera is sold as evening entertainment, and that this puts definite bounds to all attempts to transform it. We see that this entertainment has to be devoted to illusion, and must be of a ceremonial kind. Why?

In our present society the old opera cannot be just 'wished away'. Its illusions have an important social function. The drug is irreplaceable; it cannot be done without.[1]

Only in the opera does the human being have a chance to be human. His entire mental capacities have long since been ground down to a timid mistrustfulness, an envy of others, a selfish calculation. The old opera survives not just because it is old, but chiefly because the situation which it is able to meet is still the old one. This is not wholly so. And here lies the hope for the new opera. Today we can begin to ask whether opera hasn't come to such a pass that further innovations, instead of leading to the renovation of this whole form, will bring about its destruction.[2]

Perhaps *Mahagonny* is as culinary as ever – just as culinary as an opera ought to be – but one of its functions is to change society; it brings the culinary principle under discussion, it attacks the society that needs operas of such a sort; it still perches happily on the old bough, perhaps, but at least it has started (out of absent-mindedness or bad conscience) to saw it through. . . . And here you have the effect of the innovations and the song they sing.

Real innovations attack the roots.

FOR INNOVATIONS – AGAINST RENOVATION!

The opera *Mahagonny* was written three years ago, in 1927. In subsequent

[1] The life imposed on us is too hard; it brings us too many agonies, disappointments, impossible tasks. In order to stand it we have to have some kind of palliative. There seem to be three classes of these: overpowering distractions, which allow us to find our sufferings unimportant, pseudo-satisfactions which reduce them and drugs which make us insensitive to them. The pseudo-satisfactions offered by art are illusions if compared with reality, but are none the less psychologically effective for that, thanks to the part played by the imagination in our inner life. (Freud: *Das Unbehagen in der Kultur*, page 22.) Such drugs are sometimes responsible for the wastage of great stores of energy which might have been applied to bettering the human lot. (Ibid., page 28.)

[2] Such, in the opera *Mahagonny*, are those innovations which allow the theatre to present moral tableaux (showing up the commercial character both of the entertainment and of the persons entertained) and which put the spectator in a moralizing frame of mind.

works attempts were made to emphasize the didactic more and more at the expense of the culinary element. And so to develop the means of pleasure into an object of instruction, and to convert certain institutions from places of entertainment into organs of mass communication.

[From *Versuche* 2, Berlin 1930. Signed 'Brecht. Suhrkamp']

NOTE: This essay, under the title 'Notes on the Opera', followed the published text of Brecht's opera with Weill, *Aufstieg und Fall der Stadt Mahagonny*. First performed in an embryo version as a 'Songspiel' in July 1927, the full opera was given in Leipzig on 9 March 1930; i.e. after Brecht had begun writing his 'Lehrstücke', the 'subsequent works' referred to in the last paragraph. Caspar Neher, the scene designer for both productions, was a childhood friend and life-long collaborator of Brecht's. There are frequent references to him in what follows.

Besides being the first full statement of Brecht's ideas about the 'epic theatre', this essay introduces the important term '*gestisch*'. '*Gestus*,' of which '*gestisch*' is the adjective, means both gist and gesture; an attitude or a single aspect of an attitude, expressible in words or actions. Lessing used the term in his *Hamburger Dramaturgie* as something distinct from '*Geste*', or gesture proper (entry for 12 May 1767); and Weill himself seems to have preceded Brecht in its use, publishing an article 'Über den gestischen Charakter der Musik' in *Die Musik* (p. 419) in March 1929.

Weill introduces the term thus: Music, he says, is particularly important for the theatre because 'it can reproduce the *gestus* that illustrates the incident on the stage; it can even create a kind of basic *gestus* (*Grundgestus*), forcing the action into a particular attitude that excludes all doubt and misunderstanding about the incident in question.' The translator has chosen the obsolete English word 'gest', meaning 'bearing, carriage, mien' (*Shorter Oxford English Dictionary*) as the nearest manageable equivalent, together with its adjective 'gestic'.

Of the operas referred to, *Jonny spielt auf* was Ernst Křenek's opera about a Negro violinist, which included a scene in a railway station and was first performed on 11 February 1927. A factory is shown in Max Brand's *Maschinist Hopkins* (13 April 1929). The work in Latin was presumably Cocteau's and Stravinsky's *Oedipus Rex* (Berlin State Opera production in February 1928).

'Gebrauchsmusik' was a doctrine that music should perform a utilitarian function. Brecht is confusing it with its companion doctrine of 'Gemeinschaftsmusik', or amateur music played for the sake of the social virtue of playing together. Both were particularly associated with Paul Hindemith, with whom Brecht had fallen out after their collaboration on the first two Lehrstücke.

14 · The Literarization of the Theatre

(Notes to the *Threepenny Opera*)

THE READING OF PLAYS

There is no reason why John Gay's motto for his *Beggar's Opera* – nos haec novimus esse nihil – should be changed for the *Threepenny Opera*. Its publication represents little more than the prompt-book of a play wholly surrendered to theatres, and thus is directed at the expert rather than at the consumer. This doesn't mean that the conversion of the maximum number of readers or spectators into experts is not thoroughly desirable; indeed it is under way.

The *Threepenny Opera* is concerned with bourgeois conceptions not only as content, by representing them, but also through the manner in which it does so. It is a kind of report on life as any member of the audience would like to see it. Since at the same time, however, he sees a good deal that he has no wish to see; since therefore he sees his wishes not merely fulfilled but also criticized (sees himself not as the subject but as the object), he is theoretically in a position to appoint a new function for the theatre. But the theatre itself resists any alteration of its function, and so it seems desirable that the spectator should read plays whose aim is not merely to be performed in the theatre but to change it: out of mistrust of the theatre. Today we see the theatre being given absolute priority over the actual plays. The theatre apparatus's priority is a priority of means of production. This apparatus resists all conversion to other purposes, by taking any play which it encounters and immediately changing it so that it no longer represents a foreign body within the apparatus – except at those points where it neutralizes itself. The necessity to stage the new drama correctly – which matters more for the theatre's sake than for the drama's – is modified by the fact that the theatre can stage anything: it theatres it all down. Of course this priority has economic reasons.

TITLES AND SCREENS

The screens on which the titles of each scene are projected are a primitive attempt at literarizing the theatre. This literarization of the theatre needs to be developed to the utmost degree, as in general does the literarizing of all public occasions.

Literarizing entails punctuating 'representation' with 'formulation'; gives the theatre the possibility of making contact with other institutions for intellectual activities; but is bound to remain one-sided so long as the audience is taking no part in it and using it as a means of obtaining access to 'higher things'.

The orthodox playwright's objection to the titles is that the dramatist ought to say everything that has to be said in the action, that the text must express everything within its own confines. The corresponding attitude for the spectator is that he should not think about a subject, but within the confines of the subject. But this way of subordinating everything to a single idea, this passion for propelling the spectator along a single track where he can look neither right nor left, up nor down, is something that the new school of play-writing must reject. Footnotes, and the habit of turning back in order to check a point, need to be introduced into play-writing too.

Some exercise in complex seeing is needed – though it is perhaps more important to be able to think above the stream than to think in the stream. Moreover the use of screens imposes and facilitates a new style of acting. This style is the *epic style*. As he reads the projections on the screen the spectator adopts an attitude of smoking-and-watching. Such an attitude on his part at once compels a better and clearer performance as it is hopeless to try to 'carry away' any man who is smoking and accordingly pretty well occupied with himself. By these means one would soon have a theatre full of experts, just as one has sporting arenas full of experts. No chance of the actors having the effrontery to offer such people those few miserable scraps of imitation which they at present cook up in a few rehearsals 'any old how' and without the least thought! No question of their material being taken from them in so unfinished and unworked a state. The actor would have to find a quite different way of drawing attention to those incidents which had been previously announced by the titles and so deprived of any intrinsic element of surprise.

Unfortunately it is to be feared that titles and permission to smoke are not of themselves enough to lead the audience to a more fruitful use of the theatre.

ABOUT THE SINGING OF THE SONGS

When an actor sings he undergoes a change of function. Nothing is more revolting than when the actor pretends not to notice that he has left the level of plain speech and started to sing. The three levels – plain speech, heightened speech and singing – must always remain distinct, and in no case should heightened speech represent an intensification of plain speech, or singing of heightened speech. In no case therefore should singing take place where words are prevented by excess of feeling. The actor must not

1. Frank Wedekind and his wife Tilly near the Deutsches Theater,
Berlin, about 1908–12.

2. Brecht with Samson-Körner, the boxer, at work on the latter's memoirs, about 1926.

3. Fritz Kortner, 1928.

4. Reinhardt's production of *Saint Joan*, 1924, with Elisabeth Bergner (Joan), Rudolf Forster (Dauphin, at back), and Paul Hartman (Dubois).

5. Tretiakov's *Roar China* in Meyerhold's production, 1926.

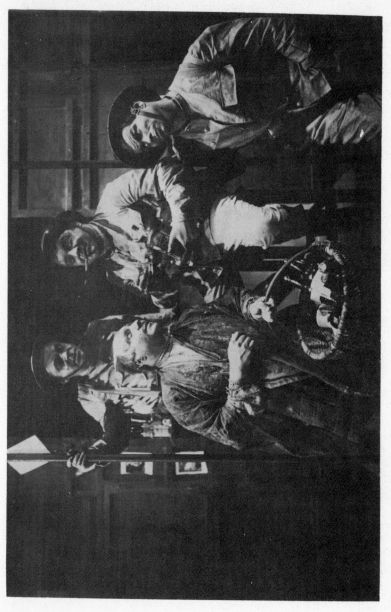

6. Erich Engel's production of *Mann ist Mann* at the Berlin Volksbühne, December 31, 1927, with Heinrich George (front) as Galy Gay, and Viktor Schwannecke, Peter Ihle, and Friedrich Gnas as the three soldiers.

7. Curtain and screens for *The Threepenny Opera*, 1928–29.

8. Scene from *Konjunktur* by Leo Lania, staged by Piscator at the Theater am Nollendorfplatz, Berlin, 1928.

9. *Der Flug der Lindberghs* at the Baden-Baden music festival, 1929.
Brecht is standing on the right.

10. Caricature of Leopold Jessner's production of *Oedipus* at the Staatstheater, 1929. Left to right: Weigel, Granach, Roland, Kortner, and Franck.

only sing but show a man singing. His aim is not so much to bring out the emotional content of his song (has one the right to offer others a dish that one has already eaten oneself?) but to show gestures that are so to speak the habits and usage of the body. To this end he would be best advised not to use the actual words of the text when rehearsing, but common everyday phrases which express the same thing in the crude language of ordinary life. As for the melody, he must not follow it blindly: there is a kind of speaking-against-the-music which can have strong effects, the results of a stubborn, incorruptible sobriety which is independent of music and rhythm. If he drops into the melody it must be an event; the actor can emphasize it by plainly showing the pleasure which the melody gives him. It helps the actor if the musicians are visible during his performance and also if he is allowed to make visible preparation for it (by straightening a chair perhaps or making himself up, etc.). Particularly in the songs it is important that 'he who is showing should himself be shown'.

WHY DOES MACHEATH HAVE TO BE ARRESTED TWICE OVER?

From the pseudo-classical German point of view the first prison scene is a diversion, but to us it is an example of rudimentary epic form. It is a diversion if, like this purely dynamic form of drama, one gives priority to the idea and makes the spectator desire an increasingly definite objective – in this case the hero's death; if one as it were creates a growing demand for the supply and, purely to allow the spectator's strong emotional participation (for emotions will only venture on to completely secure ground, and cannot survive disappointment of any sort), needs a single inevitable chain of events. The epic drama, with its materialistic standpoint and its lack of interest in any investment of its spectators' emotions, knows no objective but only a finishing point, and is familiar with a different kind of chain, whose course need not be a straight one but may quite well be in curves or even in leaps. The dynamic, idealistically-orientated kind of drama, with its interest in the individual, was in all decisive respects more radical when it began life (under the Elizabethans) than in the German pseudo-classicism of two hundred years later, which confuses dynamics of representation with the dynamics of what has to be represented, and has already put its individual 'in his place'. (The present-day successors of these successors are indescribable: dynamics of representation have changed into an ingenious and empirically-based arrangement of a jumble of effects, while the individual, now in a state of complete dissolution, still goes on being developed within his own limits, but only as parts for actors – whereas the late bourgeois novel at least considers that it has a science of psychology which has been worked out to help it analyse the individual – as though the individual had not simply collapsed long ago.) But this great kind of drama was far less radical in its purging of the material. Here the structural form didn't rule out all the individual's deviations from the straight course, as brought about by 'just life' (a part is always played here by outside relationships, with other circumstances that 'don't take place'; a far wider cross-section is taken), but used such deviations as a motive force of the play's dynamics. This friction penetrates right inside the individual, to be overcome within him. The whole weight of this kind of drama comes from the piling up of resistances. The material is not yet arranged in accordance with any wish for an easy ideal formula. Something of Baconian materialism still survives here, and the individual himself still has flesh and bones and resists the formula's demands. But whenever one comes across materialism epic forms arise in the drama, and most markedly and frequently in comedy, whose 'tone' is always 'lower' and more materialistic. Today, when the human being has to be seen as 'the sum of all social circumstances' the epic form is the only one that can embrace those processes which serve the drama as matter for a comprehensive picture of the world. Similarly man, flesh and blood man, can only be embraced through those processes by which and in course of which he exists. The new school of play-writing must systematically see to it that its form includes 'experiment'. It must be free to use connections on every side; it needs equilibrium and has a tension which governs its component parts and 'loads' them against one another. (Thus this form is anything but a revue-like sequence of sketches.)

[From *Versuche 3*, Berlin 1931. Omitting sections 'Die Hauptpersonen', 'Winke für Schauspieler' and 'Warum muss der reitende Bote reiten?']

NOTE: These notes, here cut so as to exclude three sections of less general relevance, were written subsequently to the play and published some three years after its first performance. Like the two preceding items, they form part of a series of notes and essays labelled 'On a non-aristotelian drama' which is scattered through Brecht's grey paperbound *Versuche*, starting in 1930. As Helge Hultberg points out (*Die ästhetischen Anschauungen Bertolt Brechts*, p. 100) this series was originally announced at the back of the first *Versuche* volume under the title 'On a Dialectical Drama'. The group of handwritten notes printed as 'The dialectical drama' on p. 243ff. of *Schriften zum Theater 1* is so close in theme and style to the *Mahagonny* and *Threepenny Opera* notes as to make it indeed seem possible that Brecht had a major theoretical work in mind.

The term 'dialectical' went into cold storage, to be taken out again in a somewhat different context at the end of Brecht's life (see p. 281). 'Non-aristotelian' was a better description of his theatre at this stage, referring as it does above all to the elimination of empathy and imitation (or mimesis). At the same time it recalls the distinction made by the *Poetics* (though never explicitly by Brecht) between a tragedy, which has to observe the unities of time and place, and an epic, which need not.

There is a full translation of the *Threepenny Opera* notes by Desmond Vesey in Brecht: *Plays I* (Methuen, 1950) and by Eric Bentley in *From the Modern Repertoire I* (University of Denver Press, 1949).

15 · The Film, the Novel and Epic Theatre

(From *The Threepenny Lawsuit*)

Contradictions are our hope!

SOME PRECONCEPTIONS EXAMINED

1 · 'ART CAN DO WITHOUT THE CINEMA'

We have often been told (and the court expressed the same opinion) that when we sold our work to the film industry we gave up all our rights; the buyers even purchased the right to destroy what they had bought; all further claim was covered by the money. These people felt that in agreeing to deal with the film industry we put ourselves in the position of a man who lets his laundry be washed in a dirty gutter and then complains that it has been ruined. Anybody who advises us not to make use of such new apparatus just confirms the apparatus's right to do bad work; he forgets himself out of sheer open-mindedness, for he is thus proclaiming his willingness to have nothing but dirt produced for him. At the same time he deprives us in advance of the apparatus which we need in order to produce, since this way of producing is likely more and more to supersede the present one, forcing us to speak through increasingly complex media and to express what we have to say by increasingly inadequate means. For the old forms of communication are not unaffected by the development of new ones, nor do they survive alongside them. The filmgoer develops a different way of reading stories. But the man who writes the stories is a filmgoer too. The mechanization of literary production cannot be thrown into reverse. Once instruments are used even the novelist who makes no use of them is led to wish that he could do what the instruments can: to include what they show (or could show) as part of that reality which constitutes his subject-matter; and above all, when he writes, to assume the attitude of somebody using an instrument.

For instance it makes a great difference whether the writer approaches things as if using instruments, or produces them 'from within himself'. What the film itself does, that is to say how far it makes its individuality prevail against 'art', is not unimportant in this connection. It is conceivable that other kinds of writer, such as playwrights or novelists, may for the moment be able to work in a more cinematic way than the film people. Up to a point they depend less on means of production. But they still depend on the film, its progress or regress; and the film's means of production are wholly capitalist. Today the bourgeois novel still depicts 'a world'. It does so in a purely idealistic way from within a given *Weltanschauung*: the more or less private, but in any case personal outlook of its 'creator'. Inside this world every detail of course fits exactly, though if it were taken out of its context it would not seem authentic for a minute by comparison with the 'details' of reality. What we find out about the real world is just as much as we find out about the author responsible for the unreal one; in other words we find out something about the author and nothing about the world.

The film cannot depict any world (the 'setting' in which it deals is something quite different) and lets nobody express himself (and nothing else) in a work, and no work express any person. What it provides (or could provide) is applicable conclusions about human actions in detail. Its splendid inductive method, which at any rate it facilitates, could be of infinite significance to the novel, in so far as novels still signify anything. To the playwright what is interesting is its attitude to the person performing the action. It gives life to its people, whom it classes purely according to function, simply using available types that occur in given situations and are able to adopt given attitudes in them. Character is never used as a source of motivation; these people's inner life is never the principal cause of the action and seldom its principal result; the individual is seen from outside. Literature needs the film not only indirectly but also directly. That decisive extension of its social duties which follows from the transformation of art into a paedagogical discipline entails the multiplying or the repeated changing of the means of representation. (Not to mention the Lehrstück proper, which entails supplying film apparatus to all those taking part.) This apparatus can be used better than almost anything else to supersede the old kind of un-technical, anti-technical 'glowing' art, with its religious links. The socialization of these means of production is vital for art. . . .

To understand the position we must get away from the common idea that these battles for the new institutions and apparatus only have to do with one part of art. In this view there is a part of art, its central part, which remains wholly untouched by the new possibilities of communication (radio, film, book clubs, etc.) and goes on using the old ones (printed books, freely marketed; the stage, etc.). Quite different from the other, technically-influenced part where it is a matter of creation by the apparatus itself: a wholly new business, owing its existence in the first place to certain financial calculations and thereby bound to them for ever. If works of the former sort are handed over to the apparatus they are turned into goods without further ado. This idea, leading as it does to utter fatalism, is wrong because it shuts off so-called 'sacrosanct works of art' from every process and influence of our time, treating them as sacrosanct purely because they are impervious to any development in communication. In fact, of course, the whole of art without any exception is placed in this new situation; it is as a whole, not split into parts, that it has to cope with it; it is as a whole that it turns into goods or not. The changes wrought by time leave nothing untouched, but always embrace the whole. In short, the common preconception discussed here is pernicious.

2 · A FILM MUST HAVE SOME 'HUMAN INTEREST'

This preconception is equivalent to the notion that films have got to be vulgar. Such an eminently rational view (rational because nobody is going to make any other kind of film, or look at it once made) owes its relevance to the inexorable way in which the metaphysicians of the press, with their insistence on 'art', call for profundity. It is they who want to see the 'element of fate' emphasized in all dealings between people. Fate, which used (once) to be among the great concepts, has long since become a vulgar one, where the desired 'transfiguration' and 'illumination' are achieved by reconciling oneself to circumstances – and a purely class-warfare one, where one class fixes the fate of another. As usual, our metaphysicians' demands are not hard to fulfil. It is simple to imagine everything that they reject presented in such a way that they would accept it with enthusiasm. Obviously if one were to trace certain love stories back to Romeo and Juliet, or crime stories to Macbeth, in other words to famous plays that need contain nothing else (need show no other kind of human behaviour, use no other kind of energy to govern the world's movements), then they would at once exclaim that vulgarity is determined by How and not What. But this 'it all depends how' is itself vulgar.

This beloved 'human interest' of theirs, this How (usually qualified by the word 'eternal', like some indelible dye) as applied to Othello (my wife is my property), Hamlet (better sleep on it), Macbeth (I'm destined for higher things) and co., now seems like vulgarity and nothing more when measured on a massive scale. If one insists on having it, this is the only form in which it can be had; simply to insist is vulgar. What once determined the grandeur of such passions, their non-vulgarity, was the part they had to play in society, which was a revolutionary one. Even the impact which *Potemkin* made on such people springs from the sense of outrage which they would feel if their wives were to try to serve bad meat to them (I won't stand it, I tell you!), while Chaplin is perfectly aware that he must be 'human', i.e. vulgar, if he is to achieve anything more, and to this end will alter his style in a pretty unscrupulous way (viz. the famous close-up of the doggy look which concludes *City Lights*).

What the film really demands is external action and not introspective psychology. Capitalism operates in this way by taking given needs on a massive scale, exorcizing them, organizing them and mechanizing them so as to revolutionize everything. Great areas of ideology are destroyed when capitalism concentrates on external action, dissolves everything into processes, abandons the hero as the vehicle for everything and mankind as the measure, and thereby smashes the introspective psychology of the bourgeois novel. The external viewpoint suits the film and gives it importance. For the film the principles of non-aristotelian drama (a type of drama not depending on empathy, mimesis) are immediately acceptable. Non-aristotelian effects can be seen in the Russian film *The Road to Life*, above all because the theme (re-education of neglected children by specific socialist methods) leads the spectator to establish causal relationships between the teacher's attitude and that of his pupils. Thanks to the key scenes this analysis of origins comes so to grip the spectator's interest that he 'instinctively' dismisses any motives for the children's neglect borrowed from the old empathy type of drama (unhappiness at home plus psychic trauma, rather than war or civil war). Even the use of work as a method of education arouses the spectator's scepticism, for the simple reason that it is never made clear that in the Soviet Union, in total contrast to all other countries, morality is in fact determined by work. As soon as the human being appears as an object the causal connections become decisive. Similarly in the great American comedies the human being is presented as an object, so that their audience could as well be entirely made up of Pavlovians. Behaviourism is a school of psychology that is based on the industrial producer's need to acquire means of influencing the customer; an active psychology therefore, progressive and revolutionary. Its limits are those proper to its function under capitalism (the reflexes are biological; only in certain of Chaplin's films are they social). Here again the road leads over capitalism's dead body; but here again this road is a good one.

[From *Versuche 3*, Berlin 1931. 'Der Dreigroschen-prozess', Sections III (1) and (6), i.e. 'Die Kunst braucht den Film nicht' and 'Im Film muss das Menschliche eine Rolle spielen'.]

NOTE: The above are two sections from Brecht's long account of his lawsuit over the making of Pabst's film version of *The Threepenny Opera*, which was heard in Berlin on 17 and 20 October 1930. The suit failed and Brecht lost his claim to dictate the treatment of the story, which would have been along the lines of his draft 'Die Beule' (printed in the same volume). This draft became instead the basis of *The Threepenny Novel*, the only true novel that Brecht wrote.

The emphasis on 'contradictions' in the opening quotation is new, and will become increasingly important in Brecht's writings. In Marxist language this term means the conflicting elements in any person or situation.

Nikolai Ekk's *The Road to Life*, one of the first Soviet sound films, was released on 1 June 1930. Brecht had met Eisenstein on his Berlin visit of 1929; later he came to know Chaplin in Hollywood. An earlier unpublished note on *The Gold Rush* entitled 'Less Security' ('Weniger Sicherheit', *Schriften zum Theater 2*, p.220) calls Chaplin a 'document' and praises story and theme on the ground that the average theatre would at once reject anything so simple, crude and linear. 'The cinema has no responsibilities, it doesn't have to overstrain itself. Its dramaturgy has remained so simple because a film is a matter of a few miles of celluloid in a tin box. When a man bends a saw between his knees you don't expect a fugue.' Yet another early fragment (*Schriften zum Theater 1*, pp. 163–164) on 'The theatre of the big cities' concludes: 'The only kind of art produced by these cities so far has been *fun:* Charlie Chaplin's films and jazz. Jazz is all the theatre it contains, as far as I can see.'

In 1931 Brecht helped to make the (Communist) semi-documentary film *Kuhle Wampe*, which was directed by Slatan Dudow and banned in March of the following year. Probably this came closer to his ideas than any other film with which he was associated.

16 · The Radio as an Apparatus of Communication

In our society one can invent and perfect discoveries that still have to con-quer their market and justify their existence; in other words discoveries that have not been called for. Thus there was a moment when technology was advanced enough to produce the radio and society was not yet advanced enough to accept it. The radio was then in its first phase of being a substi-tute: a substitute for theatre, opera, concerts, lectures, café music, local newspapers and so forth. This was the patient's period of halcyon youth. I am not sure if it is finished yet, but if so then this stripling who needed no certificate of competence to be born will have to start looking retrospectively for an object in life. Just as a man will begin asking at a certain age, when his first innocence has been lost, what he is supposed to be doing in the world.

As for the radio's object, I don't think it can consist merely in prettifying public life. Nor is radio in my view an adequate means of bringing back cosiness to the home and making family life bearable again. But quite apart from the dubiousness of its functions, radio is one-sided when it should be two-. It is purely an apparatus for distribution, for mere sharing out. So here is a positive suggestion: change this apparatus over from distribution to communication. The radio would be the finest possible communication apparatus in public life, a vast network of pipes. That is to say, it would be if it knew how to receive as well as to transmit, how to let the listener speak as well as hear, how to bring him into a relationship instead of isolating him. On this principle the radio should step out of the supply business and organize its listeners as suppliers. Any attempt by the radio to give a truly public character to public occasions is a step in the right direction.

Whatever the radio sets out to do it must strive to combat that lack of consequences which makes such asses of almost all our public institutions. We have a literature without consequences, which not only itself sets out to lead nowhere, but does all it can to neutralize its readers by depicting each object and situation stripped of the consequences to which they lead. We have educational establishments without consequences, working frantically to hand on an education that leads nowhere and has come from nothing.

The slightest advance in this direction is bound to succeed far more spectacularly than any performance of a culinary kind. As for the technique that needs to be developed for all such operations, it must follow the prime objective of turning the audience not only into pupils but into teachers. It is the radio's formal task to give these educational operations an interesting turn, i.e. to ensure that these interests interest people. Such an attempt by the radio to put its instruction into an artistic form would link up with the efforts of modern artists to give art an instructive character. As an example or model of the exercises possible along these lines let me repeat the explanation of *Der Flug der Lindberghs* that I gave at the Baden-Baden music festival of 1929.

[*Brecht then repeats the second, third and fifth paragraphs of 'An Example of Paedagogics'.*]

This is an innovation, a suggestion that seems utopian and that I myself admit to be utopian. When I say that the radio or the theatre 'could' do so-and-so I am aware that these vast institutions cannot do all they 'could', and not even all they want.

But it is not at all our job to renovate ideological institutions on the basis of the existing social order by means of innovations. Instead our innovations must force them to surrender that basis. So: For innovations, against renovation!

['Der Rundfunk als Kommunikationsapparat' in *Blätter des Hessischen Landestheaters*, Darmstadt, No. 16, July 1932]

NOTE: There are one or two earlier notes on the radio by Brecht, including a set of 'Suggestions for the Director of the Radio' published in the *Berliner Börsen-Courier* of 25 December 1927, which proposed the live broadcasting of law cases and Reichstag debates, as well as an increased proportion of interviews and discussion programmes. He also suggested, apparently as a new idea, that composers should be invited to write for the radio.

The present essay was published in the programme of the theatre that had first staged *Mann ist Mann* in 1926, and is headed 'From a report'. It is not known whether, when or to whom Brecht delivered this.

17 · The Question of Criteria for Judging Acting

(Notes to *Mann ist Mann*)

People interested in the ostensibly epic production of the play *Mann ist Mann* at the Staatstheater were of two opinions about the actor Lorre's performance in the leading part. Some thought his way of acting was perfectly right from the new point of view, exemplary even; others quite rejected it. I myself belong to the first group. Let me put the question in its proper perspective by saying that I saw all the rehearsals and that it was not at all due to shortcomings in the actor's equipment that his performance so disappointed some of the spectators; those on the night who felt him to be lacking in 'carrying-power' or 'the gift of making his meaning clear' could have satisfied themselves about his gifts in this direction at the early rehearsals. If these hitherto accepted hallmarks of great acting faded away at the performance (only to be replaced, in my view, by other hallmarks, of a new style of acting) this was the result aimed at by the rehearsals and is accordingly the only issue for judgment: the one point where opinions can differ.

Here is a specific question: How far can a complete change in the theatre's functions dislodge certain generally accepted criteria from their present domination of our judgment of the actor? We can simplify it by confining ourselves to two of the main objections to the actor Lorre mentioned above: his habit of not speaking his meaning clearly, and the suggestion that he acted nothing but episodes.

Presumably the objection to his way of speaking applied less in the first part of the play than in the second, with its long speeches. The speeches in question are his protest against the announcement of the verdict, his pleas before the wall when he is about to be shot, and the monologue on identity which he delivers over the coffin before its burial. In the first part it was not so obvious that his manner of speaking had been split up according to gests, but in these long summings-up the identical manner seemed monotonous and to hamper the sense. It hardly mattered in the first part that people couldn't at once recognize (feel the force of) its quality of bringing out the gest, but in the second the same failure of recognition completely destroyed the effect. For over and above the meaning of the individual sentences a quite specific basic gest was being brought out here which admittedly depended on knowing what the individual sentences meant but at the same time used this meaning only as a means to an end. The speeches' content was made up of contradictions, and the actor had not to make the spectator identify himself with individual sentences and so get caught up in contradictions, but to keep him out of them. Taken as a whole it had to be the most objective possible exposition of a contradictory internal process. Certain particularly significant sentences were therefore 'highlighted', i.e. loudly declaimed, and their selection amounted to an intellectual achievement (though of course the same could also be the result of an artistic process). This was the case with the sentences 'I insist you put a stop to it!' and 'It *was* raining yesterday evening!' By these means the sentences (sayings) were not brought home to the spectator but withdrawn from him; he was not led but left to make his own discoveries. The 'objections to the verdict' were split into separate lines by caesuras as in a poem, so as to bring out their character of adducing one argument after another; at the same time the fact that the individual arguments never followed logically on one another had to be appreciated and even applied. The impression intended was of a man simply reading a case for the defence prepared at some quite different period, without understanding what it meant as he did so. And this was indeed the impression left on any of the audience who knew how to make such observations. At first sight, admittedly, it was possible to overlook the truly magnificent way in which the actor Lorre delivered his inventory. This may seem peculiar. For generally and quite rightly the art of not being overlooked is treated as vital; and here are we, suggesting that something is magnificent which needs to be hunted for and found. All the same, the epic theatre has profound reasons for insisting on such a reversal of criteria. Part of the social transformation of the theatre is that the spectator should not be worked on in the usual way. The theatre is no longer the place where his interest is aroused but where he brings it to be satisfied. (Thus our ideas of tempo have to be revised for the epic theatre. Mental processes, e.g., demand quite a different tempo from emotional ones, and cannot necessarily stand the same speeding-up.)

We made a short film of the performance, concentrating on the principal nodal points of the action and cutting it so as to bring out the gests in a very abbreviated way, and this most interesting experiment shows surprisingly well how exactly Lorre manages in these long speeches to mime the basic meaning underlying every (silent) sentence. As for the other objection, it may be that the epic theatre, with its wholly different attitude to the individual, will simply do away with the notion of the actor who 'carries the play'; for the play is no longer 'carried' by him in the old sense. A certain capacity for coherent and unhurried development of a leading part. such as distinguished the old kind of actor, now no longer matters so much. Against that, the epic actor may possibly need an even greater range than the old stars did, for he has to be able to show his character's coherence despite, or rather by means of, interruptions and jumps. Since everything depends on the development, on the flow, the various phases must be able to be clearly seen, and therefore separated; and yet this must not be achieved mechanically. It is a matter of establishing quite new rules for the art of acting (playing against the flow, letting one's characteristics be defined by one's fellow-actors, etc.). The fact that at one point Lorre whitens his face (instead of allowing his acting to become more and more influenced by fear of death 'from within himself') may at first sight seem to stamp him as an episodic actor, but it is really something quite different. To begin with, he is helping the playwright to make a point, though there is more to it than that of course. The character's development has been very carefully divided into four phases, for which four masks are employed – the packer's face, up to the trial; the 'natural' face, up to his awakening after being shot; the 'blank page', up to his reassembly after the funeral speech; finally the soldier's face. To give some idea of our way of working: opinions differed as to which phase, second or third, called for the face to be whitened. After long consideration Lorre plumped for the third, as being characterized, to his mind, by 'the biggest decision and the biggest strain'. Between fear of death and fear of life he chose to treat the latter as the more profound.

The epic actor's efforts to make particular incidents between human beings seem striking (to use human beings as a setting), may also cause him to be misrepresented as a short-range episodist by anybody who fails to allow for his way of knotting all the separate incidents together and absorbing them in the broad flow of his performance. As against the dramatic actor, who has his character established from the first and simply exposes it to the inclemencies of the world and the tragedy, the epic actor lets his character grow before the spectator's eyes out of the way in which he behaves. 'This way of joining up', 'this way of selling an elephant', 'this way of conducting the case', do not altogether add up to a single unchangeable character but to one which changes all the time and becomes more and more clearly defined in course of 'this way of changing'. This hardly strikes the spectator who is used to something else. How many spectators can so far discard the need for tension as to see how, with this new sort of actor, the same gesture is used to summon him to the wall to change his clothes as is subsequently used to summon him there in order to be shot, and realize that the situation is similar but the behaviour different? An attitude is here required of the spectator which roughly corresponds to the reader's habit of turning back in order to check a point. Completely different economies are needed by the epic actor and the dramatic. (The actor Chaplin, incidentally, would in many ways come closer to the epic than to the dramatic theatre's requirements.)

It is possible that the epic theatre may need a larger advance loan than the ordinary theatre in order to become fully effective; this is a problem that needs attention. Perhaps the incidents portrayed by the epic actor need to be familiar ones, in which case historical incidents would be the most immediately suitable. Perhaps it may even be an advantage if an actor can be compared with other actors in the same part. If all this and a good deal more is needed to make the epic theatre effective, then it will have to be organized.

[Letter to the *Berliner Börsen-Courier*, 8 March 1931, reprinted in the Notes to *Mann ist Mann*]

NOTE: Brecht's own production of the revised *Mann ist Mann*, with Peter Lorre as the packer Galy Gay, had opened at the Staatstheater, Berlin, a month earlier. His conception of the play had greatly altered in the four and a half years since its first production at Darmstadt, and it had a short and highly controversial run in which Lorre's performance was adversely criticized. Lorre had made his name at the Volksbühne in Wedekind's *Frühlingserwachen* (as Moritz Stiefel) and Büchner's *Dantons Tod* (as Saint-Just). At the Theater am Schiffbauerdamm he had had a great success in *Die Pioniere von Ingolstadt* and played the part of a Japanese detective (? forerunner of Mr Moto) in Brecht's production of *Happy End* (1929). Fritz Lang's film *M*, which gave him his most famous part, was released in 1932.

The three speeches referred to come in scene 9, sub-sections 4 and 5 (*Stücke II*, pp. 251–2, 255 and 266–8). The silent 16 mm. film of the production was made by Carl Koch.

18 · Indirect Impact of the Epic Theatre
(Extracts from the Notes to *Die Mutter*)

I

Written in the style of the didactic pieces, but requiring actors, *Die Mutter* is a piece of anti-metaphysical, materialistic, non-aristotelian drama. This makes nothing like such a free use as does the aristotelian of the passive empathy of the spectator; it also relates differently to certain psychological effects, such as catharsis. Just as it refrains from handing its hero over to the world as if it were his inescapable fate, so it would not dream of handing the spectator over to an inspiring theatrical experience. Anxious to teach the spectator a quite definite practical attitude, directed towards changing the world, it must begin by making him adopt in the theatre a quite different attitude from what he is used to. The following are a few of the means employed in the first production of *Die Mutter* in Berlin.

II

In the first production of *Die Mutter* the stage (Caspar Neher) was not *Indirect impact* supposed to represent any real locality: it as it were took up *of the epic stage* an attitude itself towards the incidents shown; it quoted, narrated, prepared and recalled. Its sparse indication of furniture, doors, etc. was limited to objects that had a part in the play, i.e. those without which the action would have been altered or halted. A firm arrangement of iron piping slightly higher than a man was erected at varying intervals perpendicularly to the stage; other moveable horizontal pipes carrying canvasses could be slotted into it, and this allowed of quick changes. There were doors in frames hanging inside this, which could be opened and shut. A big canvas at the back of the stage was used for the projection of texts and pictorial documents which remained throughout the scene, so that this screen was also virtually part of the setting. Thus the stage not only used allusions to show actual rooms but also texts and pictures to show the great movement of ideas in which the events were taking place. The projections are in no way pure mechanical aids in the sense of being extras, they are no *pons asinorum*; they do not set out to help the spectator but to block him; they prevent his complete empathy, interrupt his being automatically carried away. They turn the impact into an *indirect* one. Thus they are organic parts of the work of art.

IV

The epic theatre uses the simplest possible groupings, such as express the *Epic method of portrayal* event's overall sense. No more 'casual', 'life-like', 'unforced' grouping; the stage no longer reflects the 'natural' disorder of things. The opposite of natural disorder is aimed at: natural order. This order is determined from a social-historical point of view. The point of view to be adopted by the production can be made more generally intelligible, though not properly characterized, if we call it that of the genre painter and the historian.

[*Specific incidents in the second scene of the play are then listed, which were brought out by the production and presented separately*. These, says Brecht], must be portrayed as emphatically and significantly as any well-known historical episodes, though without sentimentalizing them. In this epic theatre serving a non-aristotelian type of drama the actor will at the same time do all he can to make himself observed standing between the spectator and the event. This making-oneself-observed also contributes to the desired indirect impact.

V

Here are a few examples of what epic acting brought out, as shown by the *For example: a description of the first portrayal of the Mother* actress who created the part (Helene Weigel):

1. In the first scene the actress stood in a particular characteristic attitude in the centre of the stage, and spoke the sentences as if they were in the third person; and so she not only refrained from pretending in fact to be or to claim to be Vlassova (the Mother), and in fact to be speaking those sentences, but actually prevented the spectator from transferring himself to a particular room, as habit and indifference might demand, and imagining himself to be the invisible eye-witness and eavesdropper of a unique intimate occasion. Instead what she did was

openly to introduce the spectator to the person whom he would be watching acting and being acted upon for some hours.

5. The May Day demonstration was spoken as if the participants were before a police-court, but at the end the actor playing Smilgin indicated his collapse by going down on his knees; the actress playing the Mother then stooped during her final words and picked up the flag that had slipped from his hands.

6. . . . The scene where the Mother and other workers learn to read and write is one of the most difficult for the actor. The audience's laughter at one or two sentences must not prevent him from showing how difficult learning is for the old and unadaptable, thus achieving the stature of the real historical event, the fact that a proletariat which had been exploited and restricted to physical work was able to socialize knowledge and expropriate the bourgeois intellectually. This event is not to be read 'between the lines'; it is directly stated. A lot of our actors, when something has to be stated directly in a scene, get restless and at once look there for something less direct which they can represent. They fall on whatever is 'inexpressible', between the lines, because it calls for their gifts. Such an approach makes what they can and do express seem banal, and is therefore harmful. . . .

7. The Mother has to discuss her revolutionary work with her son under the enemy's nose: she deceives the prison warder by displaying what seems to him the moving, harmless attitude of the average mother. She encourages his own harmless sympathy. So this example of a quite new and active kind of mother-love is herself exploiting her knowledge of the old familiar out-of-date kind. The actress showed that the Mother is quite aware of the humour of the situation. . . .

9. In every case she picked, out of all conceivable characteristics, those whose awareness promoted the most comprehensive political treatment of the Vlassovas (i.e. special, individual and unique ones), and such as help the Vlassovas themselves in their work. It was as if she was acting to a group of politicians—but none the less an actress for that, and within the framework of art.

VII

Is non-aristotelian drama primitive, as typified by Die Mutter?

The spectator is here considered to be faced with images of men whose originals he has to deal with – i.e. make speak and act – in real life, and cannot treat as finally and exactly determined phenomena. His duty to his fellow-men consists in ranging himself with the determining factors. In this duty the drama must support him. The determining factors, such as social background, special events, etc. must be shown as alterable. By means of a certain interchange-ability of circumstances and occurrences the spectator must be given the possibility (and duty) of assembling, experimenting and abstracting. Among the differences that distinguish individuals from each other, there are quite specific ones that interest the political being who mixes with them, struggles with them and has to deal with them (e.g. those which the leaders of the class-struggle need to know). There is no point for him in stripping a given man of all his peculiarities until he stands there as Man (with a capital M), i.e. as a being who cannot be altered further. Man has to be understood in his role as man's (the spectator's) own fate. It has to be a workable definition.

VIII

In calling for a direct impact, the aesthetics of the day call for an impact
'Direct', that flattens out all social and other distinctions between
flattening, impact individuals. Plays of the aristotelian type still manage to flatten out class conflicts in this way although the individuals themselves are becoming increasingly aware of class differences. The same result is achieved even when class conflicts are the subject of such plays, and even in cases where they take sides for a particular class. A collective entity is created in the auditorium for the *duration of the entertainment*, on the basis of the 'common humanity' shared by all spectators alike. Non-aristotelian drama of *Die Mutter*'s sort is not interested in the establishment of such an entity. It divides its audience.

X

One of the chief objections made by bourgeois criticism to non-aristotelian
Resistance to plays like *Die Mutter* is based on an equally bourgeois dis-
learning and tinction between the concepts 'entertaining' and 'instruc-
contempt for
the useful tive'. In this view *Die Mutter* is possibly instructive (if only for a small section of the potential audience, the argument goes) but definitely not entertaining (not even for this small section). There is a cer-tain pleasure to be got out of looking more closely at this distinction. Surprising as it may seem, the object is to discredit learning by presenting it as not enjoyable. But in fact of course it is enjoyment that is being dis-credited by this deliberate suggestion that one learns nothing from it. One only needs to look around and see the function allotted to learning in

bourgeois society. It amounts to the buying of materially useful items of knowledge. The purchase has to take place before the individual enters the process of production. Its field is immaturity. To admit that I am still incapable of something that is a part of my profession, in other words to allow myself to be caught learning, is equivalent to confessing that I am unfit to meet competition and that I must not be allowed credit. The man who comes to the theatre for 'entertainment' refuses to let himself be 'treated like a schoolboy' once again because he remembers the fearful torments with which 'knowledge' used to be hammered into the youth of the bourgeoisie. Libellous things are being said about the learner's attitude.

In the same way most people have taken to despising the useful and the instinct for the useful ever since men first took to making use of one another exclusively by means of underhand tricks. Nowadays utility derives only from abuse of one's fellow men.

[From *Versuche 7*, Berlin 1933. Cuts as indicated below]

NOTE: *Die Mutter*, based on Gorki's novel *Mother*, was given at the Theater am Schiffbauerdamm on 17 January 1932. These notes, taken here from the first edition of the play, were later expanded to deal also with the New York production of 1935. (See p. 81ff.) The following have been cut: Section III (texts of projections); seven episodes from the play described in Section IV; items 2–4, part of 6 and 8–14 of Section V; Section VI (Choruses); most of Section VII (newspaper criticisms and Brecht's answers); Section IX (ditto); and the last paragraph of Section X.

Typical phrases from the newspaper criticisms were 'a field-day for the like-minded, more effective than speeches and newspapers; but idiotic for the outsider', and again: As theatre and as literature – terrible. As political propaganda – worth taking seriously.' Against that the Communist Party's *Rote Fahne* (which Brecht did *not* quote) saw 'a new Bert Brecht. . . . He has not yet broken all the links that tied him to his past. He will, though. He will very soon *have* to.' This was true, though not quite in the sense in which it was meant.

A note about the original production (unsigned, but presumably by Brecht himself) was included some twenty years later in the Berliner Ensemble's volume *Theaterarbeit* (p. 332). This says that the play was performed by 'a specially constituted group of professional actors and amateurs. . . .'

The form was short, direct, agitational. The production showed some features of the agit-prop theatre of those days: the pointed, sketch-like situations, the songs and choruses directed at the audience, the threadlike dramaturgy, loosely linking scenes and songs. But although both play and production owed much to the agit-prop theatre they none the less remained distinct from it. Whereas the agit-prop theatre's task was to stimulate immediate action (e.g. a strike against a wage-cut) and was liable to be overtaken by changes in the political situation, *Die Mutter* was meant to go further and teach the tactics of the class war. Moreover play and production showed real people together with a process of development, a genuine story running through the play, such as the agit-prop theatre normally lacks. Features of the agit-prop theatre were interwoven with legitimate forms of the classical German theatre (that of the youthful Schiller, Lenz, Goethe and Büchner).

'The production of *Die Mutter*,' says a somewhat similar but undated draft note (*Schriften zum Theater 2*, p. 207), 'was sponsored by great working-class organizations. The aim was to teach certain forms of political struggle to the audience. It was addressed mainly to women. About 15,000 Berlin working-class women saw the play, which was a demonstration of methods of illegal revolutionary struggle.'

As for the play's impact on this audience, another note (*Schriften zum Theater 2*, p. 213) describes it as follows:

. . . Since the audience for some of the performances was almost entirely bourgeois, while that for others (the bulk) was purely working-class, we were able to get an exact idea of the difference between their respective reactions. It was very wide. Where the workers reacted immediately to the subtlest twists in the dialogue and fell in with the most complicated assumptions without fuss, the bourgeois audience found the course of the story hard to follow and quite missed its essence. The worker – it was the working-class women who reacted with particular liveliness – was not at all put off by the extreme dryness and compression with which the various situations were sketched, but at once concentrated on the essential, on how the characters behaved in them. His reaction was in fact a political one from the first. The West-ender sat with so bored and stupid a smile as to seem positively comic; he missed the emotional embroidery and embellishment. he was used to . . .

The term 'agit-prop' derives from the Soviet Communist Party's Agitation and Propaganda department, which had performed short agitational sketches to the Red Army during the Revolution. Agit-prop groups in Germany were particularly active at this time, thanks partly to the squeezing out of the Socialists from the workers' theatrical organization (Deutscher Arbeitertheaterbund) and partly to the need to counteract the increasingly reactionary policy of the established theatres. According to Werner Hecht (*Brecht's Weg zum epischen Theater*, p. 151) Germany had over two hundred such groups in 1930.

A year after this production Hitler became Chancellor. There was no Communist revolution and no attempt at armed opposition. The Reichstag building burned down on 27 February 1933. Brecht left Germany the next day, and remained in exile until after the Second World War.

Part 2

1933-1947
(Exile: Scandinavia, U.S.A.)

If you want me to talk about the theatre it will be rather a one-sided picture. I can tell you about my ideas – I can talk about my own work just as an engineer can talk about his – but as for what other people are doing I'm not properly informed. I don't know of any modern school of playwriting; I've heard of one or two playwrights but not of any that count. The major talents aren't concerned to write for the theatre. The whole thing is stationary; we're stuck where we are.

In Germany we had great advantages: the great sums of money we were able to work with. We could always experiment and develop, because we were backed by private capital. But we came to an end long before the real collapse. Already the reaction was too strong, and our audience had lost their money. Besides, it's no more possible in the theatre than anywhere else to carry out really radical and epoch-making experiments without state subsidy, and that's something we didn't have.

I don't think there's any new school of playwriting outside Germany. At least there's none that has made its mark, and nobody in England or France is going to invest in a new and revolutionary playwright, even if he can find one, so long as the theatre remains in its present state. In Russia there's one man who's working along the right lines, Tretiakov; a play like *Roar China* shows him to have found quite new means of expression. He has the ability, and he's working steadily on. Meyerhold produced this play in Berlin with the whole Moscow Art Theatre Company before I left. There were also one or two other people trying to strike out in new directions who are hardly known here. Bruckner among others has made interesting experiments in the application of psychoanalytic theory to the stage; his *Elizabeth of England* and *Verbrecher* have been staged in Copenhagen.

Otherwise the real front-line battles were fought out mainly by Piscator, whose Theater am Nollendorfplatz was based on Marxist principles, and by myself at my Theater am Schiffbauerdamm. We denied ourselves nothing. We wrote our own texts – and I also wrote plays – or sliced up other people's in all directions, then stuck them together quite differently till they were unrecognizable. We introduced music and film and turned everything top to bottom; we made comedy out of what had originally been tragic, and vice versa. We had our characters bursting into song at the most uncalled-for moments. In short we thoroughly muddled up people's idea of the drama.

I myself took part in it all. I spent many years training my actors; I had my own composers who knew how to write exactly in my style: Eisler, Kurt

Weill and Hindemith (who was the best known). But then I was one of the few modern German playwrights who knew their way about the theatre. Most members of this profession never set foot on a stage; but I've learnt my business from the bottom, having been a producer long before any of my plays was staged. I can build a set and at a pinch take charge of my own lighting. But it's an effort, particularly when you come up against such disastrous shortcomings on the technical side as Piscator and I did. The lies collapsed when heavy objects were hung from them, the stage broke through when we put weights on it, the motors driving the various essential machinery made too much noise.

But we put our schemes into effect. We built planes at various levels on the stage, and often made them move up or down. Piscator liked to include a kind of broad treadmill in the stage, with another one rotating in the opposite direction; these would bring on his characters. Or he would hoist his actors up and down in space; now and again they would break a leg, but we were patient with them.

But then of course we had to make use of complicated machinery if we were to show modern processes on the stage. E.g. there was a play called *Petroleum*, originally written by Leo Lania but adapted by us, in which we wanted to show exactly how oil is drilled and treated. The people here were quite secondary; they were just cyphers serving a cause. And we performed a number of other plays which needed quite as complex apparatus, though it differed in each case: plays by Ernst Toller, Fleisser and myself. There was one production where Piscator adopted an entirely different method, partly for economic reasons. He staged a play called *Section 218* (this being the section of the law dealing with abortion) using a highly simplified technique. It was a huge success, but he himself didn't like it at all. As its producer he was like a bacteriologist whose microscope had been taken away from him.

Then he went gloomily off to Moscow to make films.

I don't think the traditional form of theatre means anything any longer. Its significance is purely historic; it can illuminate the way in which earlier ages regarded human relationships, and particularly relationships between men and women. Works by such people as Ibsen and Strindberg remain important historical documents, but they no longer move anybody. A modern spectator can't learn anything from them.

In modern society the motions of the individual psyche are utterly uninteresting; it was only in feudal times that a king's or a leader's passions meant anything. Today they don't. Not even Hitler's personal passions; that's not what has brought Germany to her present condition, worse luck.

Far more than he himself imagines he is the tool and not the guiding hand.

So the theatre has outlived its usefulness; it is no more able to represent modern phenomena and processes with the means available to it than the traditional kind of novelist can describe such everyday occurrences as housing shortage, export of pigs or speculation in coffee. Seen through its eyes, a little middling business man who despite all his care and effort loses his money through an unlucky stroke of business would inevitably become a 'speculator'. He would 'go bankrupt', just like that, without comment, and it would be a kind of inexplicable blow of fate, much as if a man had been struck down by pneumonia.

No, in its own field the theatre must keep up with the times and all the advances of the times, and not lag several thousand miles behind as it does at present. In the old days there was no more need for the artist to bother about science than for science to concern itself with him. But now he has to, for science has progressed so much further. Look at an aeroplane, then look at a theatrical performance. People have acquired new motives for their actions; science has found new dimensions by which to measure them; it's time for art to find new expressions.

Our time has seen amazing developments in all the sciences. We have acquired an entirely new psychology: viz. the American Dr Watson's Behaviourism. While other psychologists were proposing introspective investigation of the psyche in depth, twisting and bending human nature, this philosophy based itself solely on the human psyche's outward effects: on people's behaviour. Its theories have something in common with American business life, with the whole of modern advertising. Salesmen all over the world are trained according to its principles to influence their customers' behaviour; they learn by rule of thumb how to provide new needs for their fellow men. (Example: a man goes into a showroom, mildly infected, and comes out, severely ill, in possession of a motor-car.)

Such is our time, and the theatre must be acquainted with it and go along with it, and work out an entirely new sort of art such as will be capable of influencing modern people. The main subject of the drama must be relationships between one man and another as they exist today, and that is what I'm primarily concerned to investigate and find means of expression for. Once I've found out what modes of behaviour are most useful to the human race I show them to people and underline them. I show them in parables: if you act this way the following will happen, but if you act like that then the opposite will take place. This isn't the same thing as committed art. At most paedagogics.

But ever since the days of Bacon, the great pioneer of practical thinking, people have worked to find out how man can improve his condition, and today we know that he cannot do this purely privately. It's only by banding together and joining forces that he stands a chance. Once I take that into consideration my plays are forced to deal with political matters. Thus when a family is ruined I don't seek the reason in an inexorable fate, in hereditary weaknesses or special characteristics – it isn't only the exceptional families that get ruined – but try rather to establish how it could have been avoided by human action, how the external conditions could be altered; and that lands me back in politics again. I don't mean that all playwriting ought to be political propaganda, but I do feel that one shouldn't be satisfied with just one way of writing plays. There should be several different sorts for different purposes.

All this demands a new and special technique, and I'm not the only writer to have tried to create it. People like Georg Kaiser and his follower O'Neill have successfully applied quite new methods which are good and interesting even if their ideas don't coincide with my own. In the same way Paul Claudel in France, a severe and reactionary writer, is an original dramatist of great stature. In such ways people who have nothing new in mind have none the less done pioneering work for the new technique.

Of course those actors whom we employ have also to use a special method of representation. We need to get right away from the old naturalistic school of acting, the dramatic school with its large emotions: the school followed by people like Jannings, Poul Reumert, in short by the majority. This isn't the kind of representation that can express our time; it isn't going to sway a purely modern audience. For that one has to apply the only form of acting that I find natural: the epic, story-telling kind. It's the kind the Chinese have been using for thousands of years: among modern actors Chaplin is one of its masters.

This was the kind of acting that was always used in our theatres; you in Denmark may know a bit what I mean from *The Threepenny Opera*. The actor doesn't have to *be* the man he portrays. He has to describe his character just as it would be described in a book. If Chaplin were to play Napoleon he wouldn't even look like him; he would show objectively and critically how Napoleon would behave in the various situations the author might put him in. In my view the great comedians have always been the best character actors.

Does that give you some slight impression of my ideas? Then please end up by saying that I don't think Fascism is going to be able to put a stop to the natural development of the younger German school of playwriting, though heaven knows where it will be carried on.

[From *Exstrabladet*, Copenhagen, 20 March 1934, quoted by Helge Hultberg in *Die ästhetischen Anschauungen Bertolt Brechts*, Copenhagen 1962]

NOTE: The interviewer here was Luth Otto and the words, translated into Danish and back into German, are hardly Brecht's. One or two evident misprints have been corrected, but mistakes like the identification of Meyerhold's theatre with the Moscow Art Theatre, the misnaming of Lania's *Konjunktur* and the reference to 'my' Theater am Schiffbauerdamm have been allowed to stand. Helge Hultberg also queries Brecht's claim to have been a producer 'long before any of my plays were staged', but this seems more an exaggeration than an inaccuracy. Brecht was in fact engaged practically in the theatre for at least a year before *Trommeln in der Nacht* was put on, taking part notably (if only temporarily) in the production of Bronnen's *Vatermord* for the Berlin 'Junge Bühne' in spring 1922.

At the time of the interview Brecht had settled in Denmark, where the writer Karin Michaelis had lent him a house. He remained there till 1939, presently moving to a house of his own at Skovsbostrand near Svendborg.

Poul Reumert, the Danish actor, is referred to again on p. 141. His book *Teatrets Kunst* was published in Copenhagen in 1963.

Plays staged at the Theater am Schiffbauerdamm under E. J. Aufricht's management included *The Threepenny Opera* and *Happy End* and Marieluise Fleisser's *Die Pioniere von Ingolstadt*. *§218* was by Carl Credé.

20 · Theatre for Pleasure or Theatre for Instruction

A few years back, anybody talking about the modern theatre meant the theatre in Moscow, New York and Berlin. He might have thrown in a mention of one of Jouvet's productions in Paris or Cochran's in London, or *The Dybbuk* as given by the Habima (which is to all intents and purposes part of the Russian theatre, since Vakhtangov was its director). But broadly speaking there were only three capitals so far as modern theatre was concerned.

Russian, American and German theatres differed widely from one another, but were alike in being modern, that is to say in introducing technical and artistic innovations. In a sense they even achieved a certain stylistic resemblance, probably because technology is international (not just that part which is directly applied to the stage but also that which influences it, the film for instance), and because large progressive cities in large industrial countries are involved. Among the older capitalist countries it is the Berlin theatre that seemed of late to be in the lead. For a period all that is common to the modern theatre received its strongest and (so far) maturest expression there.

The Berlin theatre's last phase was the so-called epic theatre, and it showed the modern theatre's trend of development in its purest form. Whatever was labelled '*Zeitstück*' or '*Piscatorbühne*' or '*Lehrstück*' belongs to the epic theatre.

THE EPIC THEATRE

Many people imagine that the term 'epic theatre' is self-contradictory, as the epic and dramatic ways of narrating a story are held, following Aristotle, to be basically distinct. The difference between the two forms was never thought simply to lie in the fact that the one is performed by living beings while the other operates via the written word; epic works such as those of Homer and the medieval singers were at the same time theatrical performances, while dramas like Goethe's *Faust* and Byron's *Manfred* are agreed to have been more effective as books. Thus even by Aristotle's definition the difference between the dramatic and epic forms was attributed to their different methods of construction, whose laws were dealt with by two different branches of aesthetics. The method of construction depended on the different way of presenting the work to the public, sometimes via the stage, sometimes through a book; and independently of that there was the 'dramatic element' in epic works and the 'epic element' in dramatic. The bourgeois novel in the last century developed much that was 'dramatic', by which was meant the strong centralization of the story, a momentum that drew the separate parts into a common relationship. A particular passion of utterance, a certain emphasis on the clash of forces are hallmarks of the 'dramatic'. The epic writer Döblin provided an excellent criterion when he said that with an epic work, as opposed to a dramatic, one can as it were take a pair of scissors and cut it into individual pieces, which remain fully capable of life.

This is no place to explain how the opposition of epic and dramatic lost its rigidity after having long been held to be irreconcilable. Let us just point out that the technical advances alone were enough to permit the stage to incorporate an element of narrative in its dramatic productions. The possibility of projections, the greater adaptability of the stage due to mechanization, the film, all completed the theatre's equipment, and did so at a point where the most important transactions between people could no longer be shown simply by personifying the motive forces or subjecting the characters to invisible metaphysical powers.

To make these transactions intelligible the environment in which the people lived had to be brought to bear in a big and 'significant' way.

This environment had of course been shown in the existing drama, but only as seen from the central figure's point of view, and not as an independent element. It was defined by the hero's reactions to it. It was seen as a storm can be seen when one sees the ships on a sheet of water unfolding their sails, and the sails filling out. In the epic theatre it was to appear standing on its own.

The stage began to tell a story. The narrator was no longer missing, along with the fourth wall. Not only did the background adopt an attitude to the events on the stage – by big screens recalling other simultaneous events elsewhere, by projecting documents which confirmed or contradicted what the characters said, by concrete and intelligible figures to accompany abstract conversations, by figures and sentences to support mimed transactions whose sense was unclear – but the actors too refrained from going over wholly into their role, remaining detached from the character they were playing and clearly inviting criticism of him.

The spectator was no longer in any way allowed to submit to an experience uncritically (and without practical consequences) by means of simple empathy with the characters in a play. The production took the subject-matter and the incidents shown and put them through a process of alienation: the alienation that is necessary to all understanding. When something seems 'the most obvious thing in the world' it means that any attempt to understand the world has been given up.

What is 'natural' must have the force of what is startling. This is the only way to expose the laws of cause and effect. People's activity must simultaneously be so and be capable of being different.

It was all a great change.

The dramatic theatre's spectator says: Yes, I have felt like that too – Just like me – It's only natural – It'll never change – The sufferings of this man appal me, because they are inescapable – That's great art; it all seems the most obvious thing in the world – I weep when they weep, I laugh when they laugh.

The epic theatre's spectator says: I'd never have thought it – That's not the way – That's extraordinary, hardly believable – It's got to stop – The sufferings of this man appal me, because they are unnecessary – That's great art: nothing obvious in it – I laugh when they weep, I weep when they laugh.

THE INSTRUCTIVE THEATRE

The stage began to be instructive.

Oil, inflation, war, social struggles, the family, religion, wheat, the meat market, all became subjects for theatrical representation. Choruses enlightened the spectator about facts unknown to him. Films showed a montage of events from all over the world. Projections added statistical material. And as the 'background' came to the front of the stage so people's activity was subjected to criticism. Right and wrong courses of action were shown. People were shown who knew what they were doing, and others who did not. The theatre became an affair for philosophers, but only for such philosophers as wished not just to explain the world but also to change it. So we had philosophy, and we had instruction. And where was the amusement in all that? Were they sending us back to school, teaching us to read and write? Were we supposed to pass exams, work for diplomas?

Generally there is felt to be a very sharp distinction between learning and amusing oneself. The first may be useful, but only the second is pleasant. So we have to defend the epic theatre against the suspicion that it is a highly disagreeable, humourless, indeed strenuous affair.

Well: all that can be said is that the contrast between learning and amusing oneself is not laid down by divine rule; it is not one that has always been and must continue to be.

Undoubtedly there is much that is tedious about the kind of learning familiar to us from school, from our professional training, etc. But it must be remembered under what conditions and to what end that takes place.

It is really a commercial transaction. Knowledge is just a commodity. It is acquired in order to be resold. All those who have grown out of going to school have to do their learning virtually in secret, for anyone who admits that he still has something to learn devalues himself as a man whose knowledge is inadequate. Moreover the usefulness of learning is very much limited by factors outside the learner's control. There is unemployment, for instance, against which no knowledge can protect one. There is the division of labour, which makes generalized knowledge unnecessary and impossible. Learning is often among the concerns of those whom no amount of concern will get any forwarder. There is not much knowledge that leads to power, but plenty of knowledge to which only power can lead.

Learning has a very different function for different social strata. There are strata who cannot imagine any improvement in conditions: they find the conditions good enough for them. Whatever happens to oil they will benefit from it. And: they feel the years beginning to tell. There can't be all that many years more. What is the point of learning a lot now? They have said their final word: a grunt. But there are also strata 'waiting their turn' who are discontented with conditions, have a vast interest in the practical side of learning, want at all costs to find out where they stand, and know that they are lost without learning; these are the best and keenest learners. Similar differences apply to countries and peoples. Thus the pleasure of learning depends on all sorts of things; but none the less there is such a thing as pleasurable learning, cheerful and militant learning.

If there were not such amusement to be had from learning the theatre's whole structure would unfit it for teaching.

Theatre remains theatre even when it is instructive theatre, and in so far as it is good theatre it will amuse.

THEATRE AND KNOWLEDGE

But what has knowledge got to do with art? We know that knowledge can be amusing, but not everything that is amusing belongs in the theatre.

I have often been told, when pointing out the invaluable services that modern knowledge and science, if properly applied, can perform for art and specially for the theatre, that art and knowledge are two estimable but wholly distinct fields of human activity. This is a fearful truism, of course, and it is as well to agree quickly that, like most truisms, it is perfectly true. Art and science work in quite different ways: agreed. But, bad as it may sound, I have to admit that I cannot get along as an artist without the use of one or two sciences. This may well arouse serious doubts as to my artistic capacities. People are used to seeing poets as unique and slightly unnatural beings who reveal with a truly godlike assurance things that other people can only recognize after much sweat and toil. It is naturally distasteful to have to admit that one does not belong to this select band. All the same, it must be admitted. It must at the same time be made clear that the scientific occupations just confessed to are not pardonable side interests, pursued on days off after a good week's work. We all know how Goethe was interested in natural history, Schiller in history: as a kind of hobby, it is charitable to assume. I have no wish promptly to accuse these two of having needed these sciences for their poetic activity; I am not trying to shelter behind them; but I must say that I do need the sciences. I have to admit, however, that I look askance at all sorts of people who I know do not operate on the level of scientific understanding: that is to say, who sing as the birds sing, or as people imagine the birds to sing. I don't mean by that that I would reject a charming poem about the taste of fried fish or the delights of a boating party just because the writer had not studied gastronomy or navigation. But in my view the great and complicated things that go on in the world cannot be adequately recognized by people who do not use every possible aid to understanding.

Let us suppose that great passions or great events have to be shown which influence the fate of nations. The lust for power is nowadays held to be such a passion. Given that a poet 'feels' this lust and wants to have someone strive for power, how is he to show the exceedingly complicated machinery within which the struggle for power nowadays takes place? If his hero is a politician, how do politics work? If he is a business man, how does business work? And yet there are writers who find business and politics nothing like so passionately interesting as the individual's lust for power. How are they to acquire the necessary knowledge? They are scarcely likely to learn enough by going round and keeping their eyes open, though even then it is more than they would get by just rolling their eyes in an exalted frenzy. The foundation of a paper like the *Völkischer Beobachter* or a business like Standard Oil is a pretty complicated affair, and such things cannot be conveyed just like that. One important field for the playwright is psychology. It is taken for granted that a poet, if not an ordinary man, must be able without further instruction to discover the motives that lead a man to commit murder; he must be able to give a picture of a murderer's mental state 'from within himself'. It is taken for granted that one only has to look inside oneself in such a case; and then there's always one's imagination. . . . There are various reasons why I can no longer surrender to this agreeable hope of getting a result quite so simply. I can no longer find in myself all those motives which the press or scientific reports show to have been observed in people. Like the average judge when pronouncing sentence, I cannot without further ado conjure up an adequate picture of a murderer's mental state. Modern psychology, from psychoanalysis to behaviourism, acquaints me with facts that lead me to judge the case quite differently, especially if I bear in mind the findings of sociology and do not overlook economics and history. You will say: but that's getting complicated. I have to answer that it *is* complicated. Even if you let yourself be convinced, and agree with me that a large slice of literature is exceedingly primitive, you may still ask with profound concern: won't an evening in such a theatre be a most alarming affair? The answer to that is: no.

Whatever knowledge is embodied in a piece of poetic writing has to be wholly transmuted into poetry. Its utilization fulfils the very pleasure that the poetic element provokes. If it does not at the same time fulfil that which is fulfilled by the scientific element, none the less in an age of great discoveries and inventions one must have a certain inclination to penetrate deeper into things – a desire to make the world controllable – if one is to to be sure of enjoying its poetry.

IS THE EPIC THEATRE SOME KIND OF 'MORAL INSTITUTION'?

According to Friedrich Schiller the theatre is supposed to be a moral institution. In making this demand it hardly occurred to Schiller that by moralizing from the stage he might drive the audience out of the theatre. Audiences had no objection to moralizing in his day. It was only later that Friedrich Nietzsche attacked him for blowing a moral trumpet. To Nietzsche any concern with morality was a depressing affair; to Schiller it seemed thoroughly enjoyable. He knew of nothing that could give greater amusement and satisfaction than the propagation of ideas. The bourgeoisie was setting about forming the ideas of the nation.

Putting one's house in order, patting oneself on the back, submitting one's account, is something highly agreeable. But describing the collapse of one's house, having pains in the back, paying one's account, is indeed a depressing affair, and that was how Friedrich Nietzsche saw things a century later. He was poorly disposed towards morality, and thus towards the previous Friedrich too.

The epic theatre was likewise often objected to as moralizing too much. Yet in the epic theatre moral arguments only took second place. Its aim was less to moralize than to observe. That is to say it observed, and then the thick end of the wedge followed: the story's moral. Of course we cannot pretend that we started our observations out of a pure passion for observing and without any more practical motive, only to be completely staggered by their results. Undoubtedly there were some painful discrepancies in our environment, circumstances that were barely tolerable, and this not merely on account of moral considerations. It is not only moral considerations that make hunger, cold and oppression hard to bear. Similarly the object of our inquiries was not just to arouse moral objections to such circumstances (even though they could easily be felt – though not by all the audience alike; such objections were seldom for instance felt by those who profited by the circumstances in question) but to discover means for their elimination. We were not in fact speaking in the name of morality but in that of the victims. These truly are two distinct matters, for the victims are often told that they ought to be contented with their lot, for moral reasons. Moralists of this sort see man as existing for morality, not morality for man. At least it should be possible to gather from the above to what degree and in what sense the epic theatre is a moral institution.

CAN EPIC THEATRE BE PLAYED ANYWHERE?

Stylistically speaking, there is nothing all that new about the epic theatre. Its expository character and its emphasis on virtuosity bring it close to the old Asiatic theatre. Didactic tendencies are to be found in the medieval mystery plays and the classical Spanish theatre, and also in the theatre of the Jesuits.

These theatrical forms corresponded to particular trends of their time, and vanished with them. Similarly the modern epic theatre is linked with certain trends. It cannot by any means be practised universally. Most of the great nations today are not disposed to use the theatre for ventilating their problems. London, Paris, Tokyo and Rome maintain their theatres for quite different purposes. Up to now favourable circumstances for an epic and didactic theatre have only been found in a few places and for a short period of time. In Berlin Fascism put a very definite stop to the development of such a theatre.

It demands not only a certain technological level but a powerful movement in society which is interested to see vital questions freely aired with a view to their solution, and can defend this interest against every contrary trend.

The epic theatre is the broadest and most far-reaching attempt at large-scale modern theatre, and it has all those immense difficulties to overcome that always confront the vital forces in the sphere of politics, philosophy, science and art.

['Vergnügungstheater oder Lehrtheater?', from
Schriften zum Theater, 1957]

NOTE: This essay was unpublished in Brecht's lifetime, and its exact date and purpose are unknown. Dr Unseld, editing it for *Schriften zum Theater*, suggested that it was written 'about 1936'. Brecht's bibliographer Mr Walter Nubel thinks that notes or drafts may have existed earlier. Unlike the items that follow, it bears no evidence of Brecht's visits to Moscow and New York during 1935, and it is tempting to think of it as having been prepared for one of these, for instance as a possible contribution to that conference of producers to which Piscator invited Brecht in Moscow: what he called (in a letter of 27 January 1935, in the Brecht-Archiv) 'collecting a few good people for a constructive discussion'.

This was to take place in April, and there are fragments of a 'Brecht-Piscator conversation' in the Brecht-Archiv (334/04-05) which evidently date from then. In these Piscator is seen referring to productions by Okhlopkhov (*Aristocrats* and Serafimovitch's *Iron Stream*) and Meyerhold (*La Dame aux Camélias* and a programme of one-act plays by Tchekov), while Brecht mentions the plans for a '*Total-Theater*' which Piscator had had drawn up by Walter Gropius before 1933. So far as the present essay goes, however, all that can really be said is that some of its arguments and actual words are also to be found in the next piece.

The term here translated as 'alienation' is *Entfremdung* as used by Hegel and Marx, and not the *Verfremdung* which Brecht himself was soon to coin and make famous. The former also occurs in a short note (*Schriften zum Theater 3*, pp. 196-7) called 'Episches Theater, Entfremdung', which refers to the need for any situation to be 'alienated' if it is to be seen socially. Alfred Döblin, the friend of Brecht's referred to early in the essay, wrote *Die drei Sprünge des Wang-lun*, *Berlin Alexanderplatz* and other novels which critics of the time likened to Joyce and Dos Passos. He too was interested in the theory of epic form. The *Völkischer Beobachter* was the chief Nazi daily paper.

21 · The German Drama: pre-Hitler

The years after the World War saw the German theatre in a period of a great flowering. We had more great actors than at any other time. There were quite a number of prominent régisseurs, or directors, such as Reinhardt, Jessner, Engel, and so on, who competed sharply and interestingly with one another. Almost all plays of world literature, from *Oedipus* to *Les Affaires sont les Affaires*, from the Chinese *Chalk Circle* to Strindberg's *Miss Julie*, could be played. And they were played.

Nevertheless, for us young people the theatre had one serious flaw. Neither its highly developed stage technique nor its dramaturgy permitted us to present on the stage the great themes of our times; as, for example, the building-up of a mammoth industry, the conflict of classes, war, the fight against disease, and so on. These things could not be presented, at least not in an adequate manner. Of course, a stock exchange could be, and was, shown on the stage, or trenches, or clinics. But they formed nothing but effective background for a sort of sentimental 'magazine story' that could have taken place at any other time, though in the great periods of the theatre they would not have been found worthy of being shown on the stage. The development of the theatre so that it could master the presentation of modern events and themes, and overcome the problems of showing them, was brought about only with great labour.

One thing that helped solve the problem was the 'electrification' of the mechanics of staging plays. Within a few years after this problem of developing the modern stage had made itself felt among us, Piscator, who without doubt is one of the most important theatre men of all times, began to transform its scenic potentialities. He introduced a number of far-reaching innovations.

One of them was his use of the film and of film projections as an integral part of the settings. The setting was thus awakened to life and began to play on its own, so to speak; the film was a new, gigantic actor that helped to narrate events. By means of it documents could be shown as part of the scenic background, figures and statistics. Simultaneous events in different places could be seen together. For example, while a fight was going on between two characters for the possession of an Albanian oilfield, one could see on the screen in the background warships being launched in preparation for putting that oilfield out of commission entirely.

This was great progress. Another innovation was the introduction of moving platforms on the stage. On these moving bands that traversed the stage we played, for example, *The Good Soldier Schweik* and his famous march to Budweis, which took a half-hour and which was made great and entertaining by the actor Max Pallenberg. Pallenberg had to leave Germany at the beginning of the Third Reich and has since died. The elevator-stage on which *Der Kaufmann von Berlin* was performed made vertical action on the stage possible. New facilities for staging allowed the use of musical and graphic elements which the theatre up to this time had not been able to employ. These inspired composers of rank to write music for the theatre. The great cartoonist George Grosz made valuable contributions for the projections. His drawings for the performance of *Schweik* were published by the Malik Verlag in Berlin.

We made many experiments. I can tell of some of my own work, as I know that best. We organized small collectives of specialists in various fields to 'make' the plays; among these specialists were historians and sociologists as well as playwrights, actors and other people of the theatre. I had begun to work upon theories and experiments in a non-aristotelian drama. Some of the theories I have put down in fragments in the seven volumes of *Versuche* which were published by Gustav Kiepenheuer in Berlin. This dramaturgy does not make use of the 'identification' of the spectator with the play, as does the aristotelian, and has a different point of view also towards other psychological effects a play may have on an audience, as, for example, towards the 'catharsis'. Catharsis is not the main object of this dramaturgy.

It does not make the hero the victim of an inevitable fate, nor does it wish to make the spectator the victim, so to speak, of a hypnotic experience in the theatre. In fact, it has as a purpose the 'teaching' of the spectator a certain quite practical attitude; we have to make it possible for him to take a critical attitude while he is in the theatre (as opposed to a subjective attitude of becoming completely 'entangled' in what is going on). Some of my plays of this type of dramaturgy are *St Joan of the Stockyards*, *Mann ist Mann*, and *Die Rundköpfe und die Spitzköpfe*.

Non-aristotelian dramaturgy also investigated the field of the opera. One result of this investigation was the opera *The Rise and Fall of the City of Mahagonny*, which I wrote and to which Kurt Weill wrote the music. Theoretical comments concerning this opera may be found in the second volume of the *Versuche*. Another was *The Threepenny Opera*, which again I wrote with Weill.

At the same time, the training of a whole generation of young actors for the new style of acting, the epic style, took place. Many of these worked with us in various theatres in Berlin. The beginning of the Third Reich scattered these actors all over the world. Oskar Homolka and Fritz Kortner are in London, Carola Neher is in Moscow, and so are Alexander Granach and Ernst Busch. Helene Weigel is in Copenhagen, Peter Lorre is in Hollywood and London, Lotte Lenya (Mrs Kurt Weill) is in Zurich, and, I hear, will soon be in New York. Some of them played in the Berlin production of *Die Mutter*.

At this time, too, another series of experiments that made use of theatrical effects but that often did not need the stage in the old sense was undertaken and led to certain results. These led to the 'Lehrstücke', for which the nearest English equivalent I can find is the 'learning-play'.

Die Mutter is such a learning-play, and embodies certain principles and methods of presentation of the non-aristotelian, or epic style, as I have sometimes called it; the use of the film projection to help bring the social complex of the events taking place to the forefront; the use of music and of the chorus to supplement and vivify the action on the stage; the setting forth of actions so as to call for a critical approach, so that they would not be taken for granted by the spectator and would arouse him to think; it became obvious to him which were right actions and which were wrong ones.

Briefly, the aristotelian play is essentially static; its task is to show the world as it is. The learning-play is essentially dynamic; its task is to show the world as it changes (and also how it may be changed). It is a common truism among the producers and writers of the former type of play that the audience, once it is in the theatre, is not a number of individuals but a collective individual, a mob, which must be and can be reached only through its emotions; that it has the mental immaturity and the high emotional suggestibility of a mob. We have often seen this pointed out in treatises on the writing and production of plays. The latter theatre holds that the audience is a collection of individuals, capable of thinking and of reasoning, of making judgments even in the theatre; it treats it as individuals of mental and emotional maturity, and believes it wishes to be so regarded.

With the learning-play, then, the stage begins to be didactic. (A word of which I, as a man of many years of experience in the theatre, am not afraid.) The theatre becomes a place for philosophers, and for such philosophers as not only wish to explain the world but wish to change it.

[*Brecht then repeats p. 72, lines 8–19, and p. 73, lines 4–5*]

If there were not such entertaining learning, then the entire theatre would not be able to instruct. For theatre remains theatre even while it is didactic, and as long as it is good theatre it is also entertaining. In Germany, philosophers discussed these learning-plays, and plain people saw them and enjoyed them, and also discussed them.

I learned from these discussions. I feel myself I must still, must always, learn. From what I learned from the audiences that saw it, I rewrote *Mann ist Mann* ten times, and presented it at different times in different ways – for example, in Darmstadt in 1926, at the Berlin Volksbühne in 1927, at the Berlin Staatstheater in 1929. In studying an interesting book we must 'look back', we reread passages in order to grasp them entirely, and so too in the theatre. Revisiting a play is like rereading a page of a book. Once we know the contents of it, we can judge more closely of its meaning, of its acting, and so on. [. . .]

For some years, in carrying out my experiments, I tried, with a small staff of collaborators, to work outside the theatre, which, having for so long been forced to 'sell' an evening's entertainment, had retreated into too inflexible limits for such experiments; we tried a type of theatrical performance that could influence the thinking of all the people engaged in it. We worked with different means and in different strata of society. These experiments were theatrical performances meant not so much for the spectator as for those who were engaged in the performance. It was, so to speak, art for the producer, not art for the consumer.

I wrote, for example, plays for schools, and small operas. The *Jasager* was one of them. These plays could be performed by students. Another of these plays was *Der Lindberghflug*, a play that called for the collaboration of the schools with the radio. The radio broadcast into the schools the accompanying orchestral music and solo parts, while the classes in the schools sang the choruses and did the minor roles. For this piece Hindemith and Weill wrote music. It was done at the Baden-Baden Music Festival in 1929. The *Badener Lehrstück* is for men and women choruses, and uses also the film and clowns as performers. The music is by Hindemith. *Versuch* 12 was a learning play, *Die Massnahme*. Several workers' choruses joined in performing it. The chorus consisted of 400 singers, while several prominent actors played the solo parts. The music was by Hanns Eisler.

I might add that the experiments that we undertook at the Nollendorf Theatre and at the Schiffbauerdamm Theatre alone cost more than half a million dollars, though some plays, like *Schweik,* had continuous runs of more than six months, and *The Threepenny Opera* played for more than a year continuously, so much time and money indeed did the special machinery and the dramaturgical laboratories for these experiments need.

[From *The New York Times,* November 24, 1935, Section 9, page 1]

NOTE: There is a partial German text, written in the third person, in *Schriften zum Theater 3,* pp. 16–21. The (anonymous) translation has been slightly amended, especially with regard to titles and proper names.

Brecht had arrived in New York in mid-October. An introductory note says: 'The author of the following adapted the Theatre Union's *Mother* from the Gorki novel.' The production had opened five days earlier.

Of the actors mentioned, Carola Neher – no relation of the designer – disappeared with her husband in the USSR about 1938; it is uncertain whether she was executed or died in gaol. Alexander Granach went to Hollywood, and died in May 1945. Ernst Busch was interned in France after taking part in the Spanish war, was then handed over to the Nazis and put in a concentration camp. He is today acting with the Deutsches Theater in East Berlin, and (as guest artist) with the Berliner Ensemble. (See p. 265.) The *Chalk Circle* in Klabund's adaptation was produced by Reinhardt in October 1925; Walter Mehring's *Der Kaufmann von Berlin* by Piscator at the Theater am Nollendorfplatz on 3 September 1929, in a remarkable setting by Moholy-Nagy.

22 · Criticism of the New York Production of Die Mutter

The Theatre Union's production of the play *Mother* represents an attempt to acquaint New York workers with a hitherto unfamiliar type of play. Deriving from a non-aristotelian drama which makes use of a new, epic kind of theatre, this applies two techniques: that of the fully-evolved bourgeois theatre, and at the same time that of those small proletarian dramatic groups which worked out a novel and individual style for their own proletarian ends in Germany after the [1918] Revolution. It is unfamiliar not only to the audience but to the actors, directors and adaptors as well. Its direction requires special kinds of political knowledge and artistic capacity such as are unnecessary for the production of plays of a familiar type.

If *any* theatre is capable of going ahead of its public instead of running after it, then it is the theatre of the working class. But going ahead does not mean excluding the public from a share in what is produced. Our theatres ought to do far more than they do to organize the supervision of production by the most politically and culturally developed sections of their public. A whole series of questions that arose during the production of *Mother* could have been solved by a collaboration with the workers that would have been simple to organize. Politically-educated workers, for instance, would never have accepted the theatre's view that the big (though only seven-minute-long) anti-war propaganda scene in the third act must at all costs be cut, on the grounds that limiting the play to two hours was all-important to the public. They would at once have said: but that means having a scene (XII) which shows how the Bolshevik programme was rejected by the great bulk of the proletariat in 1914, then having the 1917 Revolution (XIV) follow immediately on it like a passively-awaited gift from heaven. It must be shown that such changes are only brought about by revolutionary work, and it must be shown how this is to be carried out. Arguing thus they would incidentally have saved the aesthetic structure of the third act, which was wrecked by the ill-conceived cutting of its main scene.

Drama of the *Mother* type both demands and permits a far higher degree of freedom for the sister arts, namely music and stage design, than any other type of play. We were extremely surprised to see the excellent designer given so little chance to carry out his aims. He had no say in the grouping and positioning of the actors, nor was he consulted about the costumes. The last-minute Russianizing of the costumes – a politically dubious operation, since it evoked a picture-book atmosphere and gave exotic local colour to the revolutionary workers' activities – was decided without his being asked.

Even the lighting was planned without him. His construction allowed the lighting mechanism and the music mechanism to be plainly seen. But as the pianos were not illuminated during the musical numbers it looked as though there had merely been no room for them anywhere else. ('But I was thinking of a plan/To dye one's whiskers green,/And always use so large a fan/ That they could not be seen ') The lighting tricks of a theatre dedicated to illusion were applied in a theatre designed to break illusion: we had an atmospheric October evening light intruding on simple walls and mechanisms which aimed at quite different effects. Eisler experienced the same treatment with his music. Because the director felt that the singers' groupings and gests were not the composer's business, some numbers were stripped of their effect by a distortion of the political sense. The chorus 'Die Partei ist in Gefahr' upset the whole production. Instead of placing the singer (or singers) near the musical apparatus or else offstage the director had the singers burst into the room when the mother lay ill, inviting her with emphatic gestures to come to the Party's aid. The individual's feeling for his party in its hour of danger was turned into an act of brutality; instead of the party's broadcast summons arousing even the mortally ill, we had a sick old woman being hounded out of her bed. The proletarian theatre must learn how to encourage the free development of the various arts it needs. It must know how to listen to artistic and political arguments and should not give the director an opportunity to 'express' his individual self.

An important question is that of simplification. A number of simplifications are necessary in order to show the attitude of the play's characters clearly enough for the spectator to grasp all its political implications. But simple does not mean primitive. In the epic theatre it is perfectly possible for a character to explain himself in a minimum of time, for instance by merely reporting: I am the teacher in this village; my work is very difficult, for I have too many pupils, and so forth. But what is possible has first to be made possible. That is where art is needed. The gest and the way of speaking here have to be carefully chosen and formed on a large scale. As the spectators' interest is directed purely towards the characters' attitudes the relevant gest must in each case be, aesthetically speaking, significant and typical. Above all, the director needs an historian's eye. The little scene where Vlassova gets her first lesson in economics, for instance, is by no means just an incident in her own life; it is an historic event: the immense pressure of misery forcing the exploited to think. They are discovering the causes of their misery. Plays of this type are so deeply concerned with the development of the life portrayed, as being a progressive process, that they really only exert their full influence when seen a second time. There are sentences uttered by the characters which are only grasped fully when one already knows how these characters will speak as the play develops. This means that incidents and sentences have to be given such a stamp that they sink into the memory.

In the Theatre Union's production of *Mother* a correct way of speaking was used for the following sentences: by Mrs Henry in the scene where the mother is lying ill (then unfortunately cuts were made here); by John Boruff as Pavel in the May Day demonstration scene, especially the passage 'Smilgin, worker, revolutionary, 15 years in the movement, on May First, 1908, at 11 o'clock in the morning, etc.'; by Millicent Green in the bible-tearing scene, when as the tenant under notice she asks for the Bible in order to prove that Christians are supposed to love their neighbours. These passages were properly spoken because they were spoken with the same sense of responsibility as a statement made for the record in a court of law, and because the gest stays in the memory.

All these are difficult artistic problems, and an initial failure or part-failure must not make our theatres lose heart. If we can improve the organization of our artistic output; if we can manage to prevent our conception of the theatre from becoming too rigid, improve our technique and make it more flexible; in short, if we can learn; then, given the incomparable alertness of our proletarian public and the undeniably fresh force of our young theatres, we may be able to construct a true proletarian art.

[Written for *New Masses*, 1935. Published in *Gesammelte Werke II*, as para. IX of the notes on the play]

NOTE: Mr Nubel has been unable to locate this article in *New Masses*, and it is doubtful if it was ever published in the U.S.

Mother was produced in Paul Peters's English translation by Theater Union at the Civic Repertory Theater, New York, on 19 November 1935. Victor Wolfson directed; Mordecai Gorelik was scene designer. Brecht made his first trip to the U.S. to see the production, and stayed about eight weeks.

He rejected the original adaptation, which 'dramatized' his characters' matter-of-fact statements along orthodox lines. In German the play opens with a long explanation by Vlassova addressed direct to the audience, much like the 'I am a teacher' etc., that he quotes (a phrase that is in fact the opening of the Nō play *Taniko* in Arthur Waley's translation). The notes give an extract from Mr Peters's adaptation which turns this into an intimate dialogue between Vlassova and her son, liberally dotted with stage directions and 'business'. A poem by Brecht, also printed as part of the notes in *Gesammelte Werke II* and subsequent editions, describes his reactions to this.

23 · On the Use of Music in an Epic Theatre

As far as my own output goes, the following plays involved application of music to the epic theatre: *Trommeln in der Nacht, Lebenslauf des asozialen Baal, Das Leben Eduards II von England, Mahagonny, The Threepenny Opera, Die Mutter, Die Rundköpfe und die Spitzköpfe*.

In the first few plays music was used in a fairly conventional way; it was a matter of songs and marches, and there was usually some naturalistic pretext for each musical piece. All the same, the introduction of music meant a certain break with the dramatic conventions of the time: the drama was (as it were) lightened, made more elegant; the theatre's offerings became more like virtuoso turns. The narrow stuffiness of the impressionistic drama and the manic lop-sidedness of the expressionists were to some extent offset by the use of music, simply because it introduced variety. At the same time, music made possible something which we had long since ceased to take for granted, namely the 'poetic theatre'. At first I wrote this music myself. Five years later, for the second Berlin production of the comedy *Mann ist Mann* at the Staatstheater, it was written by Kurt Weill. From now on music had the characteristics of art (could be valued for itself). The play involved a certain amount of knockabout comedy, and Weill introduced a 'kleine Nachtmusik' to accompany projections by Caspar Neher, also a battle- or Schlachtmusik, and a song which was sung verse by verse during the visible changes of scene. But by then the first theories had already been put forward concerning the separation of the different elements.

The most successful demonstration of the epic theatre was the production of *The Threepenny Opera* in 1928. This was the first use of theatrical music in accordance with a new point of view. Its most striking innovation lay in the strict separation of the music from all the other elements of entertainment offered. Even superficially this was evident from the fact that the small orchestra was installed visibly on the stage. For the singing of the *songs* a special change of lighting was arranged; the orchestra was lit up; the titles of the various numbers were projected on the screens at the back, for instance 'Song concerning the Insufficiency of Human Endeavour' or 'A short song allows Miss Polly Peachum to confess to her Horrified Parents that she is wedded to the Murderer Macheath'; and the actors changed their positions before the number began. There were duets, trios, solos and final choruses. The musical items, which had the immediacy of a ballad, were of a reflective and moralizing nature. The play showed the close relationship between the emotional life of the bourgeois and that of the criminal world. The criminals showed, sometimes through the music itself, that their sensations, feelings and prejudices were the same as those of the average citizen and theatregoer. One theme was, broadly speaking, to show that the only pleasant life is a comfortably-off one, even if this involves doing without certain 'higher things'. A love duet was used to argue that superficial circumstances like the social origins of one's partner or her economic status should have no influence on a man's matrimonial decisions. A trio expressed concern at the fact that the uncertainties of life on this planet apparently prevent the human race from following its natural inclinations towards goodness and decent behaviour. The tenderest and most moving love-song in the play described the eternal, indestructible mutual attachment of a procurer and his girl. The lovers sang, not without nostalgia, of their little home, the brothel. In such ways the music, just because it took up a purely emotional attitude and spurned none of the stock narcotic attractions, became an active collaborator in the stripping bare of the middleclass corpus of ideas. It became, so to speak, a muck-raker, an informer, a nark. These *songs* found a very wide public; catchwords from them cropped up in leading articles and speeches. A lot of people sang them to piano accompaniment or from the records, as they were used to doing with musical comedy hits.

This type of *song* was created on the occasion of the Baden-Baden Music Festival of 1927, where one-act operas were to be performed, when I asked Weill simply to write new settings for half-a-dozen already existing *songs*. Up to that time Weill had written relatively complicated music of a mainly psychological sort, and when he agreed to set a series of more or less banal *song* texts he was making a courageous break with a prejudice which the solid bulk of serious composers stubbornly held. The success of this attempt to apply modern music to the *song* was significant. What was the real novelty of this music, other than the hitherto unaccustomed use to which it was put?

The epic theatre is chiefly interested in the attitudes which people adopt towards one another, wherever they are socio-historically significant (typical). It works out scenes where people adopt attitudes of such a sort that the social laws under which they are acting spring into sight. For that we need to find workable definitions: that is to say, such definitions of the relevant processes as can be used in order to intervene in the processes themselves. The concern of the epic theatre is thus eminently practical. Human behaviour is shown as alterable; man himself as dependent on certain political and economic factors and at the same time as capable of altering them. To give an example: a scene where three men are hired by a fourth for a specific illegal purpose (*Mann ist Mann*) has to be shown by the epic theatre in such a way that it becomes possible to imagine the attitude of the four men other than as it is expressed there: i.e. so that one imagines either a different set of political and economic conditions under which these men would be speaking differently, or else a different approach on their part to their actual conditions, which would likewise lead them to say different things. In short, the spectator is given the chance to criticize human behaviour from a social point of view, and the scene is played as a piece of history. The idea is that the spectator should be put in a position where he can make comparisons about everything that influences the way in which human beings behave. This means, from the aesthetic point of view, that the actors' social gest becomes particularly important. The arts have to begin paying attention to the gest. (Naturally this means socially significant gest, not illustrative or expressive gest.) The gestic principle takes over, as it were, from the principle of imitation.

This marks a great revolution in the art of drama. The drama of our time still follows Aristotle's recipe for achieving what he calls catharsis (the spiritual cleansing of the spectator). In aristotelian drama the plot leads the hero into situations where he reveals his innermost being. All the incidents shown have the object of driving the hero into spiritual conflicts. It is a possibly blasphemous but quite useful comparison if one turns one's mind to the burlesque shows on Broadway, where the public, with yells of 'Take it off!', forces the girls to expose their bodies more and more. The individual whose innermost being is thus driven into the open then of course comes to stand for Man with a capital M. Everyone (including every spectator) is then carried away by the momentum of the events portrayed, so that in a performance of *Oedipus* one has for all practical purposes an auditorium full of little Oedipuses, an auditorium full of Emperor Joneses for a performance of *The Emperor Jones*. Non-aristotelian drama would at all costs avoid bundling together the events portrayed and presenting them as an inexorable fate, to which the human being is handed over helpless despite the beauty and significance of his reactions; on the contrary, it is precisely this fate that it would study closely, showing it up as of human contriving.

This survey, springing from the examination of a few unpretentious *songs*, might seem rather far-reaching if these *songs* did not represent the (likewise quite unpretentious) beginnings of a new, up-to-date theatre, or the part which music is to play in such a theatre. This music's character as a kind of gestic music can hardly be explained except by a survey to establish the social purpose of the new methods. To put it practically, gestic music is that music which allows the actor to exhibit certain basic gests on the stage. So-called 'cheap' music, particularly that of the cabaret and the operetta, has for some time been a sort of gestic music. Serious music, however, still clings to lyricism, and cultivates expression for its own sake.

The opera *Aufstieg und Fall der Stadt Mahagonny* showed the application of the new principles on a fairly large scale. I feel I should point out that in my view Weill's music for this opera is not purely gestic; but many parts of it are, enough anyway for it to represent a serious threat to the common type of opera, which in its current manifestations we can call the purely culinary opera. The theme of the opera *Mahagonny* is the cooking process itself; I have explained the reasons for this in an essay 'Anmerkungen zur Oper' in my Versuch No. 5.[1] There you will also find an argument positing

---

[1] 'The Modern Theatre is the Epic Theatre', above. Brecht's numbering of the *Versuche* can be confusing, as he gives a number to each individual item, as well as to each volume. Versuch no. 5 is in *Versuche 2*.

the impossibility of any renewal of the operatic medium in the capitalist countries, and explaining why. Any innovations introduced merely lead to opera's destruction. Composers aiming to renew the opera are bound, like Hindemith and Stravinsky, to come up against the opera apparatus.

[*Brecht here repeats from p. 34, line 6, to p. 35, line 5*]

The dangers which the apparatus can present were shown by the New York production of *Die Mutter*. Its political standpoint puts the Theatre Union in quite a different class from the theatres which had performed the opera *Mahagonny*. Yet the apparatus behaved exactly like a machine for simulating the effects of dope. Not only the play but the music too was distorted as a result, and the didactic aim was, broadly speaking, missed. Far more deliberately than in any other play of the epic theatre, the music in *Die Mutter* was designed to induce in the spectator the critical approach which has been outlined above. Eisler's music can by no means be called simple. Qua music it is relatively complicated, and I cannot think of any that is more serious. In a remarkable manner it makes possible a certain simplification of the toughest political problems, whose solution is a life and death matter for the working class. In the short piece which counters the accusation that Communism leads to chaos the friendly and explanatory gest of the music wins a hearing, as it were, for the voice of reason. The piece 'In Praise of Learning', which links the problem of learning with that of the working class's accession to power, is infected by the music with a heroic yet naturally cheerful gest. Similarly the final chorus 'In Praise of Dialectics', which might easily give the effect of a purely emotional song of triumph, has been kept in the realm of the rational by the music. (It is a frequently recurring mistake to suppose that this – epic – kind of production simply does without all emotional effects: actually, emotions are only clarified in it, steering clear of subconscious origins and carrying nobody away.)

If you imagine that the severe, yet delicate and rational gest conveyed by this music is unsuitable for a mass movement which has to face uninhibited force, oppression and exploitation, then you have misunderstood an important aspect of this fight. It is, however, clear that the effectiveness of this kind of music largely depends on the way in which it is performed. If the actors do not start by getting hold of the right gest then there is little hope that they will be able to carry out their task of stimulating a particular approach in the spectator. Our working-class theatres need careful education and strict training if they are to master the tasks proposed here and the possibilities which are here offered to them. They in turn have to carry out a certain training of their public. It is very important to keep the productive apparatus of the working-class theatre well clear of the general drug traffic conducted by bourgeois show business.

For the play *Die Rundköpfe und die Spitzköpfe*, which unlike *Die Mutter* is addressed to a 'wide' public and takes more account of purely entertainment considerations, Eisler wrote *song* music. This music too is in a certain sense philosophical. It too avoids narcotic effects, chiefly by linking the solution of musical problems to the clear and intelligible underlining of the political and philosophical meaning of each poem.

All this surely goes to show what a difficult task it is for music to fulfil the demands of an epic theatre.

Most 'advanced' music nowadays is still written for the concert hall. A single glance at the audiences who attend concerts is enough to show how impossible it is to make any political or philosophical use of music that produces such effects. We see entire rows of human beings transported into a peculiar doped state, wholly passive, sunk without trace, seemingly in the grip of a severe poisoning attack. Their tense, congealed gaze shows that these people are the helpless and involuntary victims of the unchecked lurchings of their emotions. Trickles of sweat prove how such excesses exhaust them. The worst gangster film treats its audience more like thinking beings. Music is cast in the role of Fate. As the exceedingly complex, wholly unanalysable fate of this period of the grisliest, most deliberate exploitation of man by man. Such music has nothing but purely culinary ambitions left. It seduces the listener into an enervating, because unproductive, act of enjoyment. No number of refinements can convince me that its social function is any different from that of the Broadway burlesques.

We should not overlook the fact that among the more serious composers a reaction against this demoralizing social function has already set in. The experiments being made within the musical field have taken on considerable proportions; the new music is doing all it can not only in the treatment of purely musical material but also in attracting new levels of consumer. And yet there is a whole series of problems which it has not yet been able to solve and whose solution it has not yet tackled. The art of setting epics to music, for instance, is wholly lost. We do not know to what sort of music the Odyssey and the Nibelungenlied were performed. The performance of narrative poems of any length is something that our composers can no longer render possible. Educational music is also in the doldrums; and yet there were times when music could be used to treat disease. . . . Our composers on the whole leave any observation of the effects of their music to the café proprietors. One of the few actual pieces of research which I have come across in the last ten years was the statement of a Paris restaurateur about the different orders which his customers placed under the influence of different types of music. He claimed to have noticed that specific drinks were always drunk to the works of specific composers. And it is perfectly true that the theatre would benefit greatly if musicians were able to produce music which would have a more or less exactly foreseeable effect on the spectator. It would take a load off the actors' shoulders; it would be particularly useful, for instance, to have the actors play *against* the emotion which the music called forth. (For rehearsals of works of a pretentious kind it is enough to have whatever music is available.) The silent film gave opportunities for a few experiments with music which created predetermined emotional states. I heard some interesting pieces by Hindemith, and above all by Eisler. Eisler even wrote music for conventional feature films, and extremely austere music at that.

But sound films, being one of the most blooming branches of the international narcotics traffic, will hardly carry on these experiments for long.

Another opening for modern music besides the epic theatre is provided in my view by the Lehrstück, or didactic cantata. Exceptionally interesting music for one or two examples of this class has been written by Weill, Hindemith and Eisler. (Weill and Hindemith together for a radio Lehrstück for schoolchildren, *Der Lindberghflug*; Weill for the school opera *Der Jasager*; Hindemith for the *Badener Lehrstück vom Einverständnis*; Eisler for *Die Massnahme*.)

A further consideration is that the writing of meaningful and easily comprehensible music is by no means just a matter of good will, but above all of competence and study – and study can only be undertaken in continuous contact with the masses and with other artists – not on one's own.

['Über die Verwendung von Musik für ein episches Theater', from *Schriften zum Theater*, 1957. Less sections repeated verbatim from No. 11]

NOTE: This essay, dated 1935 in *Schriften zum Theater* but evidently written after Brecht's visit to the U.S., remained unpublished in his lifetime. He is using the English word 'song' here to convey the cabaret or jazz type of song (much as we use 'Lieder' for the opposite). The 'Mahagonny songs' that Weill used to make the first version of the opera in 1927 had already been given rudimentary tunes by Brecht, just as had the songs in *Baal* and other early plays.

Film music by Hindemith was performed at the Baden-Baden Festivals of 1928 and 1929. Eisler (d. 1962) wrote the music for *Kuhle Wampe*, for Trivas's *Niemandsland*, Ivens's *A Song about Heroes*, and other films.

24 · Alienation Effects in Chinese Acting

The following is intended to refer briefly to the use of the alienation effect in traditional Chinese acting. This method was most recently used in Germany for plays of a non-aristotelian (not dependent on empathy) type as part of the attempts[1] being made to evolve an epic theatre. The efforts in question were directed to playing in such a way that the audience was hindered from simply identifying itself with the characters in the play. Acceptance or rejection of their actions and utterances was meant to take place on a conscious plane, instead of, as hitherto, in the audience's subconscious.

This effort to make the incidents represented appear strange to the public can be seen in a primitive form in the theatrical and pictorial displays at the old popular fairs. The way the clowns speak and the way the panoramas are painted both embody an act of alienation. The method of painting used to reproduce the picture of 'Charles the Bold's flight after the Battle of Murten', as shown at many German fairs, is certainly mediocre; yet the act of alienation which is achieved here (not by the original) is in no wise due to the mediocrity of the copyist. The fleeing commander, his horse, his retinue and the landscape are all quite consciously painted in such a way as to create the impression of an abnormal event, an astonishing disaster. In spite of his inadequacy the painter succeeds brilliantly in bringing out the unexpected. Amazement guides his brush.

Traditional Chinese acting also knows the alienation effect, and applies it most subtly. It is well known that the Chinese theatre uses a lot of symbols. Thus a general will carry little pennants on his shoulder, corresponding to the number of regiments under his command. Poverty is shown by patching the silken costumes with irregular shapes of different colours, likewise silken, to indicate that they have been mended. Characters are distinguished by particular masks, i.e. simply by painting. Certain gestures of the two hands signify the forcible opening of a door, etc. The stage itself remains the same, but articles of furniture are carried in during the action. All this has long been known, and cannot very well be exported.

It is not all that simple to break with the habit of assimilating a work of art as a whole. But this has to be done if just one of a large number of effects is to be singled out and studied. The alienation effect is achieved in the Chinese theatre in the following way.

Above all, the Chinese artist never acts as if there were a fourth wall

[1] Brecht uses the word 'Versuche'.

besides the three surrounding him. He expresses his awareness of being watched. This immediately removes one of the European stage's characteristic illusions. The audience can no longer have the illusion of being the unseen spectator at an event which is really taking place. A whole elaborate European stage technique, which helps to conceal the fact that the scenes are so arranged that the audience can view them in the easiest way, is thereby made unnecessary. The actors openly choose those positions which will best show them off to the audience, just as if they were *acrobats*. A further means is that the artist observes himself. Thus if he is representing a cloud, perhaps, showing its unexpected appearance, its soft and strong growth, its rapid yet gradual transformation, he will occasionally look at the audience as if to say: isn't it just like that? At the same time he also observes his own arms and legs, adducing them, testing them and perhaps finally approving them. An obvious glance at the floor, so as to judge the space available to him for his act, does not strike him as liable to break the illusion. In this way the artist separates mime (showing observation) from gesture (showing a cloud), but without detracting from the latter, since the body's attitude is reflected in the face and is wholly responsible for its expression. At one moment the expression is of well-managed restraint; at another, of utter triumph. The artist has been using his countenance as a blank sheet, to be inscribed by the gest of the body.

The artist's object is to appear strange and even surprising to the audience. He achieves this by looking strangely at himself and his work. As a result everything put forward by him has a touch of the amazing. Everyday things are thereby raised above the level of the obvious and automatic. A young woman, a fisherman's wife, is shown paddling a boat. She stands steering a non-existent boat with a paddle that barely reaches to her knees. Now the current is swifter, and she is finding it harder to keep her balance; now she is in a pool and paddling more easily. Right: that is how one manages a boat. But this journey in the boat is apparently historic, celebrated in many songs, an exceptional journey about which everybody knows. Each of this famous girl's movements has probably been recorded in pictures; each bend in the river was a well-known adventure story, it is even known which particular bend it was. This feeling on the audience's part is induced by the artist's attitude; it is this that makes the journey famous. The scene reminded us of the march to Budejovice in Piscator's production of *The Good Soldier Schweik*. Schweik's three-day-and-night march to a front which he oddly enough never gets to was seen from a completely historic point of view, as no less noteworthy a phenomenon than, for instance, Napoleon's Russian expedition of 1812. The performer's self-observation, an artful and artistic act of self-alienation, stopped the spectator from losing himself in the character completely, i.e. to the point of giving up his own identity, and lent a splendid remoteness to the events. Yet the spectator's empathy was not entirely rejected. The audience identifies itself with the actor as being an observer, and accordingly develops his attitude of observing or looking on.

The Chinese artist's performance often strikes the Western actor as cold. That does not mean that the Chinese theatre rejects all representation of feelings. The performer portrays incidents of utmost passion, but without his delivery becoming heated. At those points where the character portrayed is deeply excited the performer takes a lock of hair between his lips and chews it. But this is like a ritual, there is nothing eruptive about it. It is quite clearly somebody else's repetition of the incident: a representation, even though an artistic one. The performer shows that this man is not in control of himself, and he points to the outward signs. And so lack of control is decorously expressed, or if not decorously at any rate decorously for the stage. Among all the possible signs certain particular ones are picked out, with careful and visible consideration. Anger is naturally different from sulkiness, hatred from distaste, love from liking; but the corresponding fluctuations of feeling are portrayed economically. The coldness comes from the actor's holding himself remote from the character portrayed, along the lines described. He is careful not to make its sensations into those of the spectator. Nobody gets raped by the individual he portrays; this individual is not the spectator himself but his neighbour.

The Western actor does all he can to bring his spectator into the closest proximity to the events and the character he has to portray. To this end he persuades him to identify himself with him (the actor) and uses every energy to convert himself as completely as possible into a different type, that of the character in question. If this complete conversion succeeds then his art has been more or less expended. Once he has become the bank-clerk, doctor or general concerned he will need no more art than any of these people need 'in real life'.

This complete conversion operation is extremely exhausting. Stanislavsky puts forward a series of means – a complete system – by which what he calls 'creative mood' can repeatedly be manufactured afresh at every performance. For the actor cannot usually manage to feel for very long on end that he really is the other person; he soon gets exhausted and begins just to copy various superficialities of the other person's speech and hearing, whereupon the effect on the public drops off alarmingly. This is certainly due to the fact that the other person has been created by an 'intuitive' and accordingly murky process which takes place in the subconscious. The subconscious is not at all responsive to guidance; it has as it were a bad memory.

These problems are unknown to the Chinese performer, for he rejects complete conversion. He limits himself from the start to simply quoting the character played. But with what art he does this! He only needs a minimum of illusion. What he has to show is worth seeing even for a man in his right mind. What Western actor of the old sort (apart from one or two comedians) could demonstrate the elements of his art like the Chinese actor Mei Lan-fang, without special lighting and wearing a dinner jacket in an ordinary room full of specialists? It would be like the magician at a fair giving away his tricks, so that nobody ever wanted to see the act again. He would just be showing how to disguise oneself; the hypnotism would vanish and all that would be left would be a few pounds of ill-blended imitation, a quickly-mixed product for selling in the dark to hurried customers. Of course no Western actor would stage such a demonstration. What about the sanctity of Art? The mysteries of metamorphosis? To the Westerner what matters is that his actions should be unconscious; otherwise they would be degraded. By comparison with Asiatic acting our own art still seems hopelessly parsonical. None the less it is becoming increasingly difficult for our actors to bring off the mystery of complete conversion; their subconscious's memory is getting weaker and weaker, and it is almost impossible to extract the truth from the uncensored intuitions of any member of our class society even when the man is a genius.

For the actor it is difficult and taxing to conjure up particular inner moods or emotions night after night; it is simpler to exhibit the outer signs which accompany these emotions and identify them. In this case, however, there is not the same automatic transfer of emotions to the spectator, the same emotional infection. The alienation effect intervenes, not in the form of absence of emotion, but in the form of emotions which need not correspond to those of the character portrayed. On seeing worry the spectator may feel a sensation of joy; on seeing anger, one of disgust. When we speak of exhibiting the outer signs of emotion we do not mean such an exhibition and such a choice of signs that the emotional transference does in fact take place because the actor has managed to infect himself with the emotions portrayed, by exhibiting the outer signs; thus, by letting his voice rise, holding his breath and tightening his neck muscles so that the blood shoots to his head, the actor can easily conjure up a rage. In such a case of course the effect does not occur. But it does occur if the actor at a particular point unexpectedly shows a completely white face, which he has produced mechanically by holding his face in his hands with some white make-up on them. If the actor at the same time displays an apparently composed character, then his terror at this point (as a result of this message, or that discovery) will give rise to an alienation effect. Acting like this is healthier and in our view less unworthy of a thinking being; it demands a considerable knowledge of humanity and worldly wisdom, and a keen eye for what is socially important. In this case too there is of course a creative process at work; but it is a higher one, because it is raised to the concious level.

The alienation effect does not in any way demand an unnatural way of acting. It has nothing whatever to do with ordinary stylization. On the contrary, the achievement of an A-effect absolutely depends on lightness and naturalness of performance. But when the actor checks the truth of his performance (a necessary operation, which Stanislavsky is much concerned with in his system) he is not just thrown back on his 'natural sensibilities', but can always be corrected by a comparison with reality (is that how an angry man really speaks? is that how an offended man sits down?) and so from outside, by other people. He acts in such a way that nearly every sentence could be followed by a verdict of the audience and practically every gesture is submitted for the public's approval.

The Chinese performer is in no trance. He can be interrupted at any moment. He won't have to 'come round'. After an interruption he will go on with his exposition from that point. We are not disturbing him at the 'mystic moment of creation'; when he steps on to the stage before us the process of creation is already over. He does not mind if the setting is changed around him as he plays. Busy hands quite openly pass him what he needs for his performance. When Mei Lan-fang was playing a death scene a spectator sitting next me exclaimed with astonishment at one of his gestures. One or two people sitting in front of us turned round indignantly and sshhh'd. They behaved as if they were present at the real death of a real girl. Possibly their attitude would have been all right for a European production, but for a Chinese it was unspeakably ridiculous. In their case the A-effect had misfired.

It is not entirely easy to realize that the Chinese actor's A-effect is a transportable piece of technique: a conception that can be prised loose from the Chinese theatre. We see this theatre as uncommonly precious, its portrayal of human passions as schematized, its idea of society as rigid and wrong-headed; at first sight this superb art seems to offer nothing applicable to a realistic and revolutionary theatre. Against that, the motives and objects of the A-effect strike us as odd and suspicious.

When one sees the Chinese acting it is at first very hard to discount the feeling of estrangement which they produce in us as Europeans. One has to be able to imagine them achieving an A-effect among their Chinese spectators too. What is still harder is that one must accept the fact that when the Chinese performer conjures up an impression of mystery he seems uninterested in disclosing a mystery to us. He makes his own mystery from the mysteries of nature (especially human nature): he allows nobody to examine how he produces the natural phenomenon, nor does nature allow him to understand as he produces it. We have here the artistic counterpart of a primitive technology, a rudimentary science. The Chinese performer gets his A-effect by association with magic. 'How it's done' remains hidden; knowledge is a matter of knowing the tricks and is in the hands of a few men who guard it jealously and profit from their secrets. And yet there is already an attempt here to interfere with the course of nature; the capacity to do so leads to questioning; and the future explorer, with his anxiety to make nature's course intelligible, controllable and down-to-earth, will always start by adopting a standpoint from which it seems mysterious, incomprehensible and beyond control. He will take up the attitude of somebody wondering, will apply the A-effect. Nobody can be a mathematician who takes it for granted that 'two and two makes four'; nor is anybody one who fails to understand it. The man who first looked with astonishment at a swinging lantern and instead of taking it for granted found it highly remarkable that it should swing, and swing in that particular way rather than any other, was brought close to understanding the phenomenon by this observation, and so to mastering it. Nor must it simply be exclaimed that the attitude here proposed is all right for science but not for art. Why shouldn't art try, by its *own* means of course, to further the great social task of mastering life?

In point of fact the only people who can profitably study a piece of technique like Chinese acting's A-effect are those who need such a technique for quite definite social purposes.

The experiments conducted by the modern German theatre led to a wholly independent development of the A-effect. So far Asiatic acting has exerted no influence.

The A-effect was achieved in the German epic theatre not only by the actor, but also by the music (choruses, songs) and the setting (placards, film etc.). It was principally designed to historicize the incidents portrayed. By this is meant the following:

The bourgeois theatre emphasized the timelessness of its objects. Its representation of people is bound by the alleged 'eternally human'. Its story is arranged in such a way as to create 'universal' situations that allow

Man with a capital M to express himself: man of every period and every colour. All its incidents are just one enormous cue, and this cue is followed by the 'eternal' response: the inevitable, usual, natural, purely human response. An example: a black man falls in love in the same way as a white man; the story forces him to react with the same expression as the white man (in theory this formula works as well the other way round); and with that the sphere of art is attained. The cue can take account of what is special, different; the response is shared, there is no element of difference in it. This notion may allow that such a thing as history exists, but it is none the less unhistorical. A few circumstances vary, the environments are altered, but Man remains unchanged. History applies to the environment, not to Man. The environment is remarkably unimportant, is treated simply as a pretext; it is a variable quantity and something remarkably inhuman; it exists in fact apart from Man, confronting him as a coherent whole, whereas he is a fixed quantity, eternally unchanged. The idea of man as a function of the environment and the environment as a function of man, i.e. the breaking up of the environment into relationships between men, corresponds to a new way of thinking, the historical way. Rather than be sidetracked into the philosophy of history, let us give an example. Suppose the following is to be shown on the stage: a girl leaves home in order to take a job in a fair-sized city (Piscator's *American Tragedy*). For the bourgeois theatre this is an insignificant affair, clearly the beginning of a story; it is what one has to have been told in order to understand what comes after, or to be keyed up for it. The actor's imagination will hardly be greatly fired by it. In a sense the incident is universal: girls take jobs (in the case in question one can be keyed up to see what in particular is going to happen to her). Only in one way is it particular: this girl goes away (if she had remained what comes after would not have happened). The fact that her family lets her go is not the object of the inquiry; it is understandable (the motives are understandable). But for the historicizing theatre every-thing is different. The theatre concentrates entirely on whatever in this perfectly everyday event is remarkable, particular and demanding inquiry. What! A family letting one of its members leave the nest to earn her future living independently and without help? Is she up to it? Will what she has learnt here as a member of the family help her to earn her living? Can't families keep a grip on their children any longer? Have they become (or remained) a burden? Is it like that with every family? Was it always like that? Is this the way of the world, something that can't be affected? The fruit falls off the tree when ripe: does this sentence apply here? Do children always make themselves independent? Did they do so in every age? If so, and if it's

97

something biological, does it always happen in the same way, for the same reasons and with the same results? These are the questions (or a few of them) that the actors must answer if they want to show the incident as a unique, historical one: if they want to demonstrate a custom which leads to conclusions about the entire structure of a society at a particular (transient) time. But how is such an incident to be represented if its historic character is to be brought out? How can the confusion of our unfortunate epoch be striking? When the mother, in between warnings and moral injunctions, packs her daughter's case – a very small one – how is the following to be shown: So many injunctions and so few clothes? Moral injunctions for a lifetime and bread for five hours? How is the actress to speak the mother's sentence as she hands over such a very small case – 'There, I guess that ought to do you' – in such way that it is understood as a historic dictum? This can only be achieved if the A-effect is brought out. The actress must not make the sentence her own affair, she must hand it over for criticism, she must help us to understand its causes and protest. The effect can only be got by long training. In the New York Yiddish Theatre, a highly progressive theatre, I saw a play by S. Ornitz showing the rise of an East Side boy to be a big crooked attorney. The theatre could not perform the play. And yet there were scenes like this in it: the young attorney sits in the street outside his house giving cheap legal advice. A young woman arrives and complains that her leg has been hurt in a traffic accident. But the case has been bungled and her compensation has not yet been paid. In desperation she points to her leg and says: 'It's started to heal up.' Working without the A-effect, the theatre was unable to make use of this exceptional scene to show the horror of a bloody epoch. Few people in the audience noticed it; hardly anyone who reads this will remember that cry. The actress spoke the cry as if it were something perfectly natural. But it is exactly this – the fact that this poor creature finds such a complaint natural – that she should have reported to the public like a horrified messenger returning from the lowest of all hells. To that end she would of course have needed a special technique which would have allowed her to underline the historical aspect of a specific social condition. Only the A-effect makes this possible. Without it all she can do is to observe how she is not forced to go over entirely into the character on the stage.

In setting up new artistic principles and working out new methods of representation we must start with the compelling demands of a changing epoch; the necessity and the possibility of remodelling society loom ahead. All incidents between men must be noted, and everything must be seen from a social point of view. Among other effects that a new theatre will need for its social criticism and its historical reporting of completed transformations is the A-effect.

['Verfremdungseffekte in der chinesischen Schau-spielkunst', from *Schriften zum Theater*, 1957]

NOTE: This essay, though unpublished in German till 1949, appeared (in Mr Eric White's translation) in *Life and Letters*, London, in the winter of 1936. A pencilled note on the typescript (Brecht-Archive 332/81) says: 'This essay arose out of a performance by Mei Lan-fang's company in Moscow in spring 1935.' Brecht had seen the performance that May, during his Moscow visit, though the essay itself cannot have been completed till after his return from New York.

Almost certainly this, rather than the following item (as I wrongly suggested in my book on Brecht), is the first mention in his writings of the term 'Verfrem-dungseffekt'. That Brecht had already been feeling his way towards some such formula can be seen from his use of the term 'Entfremdung' above (p. 76), while his almost instinctive predilection for strangeness can be seen very early on in the passages quoted on pp. 19–20. The formula itself is a translation of the Russian critic Viktor Shklovskij's phrase 'Priem Ostrannenija', or 'device for making strange', and it can hardly be a coincidence that it should have entered Brecht's vocabulary after his Moscow visit. So far as Mrs Hauptmann can remember he had not spoken of 'Verfremdung' earlier, even in conversation. It was indeed virtually a neologism, for Grimm's dictionary gives only two obscure early examples for the use of 'verfremden' as a transitive verb.

According to Professor Eric Bentley the play by Samuel Ornitz was called *Haunch, Paunch and Jowl* and was performed in 1935 by the Artef Players' collective. The incident with the leg seems to anticipate the water-carrier's injury in *Der gute Mensch von Sezuan*.

Piscator's adaptation of Dreiser's *An American Tragedy* was produced by the Group Theater in New York in 1936 under the title *The Case of Clyde Griffiths*, with Lee Strasberg directing. Harold Clurman wrote of it in *The Fervent Years* (London, 1946, p. 174) that 'It was schematic in a cold way that to my mind definitely went across the American grain. . . . It was nevertheless technically intriguing and capable of being fashioned into a novel type of stage production.'

25 · Notes to Die Rundköpfe und Die Spitzköpfe
(Description of the Copenhagen production)

GENERAL

The première was given in Copenhagen on 4 November 1936 in the Riddersalen Theatre under Per Knutzon's direction. One can smoke and eat in this theatre; it holds 220. The stage is 7 metres wide, 8 metres deep and 10 metres high.

PECULIARITIES OF THE PARABLE FORM

This play, the parable type of non-aristotelian drama, demanded a considerable sacrifice of effects of illusion on the part of actors and stage set. The preparations made so as to give point to the parable had themselves to be visible. The playing had to enable and encourage the audience to draw abstract conclusions. During Missena's final speech the barrel of an enormous gun was lowered on wires so that it dangled above the banquet. The tenant farmer Callas on his way to gaol (scene 10) went right through the auditorium, telling his story over again to the spectators. [Other examples follow.]

BUILDING UP A PART (INDUCTIVE METHOD)

The parts were built up from a social point of view. The modes of behaviour shown by the actors had transparent motives of a social-historical sort. It was not the 'eternally human' that was supposed to emerge, not what any man is alleged to do at any period, but what men of specific social strata (as against other strata) do in our period (as against any other). Since actors are accustomed to rely primarily on the spectator's empathy, which means exploiting his most easily-accessible emotions, they nearly always run a whole sequence of sentences together and give a common expression to them. But with the kind of drama under consideration it is essential that each separate sentence should be treated for its social gest. The characters' unity is in no way upset by exactly reproducing their contradictory behaviour; it is only in their development that they really come to life. [Individual characters from the play are then discussed in detail.]

INFLUENCING THE AUDIENCE (BY THE INDUCTIVE METHOD)

A considerable sacrifice of the spectator's empathy does not mean sacrificing all right to influence him. The representation of human behaviour from a social point of view is meant indeed to have a decisive influence on the spectator's own social behaviour. This sort of intervention is bound to release emotional effects; they are deliberate and have to be controlled. A creation that more or less renounces empathy need not by any means be an 'unfeeling' creation, or one which leaves the spectator's feelings out of account. But it has to adopt a critical approach to his emotions, just as it does to his ideas. Emotions, instincts, impulses are generally presented as being deeper, more eternal, less easily influenced by society than ideas, but this is in no way true. The emotions are neither common to all humanity nor incapable of alteration; the instincts neither infallible nor independent of the reason; the impulses neither uncontrollable nor spontaneously engendered, and so on. But above all the actor must make certain that no worthwhile feeling is weakened when it is brought clearly and critically to the conscious level. A character's piecemeal development as he initiates more and more relationships with other characters, consolidating or expanding himself in continually new situations, produces a rich and sometimes complicated emotional curve in the spectator, a fusion of feelings and even a conflict between them.

ALIENATION

Certain incidents in the play should be treated as self-contained scenes and raised – by means of inscriptions, musical or sound effects and the actors' way of playing – above the level of the everyday, the obvious, the expected (i.e. alienated). [The four or five chief incidents in each of the play's eleven scenes are then listed.]

EXAMPLES OF ALIENATION IN THE COPENHAGEN PRODUCTION

When Nanna Callas sang her introductory song (scene 2) she stood beneath the signboard of a petty trader's shop [. . .], a commodity among other commodities, beckoning to the audience before the third verse with a mechanical prostitute's smile which she promptly switched off.

Before the fifth scene a young nun entered through the subsidiary curtain carrying a gramophone and sat down on some steps. A record of organ music accompanied the first, pious section of the scene (up to the sentence 'What will the young lady bring with her?'). The nun then got up and went out with the gramophone.

The meeting of the two de Guzmans in the eighth scene (a street in the old town) was based on Claudio's conversation with Isabella in Shakespeare's *Measure for Measure*. The scene has to be played with complete seriousness in the heightened and impassioned style of the Elizabethan theatre. The Copenhagen production alienated this style by having it rain during the scene and giving umbrellas to all appearing in it. In this way the heightened style of playing was artistically alienated. The spectator, however, having had his attention drawn to the outmoded nature of such conduct, was not as yet brought to notice that heightened means of expression are bound up with the individual conduct of the upper class. This could be achieved e.g. by having the inspector and the Hua [strong-arm men like the Nazi S.A.] who escorted the prisoner adopt a particular offhand or even amused, but at the same time slightly surprised attitude to the event.

This demonstration of historic theatrical forms continued with the ninth scene in Frau Cornamontis's café, which contained elements of the late eighteenth-century French conversation piece. Isabella had a completely white make-up in this scene.

STAGE SET AND MASKS

The basic set consisted of four ivory-coloured screens, slightly curved horizontally, which could be arranged in various ways. The lights were shown, in so far as they were movable. The two pianos were illuminated while working; their mechanism was laid open. Scene changes took place behind a small subsidiary curtain, which did not completely interrupt vision but allowed bridge scenes to be played. The setting was constructed and elaborated during the rehearsals. [A long list of props follows.]

Heads were about 20 centimetres high. The masks showed drastic distortions of nose, ears, hair and chin. The Huas had unnaturally large hands and feet.

The women's costumes were coloured and not restricted to any particular fashion; the farmers wore black trousers, linen shirts and clogs; the rich landowners Ascot get-up; Missena uniform; the small bourgeoisie ordinary suits.

SOUND EFFECTS

Recently the gramophone industry has started supplying the stage with records of real noises. These add substantially to the spectator's illusion of *not* being in a theatre. Theatres have fallen on them avidly; so that Shakespeare's *Romeo and Juliet* is now accompanied by the real noise of the mob. So far as we know the first person to make use of records was Piscator. He applied the new technique entirely correctly. In his production of the play *Rasputin* a record of Lenin's voice was played. It interrupted the performance. In another production a new technical achievement was demonstrated: the transmission by wireless of the sound of a sick man's heart. A film simultaneously showed the heart contracting. The fact that one can now get a specialist's opinion for a case of illness on a boat or in some remote place played no part in the play.

The point was simply to show how greatly human communications have been simplified by science, and that social conditions at present act as an obstacle to the full exploitation of the fact. In a parable-type play sound effects should only be used when they further the parable, not in order to evoke atmosphere and illusion. The marching feet of Iberin's troops as they enter (scene 11) can come from a record. So can the victory bells (scenes 7 and 8) and the execution bell (in scene 11). A noise that should not come from a record is that e.g. of the well at which the tenants are working (scene 3). Synthetic popular noises can accompany Iberin's entry (scene 4); while the reaction of the crowd outside the courtroom (scene 4) to the tenants' demands and the decisions of the agent, and the crowd noises at the news of victory (scene 7), can likewise be artificial.

It is best to place the record player, like the orchestra, so that it can be seen. But if such an arrangement would shock the audience unduly or give too much cause for amusement it should preferably be dropped.

> [From *Gesammelte Werke*, vol. II, London 1938.
> Less all detailed descriptions of characters and inci-
> dents from the play]

NOTE: The note must have been written shortly after the play's first perform-ance in 1936. The play itself began life about 1931 as a proposed adaptation of *Measure for Measure*. A preliminary version without songs was completed before Brecht left Germany in 1933. The songs were set by Eisler.

It is the first instance of Brecht applying the theory of 'Verfremdung' to his own work.

Piscator produced *Rasputin*, after Alexei Tolstoy, in the Theater am Nollen-dorfplatz on 12 November 1927. Brecht helped with the adaptation.

26 · On Gestic Music

DEFINITION

'Gest' is not supposed to mean gesticulation: it is not a matter of explanatory or emphatic movements of the hands, but of overall attitudes. A language is gestic when it is grounded in a gest and conveys particular attitudes adopted by the speaker towards other men. The sentence 'pluck the eye that offends thee out' is less effective from the gestic point of view that 'if thine eye offend thee, pluck it out'. The latter starts by presenting the eye, and the first clause has the definite gest of making an assumption; the main clause then comes as a surprise, a piece of advice, and a relief.

AN ARTISTIC PRINCIPLE

The musician sees this initially as an artistic principle, and not a specially interesting one. It may perhaps help him to set his texts in a particularly lively and easily assimilated way. What is more important is the fact that this principle of looking to the gest can allow him to adopt his own political attitude while making music. For that it is essential that he should be setting a social gest.

WHAT IS A SOCIAL GEST?

Not all gests are social gests. The attitude of chasing away a fly is not yet a social gest, though the attitude of chasing away a dog may be one, for instance if it comes to represent a badly dressed man's continual battle against watchdogs. One's efforts to keep one's balance on a slippery surface result in a social gest as soon as falling down would mean 'losing face'; in other words, losing one's market value. The gest of working is definitely a social gest, because all human activity directed towards the mastery of nature is a social undertaking, an undertaking between men. On the other hand a gest of pain, as long as it is kept so abstract and generalized that it does not rise above a purely animal category, is not yet a social one. But this is precisely the common tendency of art: to remove the social element in any gest. The artist is not happy till he achieves 'the look of a hunted animal'. The man then becomes just Man; his gest is stripped of any social individuality; it is an empty one, not representing any undertaking or operation among men by this particular man. The 'look of a hunted animal' can become a social gest if it is shown that particular manoeuvres by men can degrade the individual man to the level of a beast; the social gest is the gest relevant to society, the gest that allows conclusions to be drawn about the social circumstances.

HOW CAN THE COMPOSER'S ATTITUDE TO THE TEXT REFLECT HIS ATTITUDE TO THE CLASS STRUGGLE?

Suppose that the musician composing a cantata on Lenin's death has to reproduce his own attitude to the class struggle. As far as the gest goes, there are a number of different ways in which the report of Lenin's death can be set. A certain dignity of presentation means little, since where death is involved this could also be held to be fitting in the case of an enemy. Anger at 'the blind workings of providence' cutting short the lives of the best members of the community would not be a communist gest; nor would a wise resignation to 'life's irony'; for the gest of communists mourning a communist is a very special one. The musician's attitude to his text, the spokesman's to his report, shows the extent of his political, and so of his human maturity. A man's stature is shown by what he mourns and in what way he mourns it. To raise mourning to a high plane, to make it into an element of social progress: that is an artistic task.

INHUMANITY OF SUBJECT-MATTER LEFT TO ITSELF

Every artist knows that subject-matter in itself is in a sense somewhat banal, featureless, empty, and self-sufficient. It is only the social gest – criticism, craftiness, irony, propaganda, etc. – that breathes humanity into it. The pomp of the Fascists, taken at its face value, has a hollow gest, the gest of mere pomp, a featureless phenomenon: men strutting instead of walking, a certain stiffness, a lot of colour, self-conscious sticking out of chests, etc. All this could be the gest of some popular festivity, quite harmless, purely factual and therefore to be accepted. Only when the strutting takes place over corpses do we get the social gest of Fascism. This means that the artist has to adopt a definite attitude towards the fact of pomp; he cannot let it just speak only for itself, simply expressing it as the fact dictates.

A CRITERION

A good way of judging a piece of music with a text is to try out the different attitudes or gests with which the performer ought to deliver the individual sections: politely or angrily, modestly or contemptuously, approvingly or argumentatively, craftily or without calculation. For this the most suitable gests are as common, vulgar and banal as possible. In this way one can judge the political value of the musical score.

['Über gestische Musik', from *Schriften zum Theater*, 1957]

NOTE: Unpublished until after Brecht's death, this essay can hardly have been written before the mid-1930s, though the note in *Schriften zum Theater* assigns it to 1932. The *Lenin Cantata* to Brecht's words was completed in 1937, according to Volume 3 of Hanns Eisler's collected *Lieder und Kantaten*, which prints the full score.

The definition of 'gestus' or gest given here is the clearest and fullest to be found in Brecht's writings. It can perhaps be illuminated further by a short un-published fragment (Brecht-Archive 332/76) headed 'representation of sentences in a new encyclopaedia':

1. Who is the sentence of use to?
2. Who does it claim to be of use to?
3. What does it call for?
4. What practical action corresponds to it?
5. What sort of sentences result from it? What sort of sentences support it?
6. In what situation is it spoken? By whom?

See also the essay 'On Rhymeless Verse with Irregular Rhythms' below.

During 1937 Brecht propounded the idea of an international 'Diderot Society' which would circulate papers on 'theatrical science', and it is possible that some of his essays may have been written with this in mind. 'For centuries,' says his exploratory letter (*Schriften zum Theater 3*, pp. 106-10, translated in full by Mordecai Gorelik in *The Quarterly Journal of Speech*, April 1961),

> we have had international scientific societies whose business it is to organize the mutual exchange of problems and experiences. Science has its common standard, its common vocabulary, its continuity. The arts . . . have no such corresponding societies. This is because their structure is wholly individual-istic.

He planned to approach some twenty-odd people connected with different branches of the theatre in the hope that they would agree to pool their methods, knowledge and experience in this way. How many he in fact wrote to is not clear, and so far as is known the scheme is never again mentioned in his papers. The names, however, are of interest as showing the people whose views he then thought compatible with his own. Those recorded on notes, letters or drafts are: W. H. Auden, E. F. Burian, Rupert Doone, Slatan Dudow, S. M. Eisenstein, Hanns Eisler, Mordecai Gorelik, Nordahl Grieg, Georg Hoellering, Christopher Isherwood, Per Knutzon, Karl Koch, Fritz Kortner, Per Lagerquist, Per Lindberg, Archibald Macleish, Léon Moussinac, Nikolai Okhlopkhov, Erwin Piscator, Jean Renoir, Sergei Tretiakov. Naturally Brecht would have left out members of his immediate entourage and friends like Neher who were still in Germany, but even so there are some notable omissions, both of former associates like Weill and of other prominent left-wing theatre people.

27 · The Popular and the Realistic

When considering what slogans to set up for German literature today one must remember that anything with a claim to be considered as literature is printed exclusively abroad, and with few exceptions can only be read there. This gives a peculiar twist to the slogan of *Volkstümlichkeit* [or *Popularity*] *in literature*.

The writer is supposed to write for a people without living among it. When one comes to look closer, however, the gap between the writer and the people has not grown so wide as might be thought. All the same, it would be wrong, i.e. unrealistic, to see this growth as purely 'external'. Certainly a special effort is needed today in order to write in a popular way. But at the same time it has become easier: easier and more urgent. The people has clearly separated from its top layer; its oppressors and exploiters have parted company with it and become involved in a bloody war against it which can no longer be overlooked. It has become easier to take sides. Open warfare has, as it were, broken out among the 'audience'.

Nor can the demand for a realist way of writing any longer be so easily overlooked. It has become more or less self-evident. The ruling strata are using lies more openly than before, and the lies are bigger. Telling the truth seems increasingly urgent. The sufferings are greater and the number of sufferers has grown. Compared with the vast sufferings of the masses it seems trivial and even despicable to worry about petty difficulties and the difficulties of petty groups.

There is only one ally against the growth of barbarism: the people on whom it imposes these sufferings. Only the people offer any prospects. Thus it is natural to turn to them, and more necessary than ever to speak their language.

The words *Popularity* and *Realism* therefore are natural companions. It is in the interest of the people, the broad working masses, that literature should give them truthful representations of life; and truthful representations of life are in fact only of use to the broad working masses, the people; so that they have to be suggestive and intelligible to them, i.e. popular. None the less these conceptions need a thorough clean-up before being thrown into sentences where they will get smelted and put to use. It would be a mistake to treat them as fully explained, unsullied, unambiguous and without a past. ('We all know what's meant by that, no need for hairsplitting.') The German word for 'popular', *Volkstümlich*, is itself none too popular. It is unrealistic to imagine that it is. A whole series of words ending in *tum* need handling with care. One has only to think of *Brauch-tum*, *Königstum*, *Heiligtum*, and it is well known that *Volkstum* too has a quite specific ceremonious, sacramental and dubious ring which we cannot by any means overlook. We cannot overlook it, because we definitely need the conception of popularity or *Volkstümlichkeit*.

It is part of that supposedly poetic way of wording, by which the 'Volk' – more folk than people – is presented as particularly superstitious, or rather as an object of superstition. In this the folk or people appears with its immutable characteristics, its time-honoured traditions, forms of art, customs and habits, its religiosity, its hereditary enemies, its unconquerable strength and all the rest. A peculiar unity is conjured up of tormentor and tormented, exploiter and exploited, liar and victim; nor is it by any means a simple matter of the many, 'little' working people as against those on top.

The history of all the falsifications that have been operated with this conception of *Volkstum* is a long and complex story which is part of the history of the class war. We shall not embark on it but shall simply keep in mind the fact of such forgery whenever we speak of our need for popular art, meaning art for the broad masses of the people, for the many oppressed by the few, 'the people proper', the mass of producers that has so long been the object of politics and now has to become its subject. We shall remind ourselves that powerful institutions have long prevented this 'folk' from developing fully, that it has been artificially or forcibly tied down by conventions, and that the conception *Volkstümlich* has been stamped as a static one, without background or development. With this version of the conception we shall have no dealings, or rather we shall have to fight it. Our conception of 'popular' refers to the people who are not only fully involved in the process of development but are actually taking it over, forcing it, deciding it. We have in mind a people that is making history and altering the world and itself. We have in mind a fighting people and also a fighting conception of 'popularity'.

'Popular' means intelligible to the broad masses, taking over their own forms of expression and enriching them / adopting and consolidating their standpoint / representing the most progressive section of the people in such a way that it can take over the leadership: thus intelligible to other sections too / linking with tradition and carrying it further / handing on the achievements of the section now leading to the section of the people that is struggling for the lead.

We now come to the concept of 'Realism'. It is an old concept which has been much used by many men and for many purposes, and before it can be applied we must spring-clean it too. This is necessary because

11. Marieluise Fleisser's *Die Pioniere von Ingolstadt* in the Theater am Schiffbauerdamm, Berlin, 1929.

12. Erwin Piscator, 1930.

13. *Mann ist Mann* in Brecht's own production at the Staatstheater, 1931, with Peter Lorre (hatless) and (left to right) Lingen, Granach, and Heinz.

14. Charlie Chaplin in
City Lights, 1931.

15. Lotte Lenja, about 1931.

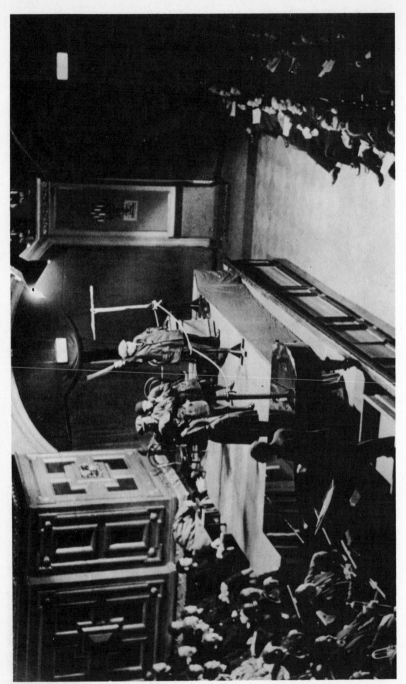

16. *Die Massnehme* in the Grosses Schauspielhaus, Berlin, 1930.

17. Rehearsal for *Happy End* in the Theater am Schiffbauerdamm, Berlin, 1929. Left to right: Erich Engel (the producer), Peter Lorre, Helene Weigel, Kurt Gerron, Carola Neher, Oskar Homolka, and Theo Lingen.

18. Fritz Sternberg, about 1932.

19. Caspar Neher's drawing of 1932 for Scene 13 of *Die Mutter*.

20. *Die Mutter* in the 1932 production, with Helene Weigel (left).

21. Ernst Busch, 1932.

when the people takes over its inheritance there has to be a process of expropriation. Literary works cannot be taken over like factories, or literary forms of expression like industrial methods. Realist writing, of which history offers many widely varying examples, is likewise conditioned by the question of how, when and for what class it is made use of: conditioned down to the last small detail. As we have in mind a fighting people that is changing the real world we must not cling to 'well-tried' rules for telling a story, worthy models set up by literary history, eternal aesthetic laws. We must not abstract the one and only realism from certain given works, but shall make a lively use of all means, old and new, tried and untried, deriving from art and deriving from other sources, in order to put living reality in the hands of living people in such a way that it can be mastered. We shall take care not to ascribe realism to a particular historical form of novel belonging to a particular period, Balzac's or Tolstoy's, for instance, so as to set up purely formal and literary criteria of realism. We shall not restrict ourselves to speaking of realism in cases where one can (e.g.) smell, look, feel whatever is depicted, where 'atmosphere' is created and stories develop in such a way that the characters are psychologically stripped down. Our conception of *realism* needs to be broad and political, free from aesthetic restrictions and independent of convention. *Realist*[1] means: laying bare society's causal network / showing up the dominant viewpoint as the viewpoint of the dominators / writing from the standpoint of the class which has prepared the broadest solutions for the most pressing problems afflicting human society / emphasizing the dynamics of development / concrete and so as to encourage abstraction.

It is a tall order, and it can be made taller. And we shall let the artist apply all his imagination, all his originality, his sense of humour and power of invention to its fulfilment. We will not stick to unduly detailed literary models or force the artist to follow over-precise rules for telling a story.

We shall establish that so-called sensuous writing (in which everything can be smelt, tasted, felt) is not to be identified automatically with realist writing, for we shall see that there are sensuously written works which are not realist, and realist works which are not sensuously written. We shall have to go carefully into the question whether the story is best developed by aiming at an eventual psychological stripping-down of the characters. Our readers may quite well feel that they have not been given the key to what is happening if they are simply induced by a combination of arts to take part in the inner emotions of our books' heroes. By taking over the

[1] To G. Lukács in particular *Das Wort* owes some most notable essays, which shed light on the concept of realism even if, in my opinion, they define it rather too narrowly.

forms of Balzac and Tolstoy without a thorough inspection we might perhaps exhaust our readers, the people, just as these writers often do. Realism is not a pure question of form. Copying the methods of these realists, we should cease to be realists ourselves.

For time flows on, and if it did not it would be a poor look-out for those who have no golden tables to sit at. Methods wear out, stimuli fail. New problems loom up and demand new techniques. Reality alters; to represent it the means of representation must alter too. Nothing arises from nothing; the new springs from the old, but that is just what makes it new.

The oppressors do not always appear in the same mask. The masks cannot always be stripped off in the same way. There are so many tricks for dodging the mirror that is held out. Their military roads are termed motor roads. Their tanks are painted to look like Macduff's bushes. Their agents can show horny hands as if they were workers. Yes: it takes ingenuity to change the hunter into the quarry. What was popular yesterday is no longer so today, for the people of yesterday were not the people as it is today.

Anybody who is not bound by formal prejudices knows that there are many ways of suppressing truth and many ways of stating it: that indignation at inhuman conditions can be stimulated in many ways, by direct description of a pathetic or matter-of-fact kind, by narrating stories and parables, by jokes, by over- and understatement. In the theatre reality can be represented in a factual or a fantastic form. The actors can do without (or with the minimum of) makeup, appearing 'natural', and the whole thing can be a fake; they can wear grotesque masks and represent the truth. There is not much to argue about here: the means must be asked what the end is. The people knows how to ask this. Piscator's great experiments in the theatre (and my own), which repeatedly involved the exploding of conventional forms, found their chief support in the most progressive cadres of the working class. The workers judged everything by the amount of truth contained in it; they welcomed any innovation which helped the representation of truth, of the real mechanism of society; they rejected whatever seemed like playing, like machinery working for its own sake, i.e. no longer, or not yet, fulfilling a purpose. The workers' arguments were never literary or purely theatrical. 'You can't mix theatre and film': that sort of thing was never said. If the film was not properly used the most one heard was: 'that bit of film is unnecessary, it's distracting'. Workers' choruses spoke intricate rhythmical verse parts ('if it rhymed it'd all slip down like butter, and nothing would stick') and sang difficult (unaccustomed) compositions by Eisler ('it's got some guts in it'). But we had to alter particular lines whose sense was wrong or hard to arrive at. When there were certain subtleties (irregularities, complexities) in marching songs which had rhymes to make them easier to learn and simple rhythms to 'put them across' better, then they said: 'that's amusing, there was a sort of twist in that'. They had no use for anything played out, trivial, so ordinary that one doesn't need to think ('there's nothing in it'). If an aesthetic was needed, here it was. I shall never forget how one worker looked at me when I answered his request to include something extra in a song about the USSR ('It must go in – what's the point otherwise?') by saying that it would wreck the artistic form: he put his head on one side and smiled. At this polite smile a whole section of aesthetic collapsed. The workers were not afraid to teach us, nor were they afraid to learn.

I speak from experience when I say that one need never be frightened of putting bold and unaccustomed things before the proletariat, so long as they have to do with reality. There will always be educated persons, connoisseurs of the arts, who will step in with a 'The people won't understand that'. But the people impatiently shoves them aside and comes to terms directly with the artist. There is highly cultured stuff made for minorities, designed to form minorities: the two thousandth transformation of some old hat, the spicing-up of a venerable and now decomposing piece of meat. The proletariat rejects it ('they've got something to worry about') with an incredulous, somewhat reflective shake of the head. It is not the spice that is being rejected, but the meat; not the two thousandth form, but the old hat. When they themselves took to writing and acting they were compellingly original. What was known as 'agit-prop' art, which a number of second-rate noses were turned up at, was a mine of novel artistic techniques and ways of expression. Magnificent and long-forgotten elements from periods of truly popular art cropped up there, boldly adapted to the new social ends. Daring cuts and compositions, beautiful simplifications (alongside misconceived ones): in all this there was often an astonishing economy and elegance and a fearless eye for complexity. A lot of it may have been primitive, but it was never primitive with the kind of primitivity that affected the supposedly varied psychological portrayals of bourgeois art. It is very wrong to make a few misconceived stylizations a pretext for rejecting a style of representation which attempts (so often successfully) to bring out the essential and to encourage abstraction. The sharp eyes of the workers saw through naturalism's superficial representation of reality. When they said in *Fuhrmann Henschel*, 'that's more than we want to know about it' they were in fact wishing they could get a more exact representation of the real social forces operating under the immediately visible surface. To quote from my own experience: they were not put off by the fantastic costumes and the apparently unreal setting of *The Threepenny Opera*. They were not narrow; they hated narrowness (their living quarters were narrow). They were generous; their employers were stingy. They thought it possible to dispense with some things that the artists felt to be essential, but they were amiable enough about it; they were not against superfluity: they were against certain superfluous people. They did not muzzle the threshing ox, though they saw to it that he threshed. 'The universally-applicable creative method': they didn't believe in that sort of thing. They knew that they needed many different methods in order to reach their objective. If you want an aesthetic, there you are.

So the criteria for the popular and the realistic need to be chosen not only with great care but also with an open mind. They must not be deduced from existing realist works and existing popular works, as is often the case. Such an approach would lead to purely formalistic criteria, and questions of popularity and realism would be decided by form.

One cannot decide if a work is realist or not by finding out whether it resembles existing, reputedly realist works which must be counted realist for their time. In each individual case the picture given of life must be compared, not with another picture, but with the actual life portrayed. And likewise where popularity is concerned there is a wholly formalistic procedure that has to be guarded against. The intelligibility of a work of literature is not ensured exclusively by its being written in exactly the same way as other works which people have understood. These other works too were not invariably written just like the works before them. Something was done towards their understanding. In the same way we must do something for the understanding of the new works. Besides *being popular* there is such a thing as *becoming popular*.

If we want a truly popular literature, alive and fighting, completely gripped by reality and completely gripping reality, then we must keep pace with reality's headlong development. The great working masses of the people are on the move. The activity and brutality of their enemies proves it.

['Volkstümlichkeit und Realismus', from *Sinn und Form*, Potsdam, 1958, No. 4. Also *Schriften zum Theater 4*, pp. 149–61]

NOTE: From July 1936 to its last number in March 1939, Brecht was one of the three editors of *Das Wort*, a monthly German-language review published in Moscow, where Willi Bredel was in charge. During 1937 its columns were opened to the debate on realism and expressionism which had been raging among the German émigrés ever since Georg Lukács first raised the subject in January 1934 in *Internationale Literatur* (*Deutsche Blätter*), the largely similar Moscow review

DAS WORT

LITERARISCHE MONATSSCHRIFT

REDAKTION: BERTOLT BRECHT, LION FEUCHTWANGER, WILLI BREDEL

1

JOURGAZ-VERLAG MOSKAU / 2. JAHR 1937

edited by Johannes R. Becher to which Brecht also contributed. The debate began with two attacks on Gottfried Benn by Klaus Mann and Alfred Kurella (the main cultural politician in East Germany today, writing then under the name Bernhard Ziegler), who were followed in the second and third issues of 1938 by Herwarth Walden, Bela Balász, Gustav von Wangenheim and others. In the April number Professor Lukács wrote about the realist novel, quoting Balzac and Tolstoy as models, praising Rolland and the two Manns and singling out Gorky as the 'leading author of the world's literature in our day' (p. 90). In June he attacked the pro-Expressionist views of Ernst Bloch – Professor Bloch's own articles are reprinted in his *Erbschaft dieser Zeit* (Suhrkamp, Frankfurt, 1962) – in an article called 'Es geht um den Realismus' ('It's realism that's at stake'), where he denounced the principle of montage, criticized Joyce as a 'surrealist' and patted Brecht on the back for the new realistic tone of the scene 'Der Spitzel' ('The Informer') from *Furcht und Elend des Dritten Reiches*: one of his least typical works. Kurella then summed up (both his essays are reprinted in his *Zwischendurch*, Aufbau-Verlag, East Berlin, 1961).

Brecht's reaction was to write two articles, neither of which in fact appeared in *Das Wort*: this one and another called 'Weite und Vielfalt der realistischen Schreibweise' whose manuscript bears the pencilled date 'July 1938, Skovsbostrand'. It was first published in *Versuche 13* (1954) and goes straight to the point:

> As a result no doubt of a number of essays concentrating on a particular way of realistic writing – that of the bourgeois novel – readers of *Das Wort* have recently expressed their concern that this review may be restricting realism in literature within too narrow boundaries. One or two articles may have laid down unduly formal criteria for realist writing, and as a result several readers came to interpret this as meaning that a book is written realistically when it is 'written in the same way as the bourgeois novels of the last century'.

The article goes on to quote Shelley as an even better realist than Balzac, printing all but the opening stanza of 'The Mask of Anarchy' (which Brecht himself used later as the model for his ballad 'Freiheit und Democracy') with a line-by-line translation. Cervantes, Swift, Grimmelshausen, Dickens, Voltaire and Hašek are cited as further realists who adopted quite different forms from Tolstoy and Balzac. 'Realism is not a matter of form,' says Brecht.

> Tying a great conception like Realism to a few names is dangerous, however famous they may be, and so is the bundling together of a few forms to make a universally-applicable creative method, even if those forms are useful in themselves. Literary forms have to be checked against reality, not against aesthetics – even realist aesthetics. There are many ways of suppressing truth, and many ways of stating it.

Lukács had claimed that it was his object 'to show the connection between the Popular Front [this having become Communist policy at the Seventh Comintern Congress of 1935], popularity of literature, and true realism'. The modern reader may be more inclined to notice the evident connection between his arguments and the new politico-aesthetic doctrine of Socialist Realism, a 'universally-applicable creative method' if ever there was one, as laid down at the Soviet Writers' Congress of 1934; it is no coincidence that its spokesman A. A. Zhdanov was also insistent on 'popularity'. How far Brecht himself had the new doctrine in mind is not clear; he never explicitly said a word against it either then or later – see p. 269 for his own definition of the term – though the Soviet artists whose work he admired, and the concept of Alienation itself, were all now to be condemned in Russia as 'formalistic' – a word which Brecht himself uses in almost the opposite sense. Worse still, Tretiakov, who had written about Brecht and been adapted by him, disappeared in the Soviet purges around this time, and soon Meyerhold's arrest and death were to follow.

It is interesting that Brecht's two (for some reason) unpublished ripostes should have come at the end of his own brief period of more or less orthodox realistic writing (*Señora Carrar's Rifles* and *Furcht und Elend*). A few months more, and even the first version of *Galileo*, which he provisionally finished on 23 November, began to seem to him too conservative. 'Technically a step backwards,' says a diary note of 25 February 1939, 'just like *Señora Carrar's Rifles*. Too opportunist.' *Señora Carrar's Rifles*, according to Brecht's own note at the end of the play, is 'Aristotelian (empathy-) drama'. It is the only one of his works of which he said this.

28 · On Rhymeless Verse with Irregular Rhythms

Sometimes on publishing unrhymed verse I was asked how on earth I could present such stuff as verse; this happened most recently with my 'German Satires'. It is a fair question, as it is usual for verse which does without rhyme to offer at least a solid rhythm. Many of my most recent works in verse have had neither rhyme nor any regular solid rhythm. The reason I give for labelling them verse is: because they have a kind of (shifting, syncopated, gestic) rhythm, even if not a regular one. My first book of poems contained virtually nothing but songs and ballads, and the verse forms were fairly regular; they were nearly all supposed to be singable, and in the simplest possible way: I set them to music myself. There was only one poem without rhymes, and it was rhythmically regular; the rhymed poems on the other hand nearly all had irregular rhythms. In the nineteen stanzas of the 'Ballad of the Dead Soldier' there were nine different scansions of the second line: [The examples quoted are from stanzas 1–6, 14, 15 and 18]. After that I wrote a play (*Im Dickicht der Städte*) making use of Arthur Rimbaud's heightened prose (from his *Une Saison en Enfer*).

For another play (*Edward II*) I had to tackle the problem of iambics. I had been struck with the greater force of the actors' delivery when they used the almost unreadable 'stumbling' verses of the old Schlegel and Tieck Shakespeare translation rather than Rothe's smooth new one. How much better it expressed the tussle of thoughts in the great monologues! How much richer the structure of the verse! The problem was simple: I needed elevated language, but was brought up against the oily smoothness of the usual five-foot iambic metre. I needed rhythm, but not the usual jingle. I went about it like this. Instead of:

> I heard the drumbeats ring across the swamp
> Horses and weapons sank before my eyes
> And now my head is turning. Are they all
> Now drowned and dead? Does only noise still hang
> Hollow and idle on the air? But I
> Should not be running. . . .

I wrote:

> After those drumbeats, the swamp gulping
> Weapons and horses, all turns
> In my mother's son's head. Stop panting! Are all
> Drowned and dead, leaving just noise
> Hanging on the air? I will not
> Run further.

This gave the jerky breath of a man running, and such syncopation did more to show the speaker's conflicting feelings. My political knowledge in those days was disgracefully slight, but I was aware of huge inconsistencies in people's social life, and I didn't think it my task formally to iron out all the discordances and interferences of which I was strongly conscious. I caught them up in the incidents of my plays and in the verses of my poems; and did so long before I had recognized their real character and causes. As can be seen from the texts it was a matter not just of a formal 'kicking against the pricks' – of a protest against the smoothness and harmony of conventional poetry – but already of an attempt to show human dealings as contradictory, fiercely fought over, full of violence.

I could be still freer in my approach when I wrote opera, Lehrstück or cantata for modern composers. There I gave up iambics entirely and applied firm but irregular rhythms. Composers of the most varied schools assured me, and I myself could see, that they were admirably suited for music.

After that, alongside ballads and mass choruses with rhymes and regular (or almost regular) rhythms, I wrote more and more poems with no rhymes and with irregular rhythms. It must be remembered that the bulk of my work was designed for the theatre; I was always thinking of actual delivery. And for this delivery (whether of prose or of verse) I had worked out a quite definite technique. I called it 'gestic'.

This meant that the sentence must entirely follow the gest of the person speaking. Let me give an example. The Bible's sentence 'pluck out the eye that offends thee' is based on a gest – that of commanding – but it is not entirely gestically expressed, as 'that offends thee' has a further gest which remains unexpressed, namely that of explanation. Purely gestically expressed the sentence runs 'if thine eye offends thee, pluck it out' (and this is how it was put by Luther, who 'watched the people's mouth'). It can be seen at a glance that this way of putting it is far richer and cleaner from a gestic point of view. The first clause contains an assumption, and its peculiarity and specialness can be fully expressed by the tone of voice. Then there is a little pause of bewilderment, and only then the devastating proposal. The gestic way of putting things can of course quite well apply within a regular rhythm (or in a rhymed poem). Here is an example showing the difference:

> Haven't you seen the child, unconscious yet of affection
> Warming and cherishing him, who moves from one arm to another
> Dozing, until the call of passion awakens the stripling
> And with consciousness' flame the dawning world is illumined?
>
> (Schiller: *Der philosophische Egoist*)

And:

> Nothing comes from nothing; not even the gods can deny it.
> So constrained by fear our poor mortality, always;
> So many things it sees appearing on earth or in heaven,
> Moved by some basic cause that itself is unable to compass,
> That it assumes some Power alone can be their creator.
> But when we've seen for ourselves that nothing can come out of nothing,
> Then we shall understand just what we are asking: the reason
> Why all these things arose without divine intervention.
>
> (Lucretius: *De rerum natura*)

The lack of gestic elements in Schiller's poem and the wealth of them in Lucretius's can be easily confirmed by repeating the verses and observing how often one's own gest changes in the process.

I began speaking of the gestic way of putting things for the reason that, although this can be achieved within our regular rhythmical framework, it seems to me at present that irregular rhythms must further the gestic way of putting things. I remember two observations helping me to work out irregular rhythms. The first related to those short shouted choruses at workers' demonstrations, which I first heard one Christmas Eve. A band of proletarians was marching through the respectable Western districts of

Berlin shouting the sentence 'We're hungry': 'Wir haben Hunger'. The rhythm was this:

Wir haben Hunger

I subsequently heard other similar choruses, just with an easily-spoken and disciplined text. One of them ran 'Help yourselves: vote for Thälmann'.

Helft euch selber, wählt Thälmann.

Another experience of rhythm with a popular origin was the cry of 'Text-book for the opera *Fratella* to be given on the radio tonight' which I heard a Berlin streetseller calling as he sold libretti outside the Kaufhaus des Westens. He gave it the following rhythm:

Textbuch für die Oper Fratella welche heute Abend im Rundfunk
gehört wird

He continually varied the pitch and the volume, but stuck inflexibly to the rhythm.

The newspaper-seller's technique of rhythmical cries is easily studied. But irregular rhythms are also used in written matter, whenever it is a question of more or less dinning something in.

[Two advertising slogans are then quoted and scanned]

These experiences were applied to the development of irregular rhythms. What do these irregular rhythms look like, then? Here is an example from the 'German Satires': the two last verses from 'Die Jugend und das Dritte Reich'. First

> Ja, wenn die Kinder Kinder blieben, dann
> Könnte man ihnen immer Märchen erzählen
> Da sie aber älter werden
> Kann man es nicht.
> [Ah yes, if children only remained children, then
> One could always tell them stories
> But since they grow older
> One cannot.]

How does one read that? We start by superimposing it on a regular rhythm.

Ja, wenn die Kinder Kinder blieben, dann
Könnte man ihnen immer Märchen erzählen
Da sie aber älter werden
Kann man es nicht.

The missing syllables [Brecht says 'feet', but clearly syllables are meant] must be allowed for when speaking either by prolonging the previous syllable ('foot') or by pauses. The division into lines helps that. I picked this particular verse because if one splits its second line in two:

> Könnte man ihnen
> Immer Märchen erzählen

it becomes still easier to read, so that the principle can be studied in a borderline case. The effect on sound and emphasis of this division can be seen if the last verse:

> When the régime rubs its hands and speaks of Youth
> It is like a man, who
> Looking at the snowy hillside, rubs his hands and says:
> How cold it'll be this summer, with
> So much snow.

is divided differently, thus:

> When the régime rubs its hands and speaks of Youth
> It is like a man
> Who, looking at the snowy hillside, rubs his hands and says:
> How cold it'll be this summer
> With so much snow.

This way of writing it can in fact be read rhythmically too. But the qualitative difference hits the eye. In general, it must be admitted, this free way of treating verse strongly tempts the writer to be formless: rhythm isn't even guaranteed to the same extent as with a regular rhythmical scheme (though with this the right number of feet does not necessarily produce rhythm). The proof of the pudding is simply in the eating.

It must also be admitted that at the moment the reading of irregular rhythms presents one or two difficulties. This seems to me no criticism of it. Our ear is certainly in course of being physiologically transformed. Our acoustic environment has changed immensely. An episode in an American feature film, when the dancer Astaire tap-danced to the sounds of a machine-room, showed the astonishingly close relationship between the new noises and the percussive rhythms of jazz. Jazz signified a broad flow of popular musical elements into modern music, whatever our commercialized world may have made of it since. Its connection with the freeing of the Negroes is well known.

The extremely healthy campaign against Formalism has made possible the productive development of artistic forms by showing that the development of social content is an absolutely essential precondition for it. Unless it adapts itself to this development of content and takes orders from it, any formal innovation will remain wholly unfruitful.

The 'German Satires' were written for the German Freedom Radio. It was a matter of projecting single sentences to a distant, artificially scattered audience. They had to be cut down to the most concise possible form and to be reasonably invulnerable to interruptions (by jamming). Rhyme seemed to me to be unsuitable, as it easily makes a poem seem self-contained, lets it glide past the ear. Regular rhythms with their even cadence fail in the same way to cut deep enough, and they impose circumlocutions; a lot of everyday expressions won't fit them; what was needed was the tone of direct and spontaneous speech. I thought rhymeless verse with irregular rhythms seemed suitable.

['Über reimlose Lyrik mit unregelmässigen Rhythmen' from *Das Wort*, Moscow, 1939, No. 3]

NOTE: This essay appeared in the final number of *Das Wort*. The verse examples have been turned into English wherever a translation can still carry Brecht's point. The 'German Satires' appeared in the *Svendborger Gedichte* (London 1939), now incorporated in *Gedichte 3* (Frankfurt, 1961). The anti-Nazi Freedom Radio operated from Czechoslovakia in the later 1930s.

Brecht's first book of poems was *Die Hauspostille* (Berlin 1927; Frankfurt 1951). He adapted *Edward II* from Marlowe in collaboration with Feuchtwanger; the lines quoted are from Gaveston's speech just before his capture, and bear little relation to Marlowe's 'Yet, lusty lords, I have escaped your hands', etc. Rothe is the modern translator whose versions were used by Reinhardt; his book *Shakespeare als Provokation* appeared in 1962. Thälmann was Communist candidate for the presidency in 1932. The Kaufhaus des Westens is a big Berlin store.

This indication that Brecht approved of the anti-Formalist campaign of the 1930s, given his own interpretation of 'Formalism', is the only indication that he approved of it at all.

The great majority of the *Svendborger Gedichte* are written in the style described, as well as the whole of *Lucullus* (on which he was working at this time), *Antigone* (1947) and many verse sections of other plays. For the connection between Brecht's poems and their musical settings see also pp. 4, 85 and 104-5.

29 · The Street Scene
A Basic Model for an Epic Theatre

In the decade and a half that followed the World War a comparatively new way of acting was tried out in a number of German theatres. Its qualities of clear description and reporting and its use of choruses and projections as a means of commentary earned it the name of 'epic'. The actor used a somewhat complex technique to detach himself from the character portrayed; he forced the spectator to look at the play's situations from such an angle that they necessarily became subject to his criticism. Supporters of this epic theatre argued that the new subject-matter, the highly involved incidents of the class war in its acutest and most terrible stage, would be mastered more easily by such a method, since it would thereby become possible to portray social processes as seen in their causal relationships. But the result of these experiments was that aesthetics found itself up against a whole series of substantial difficulties.

It is comparatively easy to set up a basic model for epic theatre. For practical experiments I usually picked as my example of completely simple, 'natural' epic theatre an incident such as can be seen at any street corner: an eyewitness demonstrating to a collection of people how a traffic accident took place. The bystanders may not have observed what happened, or they may simply not agree with him, may 'see things a different way'; the point is that the demonstrator acts the behaviour of driver or victim or both in such a way that the bystanders are able to form an opinion about the accident.

Such an example of the most primitive type of epic theatre seems easy to understand. Yet experience has shown that it presents astounding difficulties to the reader or listener as soon as he is asked to see the implications of treating this kind of street corner demonstration as a basic form of major theatre, theatre for a scientific age. What this means of course is that the epic theatre may appear richer, more intricate and complex in every particular, yet to be major theatre it need at bottom only contain the same elements as a street-corner demonstration of this sort; nor could it any longer be termed epic theatre if any of the main elements of the street-corner demonstration were lacking. Until this is understood it is impossible really to understand what follows. Until one understands the novelty, un-familiarity and direct challenge to the critical faculties of the suggestion that street-corner demonstration of this sort can serve as a satisfactory basic model of major theatre one cannot really understand what follows.

Consider: the incident is clearly very far from what we mean by an artistic one. The demonstrator need not be an artist. The capacities he needs to achieve his aim are in effect universal. Suppose he cannot carry out some particular movement as quickly as the victim he is imitating; all he need do is to explain that *he* moves three times as fast, and the demonstration neither suffers in essentials nor loses its point. On the contrary it is important that he should not be too perfect. His demonstration would be spoilt if the bystanders' attention were drawn to his powers of transformation. He has to avoid presenting himself in such a way that someone calls out 'What a lifelike portrayal of a chauffeur!' He must not 'cast a spell' over anyone. He should not transport people from normality to 'higher realms'. He need not dispose of any special powers of suggestion.

It is most important that one of the main features of the ordinary theatre should be excluded from our street scene: the engendering of illusion. The street demonstrator's performance is essentially repetitive. The event has taken place; what you are seeing now is a repeat. If the scene in the theatre follows the street scene in this respect then the theatre will stop pretending not to be theatre, just as the street-corner demonstration admits it is a demonstration (and does not pretend to be the actual event). The element of rehearsal in the acting and of learning by heart in the text, the whole machinery and the whole process of preparation: it all becomes plainly apparent. What room is left for experience? Is the reality portrayed still experienced in any sense?

The street scene determines what kind of experience is to be prepared for the spectator. There is no question but that the street-corner demonstrator has been through an 'experience', but he is not out to make his demonstration serve as an 'experience' for the audience. Even the experience of the driver and the victim is only partially communicated by him, and he by no means tries to turn it into an enjoyable experience for the spectator, however lifelike he may make his demonstration. The demonstration would become no less valid if he did not reproduce the fear caused by the accident; on the contrary it would lose validity if he did. He is not interested in creating pure emotions. It is important to understand that a theatre which follows his lead in this respect undergoes a positive change of function.

One essential element of the street scene must also be present in the theatrical scene if this is to qualify as epic, namely that the demonstration should have a socially practical significance. Whether our street demonstrator is out to show that one attitude on the part of driver or pedestrian makes an accident inevitable where another would not, or whether he is demonstrating with a view to fixing the responsibility, his demonstration has a practical purpose, intervenes socially.

The demonstrator's purpose determines how thoroughly he has to imitate. Our demonstrator need not imitate every aspect of his characters' behaviour, but only so much as gives a picture. Generally the theatre scene will give much fuller pictures, corresponding to its more extensive range of interest. How do street scene and theatre scene link up here? To take a point of detail, the victim's voice may have played no immediate part in the accident. Eye-witnesses may disagree as to whether a cry they heard ('Look out!') came from the victim or from someone else, and this may give our demonstrator a motive for imitating the voice. The question can be settled by demonstrating whether the voice was an old man's or a woman's, or merely whether it was high or low. Again, the answer may depend on whether it was that of an educated person or not. Loud or soft may play a great part, as the driver could be correspondingly more or less guilty. A whole series of characteristics of the victim ask to be portrayed. Was he absent-minded? Was his attention distracted? If so, by what? What, on the evidence of his behaviour, could have made him liable to be distracted by just that circumstance and no other? Etc., etc. It can be seen that our street-corner demonstration provides opportunities for a pretty rich and varied portrayal of human types. Yet a theatre which tries to restrict its essential elements to those provided by our street scene will have to acknowledge certain limits to imitation. It must be able to justify any outlay in terms of its purpose.[1]

The demonstration may for instance be dominated by the question of compensation for the victim, etc. The driver risks being sacked from his job, losing his licence, going to prison; the victim risks a heavy hospital bill, loss of job, permanent disfigurement, possibly unfitness for work.

---

[1] We often come across demonstrations of an everyday sort which are more thorough imitations than our street-corner accident demands. Generally they are comic ones. Our next-door neighbour may decide to 'take off' the rapacious behaviour of our common landlord. Such an imitation is often rich and full of variety. Closer examination will show however that even so apparently complex an imitation concentrates on one specific side of the landlord's behaviour. The imitation is summary or selective, deliberately leaving out those occasions where the landlord strikes our neighbour as 'perfectly sensible', though such occasions of course occur. He is far from giving a rounded picture; for that would have no comic impact at all. The street scene, perforce adopting a wider angle of vision, at this point lands in difficulties which must not be underestimated. It has to be just as successful in promoting criticism, but the incidents in question are far more complex. It must promote positive as well as negative criticism, and as part of a single process. You have to understand what is involved in winning the audience's approval by means of a critical approach. Here again we have a precedent in our street scene, i.e. in any demonstration of an everyday sort. Next-door neighbour and street demonstrator can reproduce their subject's 'sensible' or his 'senseless' behaviour alike, by submitting it for an opinion. When it crops up in the course of events, however (when a man switches from being sensible to being senseless, or the other way round), then they usually need some form of commentary in order to change the angle of their portrayal. Hence, as already mentioned, certain difficulties for the theatre scene. These cannot be dealt with here.

This is the area within which the demonstrator builds up his characters. The victim may have had a companion; the driver may have had his girl sitting alongside him. That would bring out the social element better and allow the characters to be more fully drawn.

Another essential element in the street scene is that the demonstrator should derive his characters entirely from their actions. He imitates their actions and so allows conclusions to be drawn about them. A theatre that follows him in this will be largely breaking with the orthodox theatre's habit of basing the actions on the characters and having the former exempted from criticism by presenting them as an unavoidable consequence deriving by natural law from the characters who perform them. To the street demonstrator the character of the man being demonstrated remains a quantity that need not be completely defined. Within certain limits he may be like this or like that; it doesn't matter. What the demonstrator is concerned with are his accident-prone and accident-proof qualities.[1] The theatrical scene may show more fully-defined individuals. But it must then be in a position to treat their individuality as a special case and outline the field within which, once more, its most socially relevant effects are produced. Our street demonstrator's possibilities of demonstration are narrowly restricted (indeed, we chose this model so that the limits should be as narrow as possible). If the essential elements of the theatrical scene are limited to those of the street scene then its greater richness must be an enrichment only. The question of border-line cases becomes acute.

Let us take a specific detail. Can our street demonstrator, say, ever become entitled to use an excited tone of voice in repeating the driver's statement that he has been exhausted by too long a spell of work? (In theory this is no more possible than for a returning messenger to start telling his fellow-countrymen of his talk with the king with the words 'I saw the bearded king'.) It can only be possible, let alone unavoidable, if one imagines a street-corner situation where such excitement, specifically about this aspect of the affair, plays a particular part. (In the instance above this would be so if the king had sworn never to cut his beard off until ... etc.) We have to find a point of view for our demonstrator that allows him to submit this excitement to criticism. Only if he adopts a quite definite point of view can he be entitled to imitate the driver's excited voice; e.g. if he blames drivers as such for doing too little to reduce their hours of work. ('Look at him. Doesn't even belong to a union, but gets worked up soon enough when an accident happens. "Ten hours I've been at the wheel." ')

[1] The same situation will be produced by all those people whose characters fulfil the conditions laid down by him and show the features that he imitates.

Before it can get as far as this, i.e. be able to suggest a point of view to the actor, the theatre needs to take a number of steps. By widening its field of vision and showing the driver in other situations besides that of the accident the theatre in no way exceeds its model; it merely creates a further situation on the same pattern. One can imagine a scene of the same kind as the street scene which provides a well-argued demonstration showing how such emotions as the driver's develop, or another which involves making comparisons between tones of voice. In order not to exceed the model scene the theatre only has to develop a technique for submitting emotions to the spectator's criticism. Of course this does not mean that the spectator must be barred on principle from sharing certain emotions that are put before him; none the less to communicate emotions is only one particular form (phase, consequence) of criticism. The theatre's demonstrator, the actor, must apply a technique which will let him reproduce the tone of the subject demonstrated with a certain reserve, with detachment (so that the spectator can say: 'He's getting excited – in vain, too late, at last. . . .' etc.). In short, the actor must remain a demonstrator; he must present the person demonstrated as a stranger, he must not suppress the '*he* did that, *he* said that' element in his performance. He must not go so far as to be wholly transformed into the person demonstrated.

One essential element of the street scene lies in the natural attitude adopted by the demonstrator, which is two-fold; he is always taking two situations into account. He behaves naturally as a demonstrator, and he lets the subject of the demonstration behave naturally too. He never forgets, nor does he allow it to be forgotten, that he is not the subject but the demonstrator. That is to say, what the audience sees is not a fusion between demonstrator and subject, not some third, independent, uncontradictory entity with isolated features of (a) demonstrator and (b) subject, such as the orthodox theatre puts before us in its productions.[1] The feelings and opinions of demonstrator and demonstrated are not merged into one.

We now come to one of those elements that are peculiar to the epic theatre, the so-called A-effect (alienation effect). What is involved here is, briefly, a technique of taking the human social incidents to be portrayed and labelling them as something striking, something that calls for explanation, is not to be taken for granted, not just natural. The object of this 'effect' is to allow the spectator to criticize constructively from a social point of view. Can we show that this A-effect is significant for our street demonstrator?

We can picture what happens if he fails to make use of it. The following situation could occur. One of the spectators might say: 'But if the victim

[1] Most clearly worked out by Stanislavsky.

125

stepped off the kerb with his right foot, as you showed him doing. . . .' The demonstrator might interrupt saying: 'I showed him stepping off with his left foot.' By arguing which foot he really stepped off with in his demonstration, and, even more, how the victim himself acted, the demonstration can be so transformed that the A-effect occurs. The demonstrator achieves it by paying exact attention this time to his movements, executing them carefully, probably in slow motion; in this way he alienates the little sub-incident, emphasizes its importance, makes it worthy of notice. And so the epic theatre's alienation effect proves to have its uses for our street demonstrator too; in other words it is also to be found in this small everyday scene of natural street-corner theatre, which has little to do with art. The direct changeover from representation to commentary that is so characteristic of the epic theatre is still more easily recognized as one element of any street demonstration. Wherever he feels he can the demonstrator breaks off his imitation in order to give explanations. The epic theatre's choruses and documentary projections, the direct addressing of the audience by its actors, are at bottom just this.

It will have been observed, not without astonishment I hope, that I have not named any strictly artistic elements as characterizing our street scene and, with it, that of the epic theatre. The street demonstrator can carry out a successful demonstration with no greater abilities than, in effect, anybody has. What about the epic theatre's value as art?

The epic theatre wants to establish its basic model at the street corner, i.e. to return to the very simplest 'natural' theatre, a social enterprise whose origins, means and ends are practical and earthly. The model works without any need of programmatic theatrical phrases like 'the urge to self-expression', 'making a part one's own', 'spiritual experience', 'the play instinct', 'the story-teller's art', etc. Does that mean that the epic theatre isn't concerned with art?

It might be as well to begin by putting the question differently, thus: can we make use of artistic abilities for the purposes of our street scene? Obviously yes. Even the street-corner demonstration includes artistic elements. Artistic abilities in some small degree are to be found in any man. It does no harm to remember this when one is confronted with great art. Undoubtedly what we call artistic abilities can be exercised at any time within the limits imposed by our street scene model. They will function as artistic abilities even though they do not exceed these limits (for instance, when there is meant to be no complete transformation of demonstrator into subject). And true enough, the epic theatre is an extremely artistic affair, hardly thinkable without artists and virtuosity, imagination, humour and fellow-feeling; it cannot be practised without all these and much else too. It has got to be entertaining, it has got to be instructive. How then can art be developed out of the elements of the street scene, without adding any or leaving any out? How does it evolve into the theatrical scene with its fabricated story, its trained actors, its lofty style of speaking, its make-up, its team performance by a number of players? Do we need to add to our elements in order to move on from the 'natural' demonstration to the 'artificial'?

Is it not true that the additions which we must make to our model in order to arrive at epic theatre are of a fundamental kind? A brief examination will show that they are not. Take the *story*. There was nothing fabricated about our street accident. Nor does the orthodox theatre deal only in fabrications; think for instance of the historical play. None the less a story can be performed at the street corner too. Our demonstrator may at any time be in a position to say: 'The driver was guilty, because it all happened the way I showed you. He wouldn't be guilty if it had happened the way I'm going to show you now.' And he can fabricate an incident and demonstrate it. Or take the fact that the text is learnt by heart. As a witness in a court case the demonstrator may have written down the subject's exact words, learnt them by heart and rehearsed them; in that case he too is performing a text he has learned. Or take a rehearsed programme by several players: it doesn't always have to be artistic purposes that bring about a demonstration of this sort; one need only think of the French police technique of making the chief figures in any criminal case re-enact certain crucial situations before a police audience. Or take making-up. Minor changes in appearance – ruffling one's hair, for instance – can occur at any time within the framework of the non-artistic type of demonstration. Nor is make-up itself used solely for theatrical purposes. In the street scene the driver's moustache may be particularly significant. It may have influenced the testimony of the possible girl companion suggested earlier. This can be represented by our demonstrator making the driver stroke an imaginary moustache when prompting his companion's evidence. In this way the demonstrator can do a good deal to discredit her as a witness. Moving on to the use of a real moustache in the theatre, however, is not an entirely easy transition, and the same difficulty occurs with respect to *costume*. Our demonstrator may under given circumstances put on the driver's cap – for instance if he wants to show that he was drunk: (he had it on crooked) – but he can only do so conditionally, under these circumstances; (see what was said about borderline cases earlier). However, where there is a demonstration by several demonstrators of the kind referred to above we can have costume so that the various characters can be distinguished. This again is only a limited use of costume. There must be no question of creating an illusion that the demonstrators really are these characters. (The epic theatre can counteract this illusion by especially exaggerated costume or by garments that are somehow marked out as objects for display.) Moreover we can suggest another model as a substitute for ours on this point: the kind of street demonstration given by hawkers. To sell their neckties these people will portray a badly-dressed and a well-dressed man; with a few props and technical tricks they can perform significant little scenes where they submit essentially to the same restrictions as apply to the demonstrator in our street scene: (they will pick up tie, hat, stick, gloves and give certain significant imitations of a man of the world, and the whole time they will refer to him as '*he*'!) With hawkers we also find *verse* being used within the same framework as that of our basic model. They use firm irregular rhythms to sell braces and newspapers alike.

Reflecting along these lines we see that our basic model will work. The elements of natural and of artificial epic theatre are the same. Our street-corner theatre is primitive; origins, aims and methods of its performance are close to home. But there is no doubt that it is a meaningful phenomenon with a clear social function that dominates all its elements. The performance's origins lie in an incident that can be judged one way or another, that may repeat itself in different forms and is not finished but is bound to have consequences, so that this judgment has some significance. The object of the performance is to make it easier to give an opinion on the incident. Its means correspond to that. The epic theatre is a highly skilled theatre with complex contents and far-reaching social objectives. In setting up the street scene as a basic model for it we pass on the clear social function and give the epic theatre criteria by which to decide whether an incident is meaningful or not. The basic model has a practical significance. As producer and actors work to build up a performance involving many difficult questions – technical problems, social ones – it allows them to check whether the social function of the whole apparatus is still clearly intact.

['Die Strassenszene, Grundmodell eines epischen Theaters', from *Versuche 10*, 1950]

NOTE: Originally stated to have been written in 1940, but now ascribed by Werner Hecht to June 1938. This is an elaboration of a poem 'Über alltägliches Theater' which is supposed to have been written in 1930 and is included as one of the 'Gedichte aus dem Messingkauf' in *Theaterarbeit*, *Versuche 14* and *Gedichte 3*. The notion of the man at the street-corner miming an accident is already developed at length there, and it also occurs in the following undated scheme (*Schriften zum Theater 4*, pp. 51–2):

EXERCISES FOR ACTING SCHOOLS

(a) Conjuring tricks, including attitude of spectators.

(b) For women: folding and putting away linen. Same for men.

(c) For men: varying attitudes of smokers. Same for women.

(d) Cat playing with a hank of thread.

(e) Exercises in observation.

(f) Exercises in imitation.

(g) How to take notes. Noting of gestures, tones of voice.

(h) Exercises in imagination. Three men throwing dice for their life. One loses. Then: they all lose.

(i) Dramatizing an epic. Passages from the Bible.

(k) For everybody: repeated exercises in production. Essential to show one's colleagues.

(l) Exercises in temperament. Situation: two women calmly folding linen. They feign a wild and jealous quarrel for the benefit of their husbands; the husbands are in the next room.

(m) They come to blows as they fold their linen in silence.

(n) Game (l) turns serious.

(o) Quick-change competition. Behind a screen; open.

(p) Modifying an imitation, simply described so that others can put it into effect.

(q) Rhythmical (verse-) speaking with tap-dance.

(r) Eating with outsize knife and fork. Very small knife and fork.

(s) Dialogue with gramophone: recorded sentences, free answers.

(t) Search for 'nodal points'.

(u) Characterization of a fellow-actor.

(v) Improvisation of incidents. Running through scenes in the style of a report, no text.

(w) The street accident. Laying down limits of justifiable imitation.

(x) Variations: a dog went into the kitchen. [A traditional song]

(y) Memorizing first impressions of a part.

Werner Hecht suggests that these exercises, like those cited on p. 147, may relate to lessons given by Helene Weigel at a Finnish theatre school.

30 · On Experimental Theatre

For at least two generations the serious European drama has been passing through a period of experiment. So far the various experiments conducted have not led to any definite and clearly established result, nor is the period itself over. In my view these experiments were pursued along two lines which occasionally intersected but can none the less be followed separately. They are defined by the two functions of *entertainment* and *instruction*; that is to say that the theatre organized experiments to increase its ability to amuse, and others which were intended to raise its value as education.

[Brecht then lists various experiments from Antoine on, designed to increase the theatre's capacity to entertain, and singles out Vakhtanghov and the constructivist Meyerhold – who 'took over from the asiatic theatre certain dance-like forms and created a whole choreography for the drama' – Reinhardt, with his open-air productions of *Faust*, *Jedermann* and *Midsummer Night's Dream*, and his seating of actors among the audience in Büchner's *Danton's Death*; Okhlopkov, and the elaboration of crowd scenes by Stanislavsky, Reinhardt and Jessner. But 'on the whole the theatre has not been brought up to modern technological standards'.

The second line he sees as pursued primarily by the playwrights, instancing Ibsen, Tolstoy, Strindberg, Gorki, Tchekov, Hauptmann, Shaw, Georg Kaiser and Eugene O'Neill, and mentioning his own *Threepenny Opera* as 'a parable type plus ideology-busting'. Piscator's theatre was 'the most radical' of all such attempts. 'I took part in all his experiments, and every single one was aimed to increase the theatre's value as education.']

These discoveries [he goes on] have not yet been taken up by the international theatre; this electrification of the stage has been virtually forgotten; the whole ingenious machinery is rusting up, and grass is growing over it. Why is that?

The breakdown of this eminently political theatre must be attributed to political causes. The increase in the theatre's value as political education clashed with the growth of political reaction. But for the moment we shall restrict ourselves to seeing how its crisis developed in aesthetic terms.

Piscator's experiments began by causing complete theatrical chaos. While they turned the stage into a machine-room, the auditorium became a public meeting. Piscator saw the theatre as a parliament, the audience as a legislative body. To this parliament were submitted in plastic form all the great public questions that needed an answer. Instead of a Deputy speaking about certain intolerable social conditions there was an artistic copy of these conditions. It was the stage's ambition to supply images, statistics, slogans which would enable its parliament, the audience, to reach political decisions. Piscator's stage was not indifferent to applause, but it preferred a discussion. It didn't want only to provide its spectator with an experience but also to squeeze from him a practical decision to intervene actively in life. Every means was justified which helped to secure this. The technical side of the stage became extremely complicated. Piscator's stage manager had before him a book that was as different from that of Reinhardt's stage manager as the score of a Stravinsky opera is from a lute-player's part. The mechanism on the stage weighed so much that the stage of the Nollendorftheater had to be reinforced with steel and concrete supports; so much machinery was hung from the dome that it began to give way. Aesthetic considerations were entirely subject to political. Away with painted scenery if a film could be shown that had been taken on the spot and had the stamp of documentary realism. Up with painted cartoons, if the artist (e.g. George Grosz) had something to say to the parliamentary audience. Piscator was even ready to do wholly without actors. When the former German Emperor had his lawyers protest at Piscator's plan to let an actor portray him on his stage, Piscator just asked if the Emperor wouldn't be willing to appear in person; he even offered him a contract. In short, the end was such a vast and important one that all means seemed justified. And the plays themselves were prepared in much the same way as the performance. A whole staff of playwrights worked together on a single play, and their work was supported and checked by a staff of experts, historians, economists, statisticians.

Piscator's experiments broke nearly all the conventions. They intervened to transform the playwright's creative methods, the actor's style of representation, and the work of the stage designer. *They were striving towards an entirely new social function for the theatre.*

Bourgeois revolutionary aesthetics, founded by such great figures of the Enlightenment as *Diderot* and *Lessing*, defines the theatre as a place of entertainment and instruction. During the Enlightenment, a period which saw the start of a tremendous upsurge of the European theatre, there was no conflict between these two things. Pure amusement, provoked even by objects of tragedy, struck men like Diderot as utterly hollow and unworthy unless it added something to the spectators' knowledge, while elements of instruction, in artistic form of course, seemed in no wise to detract from the amusement; in these men's view they gave depth to it.

If we now look at the theatre of our day we shall find an increasingly marked conflict between the two elements which go to make it up, together with its plays – entertainment and instruction. Today there is an opposition here. That 'assimilation of art to science' which gave naturalism its social influence undoubtedly hamstrung some major artistic capacities, notably the imagination, the sense of play and the element of pure poetry. Its artistic aspects were clearly harmed by its instructive side.

The expressionism of the postwar period showed the World as Will and Idea and led to a special kind of solipsism. It was the theatre's answer to the great crisis of society, just as the doctrines of Mach were philosophy's. It represented art's revolt against life: here the world existed purely as a vision, strangely distorted, a monster conjured up by perturbed souls. Expressionism vastly enriched the theatre's means of expression and brought aesthetic gains that still have to be fully exploited, but it proved quite incapable of shedding light on the world as an object of human activity. The theatre's educative value collapsed.

In Piscator's productions or in *The Threepenny Opera* the educative elements were so to speak *built in*: they were not an organic consequence of the whole, but stood in contradiction to it; they broke up the flow of the play and its incidents, they prevented empathy, they acted as a cold douche for those whose sympathies were becoming involved. I hope that the moralizing parts of *The Threepenny Opera* and the educative songs are reasonably entertaining, but it is certain that the entertainment in question is different from what one gets from the more orthodox scenes. The play has a double nature. Instruction and entertainment conflict openly. With Piscator it was the actor and the machinery that openly conflicted.

This is quite apart from the fact that such productions split the audience into at least two mutually hostile social groups, and thus put a stop to any common experience of art. The fact is a political one. Enjoyment of learning depends on the class situation. Artistic appreciation depends on one's political attitude, which can accordingly be stimulated and adopted. But even if we restrict ourselves to the section of the audience which agreed politically we see the sharpening of the conflict between ability to entertain and educative value. Here is a new and quite specific kind of learning, and it can no longer be reconciled with a specific old kind of entertainment. At one (later) stage of the experiments the result of any fresh increase in educative value was an immediate decrease in ability to entertain. ('This isn't theatre, it's secondary-school stuff.') Conversely, emotional acting's effects on the nerves was a continual menace to the production's educative value. (It often helped the educational effect to have bad actors instead of good ones.) In other words, the greater the grip on the audience's nerves, the less chance there was of its learning. The more we induced the audience to identify its own experiences and feelings with the production, the less it learned; and the more there was to learn, the less the artistic enjoyment.

Here was a crisis: half a century's experiments, conducted in nearly every civilized country, had won the theatre brand-new fields of subject-matter and types of problem, and made it a factor of marked social importance. At the same time they had brought the theatre to a point where any further development of the intellectual, social (political) experience must wreck the artistic experience. And yet, without further development of the former, the latter occurred less and less often. A technical apparatus and a style of acting had been evolved which could do more to stimulate illusions than to give experiences, more to intoxicate than to elevate, more to deceive than to illumine.

What was the good of a constructivist stage if it was socially unconstructive; of the finest lighting equipment if it lit nothing but childish and twisted representations of the world; of a suggestive style of acting if it only served to tell us that A was B? What use was the whole box of tricks if all it could do was to offer artificial surrogates for real experience? Why this eternal ventilating of problems that were always left unsolved? This titillation not only of the nerves but of the brain? We couldn't leave it at that.

The development tended towards a fusion of the two functions, instruction and entertainment. If such preoccupations were to have any social meaning, then they must eventually enable the theatre to project a picture of the world by artistic means: models of men's life together such as could help the spectator to understand his social environment and both rationally and emotionally to master it.

[Brecht goes on, in terms that anticipate the Short Organum and perhaps reflect his work on the first version of *Galileo*, to lament man's failure to understand the laws governing his life in society. His knowledge of these has not kept pace with his scientific knowledge, so that 'nowadays nearly every new discovery is greeted with a shout of triumph which transforms itself into a shout of fear'. (Cf. the long speech in Scene 14 of *Galileo*.) But art ought to be able to give 'a workable picture of the world'.

As it is, he argues, art gets its effects more by empathy than by accuracy. He attacks empathy on the same grounds as before, and describes the attempt to stave it off by methods of 'alienation'. This technique was developed at the Theater am Schiffbauerdamm in Berlin with 'the most talented of the younger generation of actors . . . Weigel, Peter Lorre, Oskar Homolka, (Carola) Neher and Busch', and also with amateur groups, workers' choruses, etc.]

This all represented a continuation of previous experiments, in particular of Piscator's theatre. Already in his last experiments the logical development of the technical apparatus had at last allowed the machinery to be mastered and led to a beautiful simplicity of performance. The so-called *epic* style of production which we developed at the Schiffbauerdamm Theater proved its artistic merits relatively soon, and the *non-aristotelian school of playwriting* tackled the large-scale treatment of large-scale social objects. There was some prospect of changing the choreographic and grouping aspects of Meyerhold's school from artifice into art, of transforming the Stanislavsky school's naturalistic elements into realism. Speech was related to gestics; both everyday language and verse speaking were shaped according to the so-called *gestic principle*. A complete revolution took place in stage design. By a free manipulation of Piscator's principles it became possible to design a setting that was both instructive and beautiful. Symbolism and illusion could be more or less dispensed with, and the *Neher principle* of building the set according to the requirements established at the actors' rehearsals allowed the designer to profit by the actors' performance and influence it in turn. The playwright could work out his experiments in uninterrupted collaboration with actor and stage designer; he could influence and be influenced. At the same time the painter and the composer regained their independence, and were able to express their view of the theme by their own artistic means. The integrated work of art (or 'Gesamtkunstwerk') appeared before the spectator as a bundle of separate elements.

From the start the *classical repertoire* supplied the basis of many of these experiments. The artistic means of alienation made possible a broad approach to the living works of dramatists of other periods. Thanks to them such valuable old plays could be performed without either jarring modernization or museum-like methods, and in an entertaining and instructive way.

It plainly has a particularly good effect on the contemporary amateur theatre (worker, student and child actors) when it is no longer forced to work by hypnosis. It seems conceivable that a line may be drawn between the playing of amateur actors and professionals without one of the theatre's basic functions having to be sacrificed.

Such very different ways of acting as those of, say, the Vakhtangov or Okhlopkov companies and the workers' groups can be reconciled on this new foundation. The variegated experiments of half a century seem to have acquired a basis that allows them to be exploited.

None the less these experiments are not so easy to describe, and I am forced here simply to state our belief that we can indeed encourage artistic understanding on the basis of alienation. This is not very surprising, as the theatre of past periods also, technically speaking, achieved results with alienation effects – for instance the Chinese theatre, the Spanish classical theatre, the popular theatre of Brueghel's day and the Elizabethan theatre.

So is this new style of production *the* new style; is it a complete and comprehensible technique, the final result of every experiment? Answer: no. It is *a* way, the one that *we* have followed. The effort must be continued. The problem holds for all art, and it is a vast one. The solution here aimed at is only *one* of the conceivable solutions to the problem, which can be expressed so: How can the theatre be both instructive and entertaining? How can it be divorced from spiritual dope traffic and turned from a home of illusions to a home of experiences? How can the unfree, ignorant man of our century, with his thirst for freedom and his hunger for knowledge; how can the tortured and heroic, abused and ingenious, changeable and world-changing man of this great and ghastly century obtain his own theatre which will help him to master the world and himself?

['Über experimentelles Theater', from *Theater der Zeit*, East Berlin, 1959, No. 4. Also *Schriften zum Theater 3*, pp. 79–106. Two long passages have been summarized to save repetition of Brecht's arguments]

NOTE: This lecture is published in full in another translation in *The Tulane Drama Review* for Autumn 1961. Brecht delivered it to a student theatre in Stockholm in May 1939, revising it and repeating it in Helsinki in October 1940 (by which time he had temporarily settled in Finland). A draft version (Brecht-Archive 60/06-10) shows that he was conscious of addressing 'a scientifically-trained body, not just ordinary theatre lovers'.

Here is the first indication that Brecht wanted to strike a balance between didacticism and entertainment. Ever since the *Lehrstücke* his theoretical writing had been consistently on the side of the former; thus compare this essay with 'Theatre for Pleasure or Theatre for Instruction' (p. 69ff.), where learning is supposed to contain its own amusement. Soon, however, he was writing in his diary (12 January 1941, quoted in Mittenzwei, *Bertolt Brecht*, East Berlin, 1962, p. 332):

It must never be forgotten that *non-aristotelian theatre* is only *one* form of theatre; it furthers specific social aims and has no claims to monopoly as far as the theatre in general is concerned. I myself can use both aristotelian and non-aristotelian theatre in certain productions.

It was the period of his greatest plays – the first version of *Galileo* was finished in November 1938, *Mother Courage* by the end of 1939, *The Good Person of Szechwan* 'more or less finished' in June 1940 – and he was heading for the theoretical compromise of the 'Short Organum'.

31 · Short Description of a New Technique of Acting which Produces an Alienation Effect

What follows represents an attempt to describe a technique of acting which was applied in certain theatres (1) with a view to taking the incidents portrayed and alienating them from the spectator. The aim of this technique, known as the alienation effect, was to make the spectator adopt an attitude of inquiry and criticism in his approach to the incident. The means were artistic.

The first condition for the A-effect's application to this end is that stage and auditorium must be purged of everything 'magical' and that no 'hypnotic tensions' should be set up. This ruled out any attempt to make the stage convey the flavour of a particular place (a room at evening, a road in the autumn), or to create atmosphere by relaxing the tempo of the conversation. The audience was not 'worked up' by a display of temperament or 'swept away' by acting with tautened muscles; in short, no attempt was made to put it in a trance and give it the illusion of watching an ordinary unrehearsed event. As will be seen presently, the audience's tendency to plunge into such illusions has to be checked by specific artistic means (3).

The first condition for the achievement of the A-effect is that the actor must invest what he has to show with a definite gest of showing. It is of course necessary to drop the assumption that there is a fourth wall cutting the audience off from the stage and the consequent illusion that the stage action is taking place in reality and without an audience. That being so, it is possible for the actor in principle to address the audience direct.

It is well known that contact between audience and stage is normally made on the basis of empathy. Conventional actors devote their efforts so exclusively to bringing about this psychological operation that they may be said to see it as the principal aim of their art (5). Our introductory remarks will already have made it clear that the technique which produces an A-effect is the exact opposite of that which aims at empathy. The actor applying it is bound not to try to bring about the empathy operation.

Yet in his efforts to reproduce particular characters and show their behaviour he need not renounce the means of empathy entirely. He uses these means just as any normal person with no particular acting talent would use them if he wanted to portray someone else, i.e. show how he behaves. This showing of other people's behaviour happens time and again in ordinary life (witnesses of an accident demonstrating to newcomers how the victim behaved, a facetious person imitating a friend's walk, etc.), without those involved making the least effort to subject their spectators to an illusion. At the same time they do feel their way into their characters' skins with a view to acquiring their characteristics.

As has already been said, the actor too will make use of this psychological operation. But whereas the usual practice in acting is to execute it during the actual performance, in the hope of stimulating the spectator into a similar operation, he will achieve it only at an earlier stage, at some time during rehearsals.

To safeguard against an unduly 'impulsive', frictionless and uncritical creation of characters and incidents, more reading rehearsals can be held than usual. The actor should refrain from living himself into the part prematurely in any way, and should go on functioning as long as possible as a reader (which does not mean a reader-aloud). An important step is memorizing one's first impressions.

When reading his part the actor's attitude should be one of a man who is astounded and contradicts. Not only the occurrence of the incidents, as he reads about them, but the conduct of the man he is playing, as he experiences it, must be weighed up by him and their peculiarities understood; none can be taken as given, as something that 'was bound to turn out that way', that was 'only to be expected from a character like that'. Before memorizing the words he must memorize what he felt astounded at and where he felt impelled to contradict. For these are dynamic forces that he must preserve in creating his performance.

When he appears on the stage, besides what he actually is doing he will at all essential points discover, specify, imply what he is not doing; that is to say he will act in such a way that the alternative emerges as clearly as possible, that his acting allows the other possibilities to be inferred and only represents one out of the possible variants. He will say for instance 'You'll pay for that', and not say 'I forgive you'. He detests his children; it is not the case that he loves them. He moves down stage left and not up stage right. Whatever he doesn't do must be contained and conserved in what he does. In this way every sentence and every gesture signifies a decision; the character remains under observation and is tested. The technical term for this procedure is 'fixing the "not . . . but"'.

The actor does not allow himself to become completely transformed on the stage into the character he is portraying. He is not Lear, Harpagon, Schweik; he shows them. He reproduces their remarks as authentically as he can; he puts forward their way of behaving to the best of his abilities and knowledge of men; but he never tries to persuade himself (and thereby others) that this amounts to a complete transformation. Actors will know what it means if I say that a typical kind of acting without this complete transformation takes place when a producer or colleague shows one how to play a particular passage. It is not his own part, so he is not completely transformed; he underlines the technical aspect and retains the attitude of someone just making suggestions.

Once the idea of total transformation is abandoned the actor speaks his part not as if he were improvising it himself but like a quotation (7). At the same time he obviously has to render all the quotation's overtones, the remark's full human and concrete shape; similarly the gesture he makes must have the full substance of a human gesture even though it now represents a copy.

Given this absence of total transformation in the acting there are three aids which may help to alienate the actions and remarks of the characters being portrayed:

1. Transposition into the third person.
2. Transposition into the past.
3. Speaking the stage directions out loud.

Using the third person and the past tense allows the actor to adopt the right attitude of detachment. In addition he will look for stage directions and remarks that comment on his lines, and speak them aloud at rehearsal ('He stood up and exclaimed angrily, not having eaten: . . .', or 'He had never been told so before, and didn't know if it was true or not', or 'He smiled, and said with forced nonchalance: . . .'). Speaking the stage directions out loud in the third person results in a clash between two tones of voice, alienating the second of them, the text proper. This style of acting is further alienated by taking place on the stage after having already been outlined and announced in words. Transposing it into the past gives the speaker a standpoint from which he can look back at his sentence. The sentence too is thereby alienated without the speaker adopting an unreal point of view; unlike the spectator, he has read the play right through and is better placed to judge the sentence in accordance with the ending, with its consequences, than the former, who knows less and is more of a stranger to the sentence.

This composite process leads to an alienation of the text in the rehearsals which generally persists in the performance too (9). The directness of the relationship with the audience allows and indeed forces the actual speech delivery to be varied in accordance with the greater or smaller significance attaching to the sentences. Take the case of witnesses addressing a court. The underlinings, the characters' insistence on their remarks, must be developed as a piece of effective virtuosity. If the actor turns to the audience it must be a whole-hearted turn rather than the asides and soliloquizing technique of the old-fashioned theatre. To get the full A-effect from the poetic medium the actor should start at rehearsal by paraphrasing the verse's content in vulgar prose, possibly accompanying this by the gestures designed for the verse. A daring and beautiful handling of verbal media will alienate the text. (Prose can be alienated by translation into the actor's native dialect.)

Gesture will be dealt with below, but it can at once be said that everything to do with the emotions has to be externalized; that is to say, it must be developed into a gesture. The actor has to find a sensibly perceptible outward expression for his character's emotions, preferably some action that gives away what is going on inside him. The emotion in question must be brought out, must lose all its restrictions so that it can be treated on a big scale. Special elegance, power and grace of gesture bring about the A-effect.

A masterly use of gesture can be seen in Chinese acting. The Chinese actor achieves the A-effect by being seen to observe his own movements.

Whatever the actor offers in the way of gesture, verse structure, etc., must be finished and bear the hallmarks of something rehearsed and rounded-off. The impression to be given is one of ease, which is at the same time one of difficulties overcome. The actor must make it possible for the audience to take his own art, his mastery of technique, lightly too. He puts an incident before the spectator with perfection and as he thinks it really happened or might have happened. He does not conceal the fact that he has rehearsed it, any more than an acrobat conceals his training, and he emphasizes that it is his own (actor's) account, view, version of the incident.

Because he doesn't identify himself with him he can pick a definite attitude to adopt towards the character whom he portrays, can show what he thinks of him and invite the spectator, who is likewise not asked to identify himself, to criticize the character portrayed.

The attitude which he adopts is a socially critical one. In his exposition of the incidents and in his characterization of the person he tries to bring out those features which come within society's sphere. In this way his performance becomes a discussion (about social conditions) with the audience he is addressing. He prompts the spectator to justify or abolish these conditions according to what class he belongs to (13).

The object of the A-effect is to alienate the social gest underlying every incident. By social gest is meant the mimetic and gestural expression of the social relationships prevailing between people of a given period (14).

It helps to formulate the incident for society, and to put it across in such a way that society is given the key, if titles are thought up for the scenes. These titles must have a historical quality.

This brings us to a crucial technical device: historicization.

The actor must play the incidents as historical ones. Historical incidents are unique, transitory incidents associated with particular periods. The conduct of the persons involved in them is not fixed and 'universally human'; it includes elements that have been or may be overtaken by the course of history, and is subject to criticism from the immediately following period's point of view. The conduct of those born before us is alienated[1] from us by an incessant evolution.

It is up to the actor to treat present-day events and modes of behaviour with the same detachment as the historian adopts with regard to those of the past. He must alienate these characters and incidents from us.

Characters and incidents from ordinary life, from our immediate surroundings, being familiar, strike us as more or less natural. Alienating them helps to make them seem remarkable to us. Science has carefully developed a technique of getting irritated with the everyday, 'self-evident', universally accepted occurrence, and there is no reason why this infinitely useful attitude should not be taken over by art (17). It is an attitude which arose in science as a result of the growth in human productive powers. In art the same motive applies.

As for the emotions, the experimental use of the A-effect in the epic theatre's German productions indicated that this way of acting too can stimulate them, though possibly a different class of emotion is involved from those of the orthodox theatre (18). A critical attitude on the audience's part is a thoroughly artistic one (19). Nor does the actual practice of the A-effect seem anything like so unnatural as its description. Of course it is a way of acting that has nothing to do with stylization as commonly practised. The main advantage of the epic theatre with its A-effect, intended purely to show the world in such a way that it becomes manageable, is precisely its quality of being natural and earthly, its humour and its renunciation of all the mystical elements that have stuck to the orthodox theatre from the old days.

[1] *Entfremdet.*

Appendix

[selected notes]

1. *Edward II* after Marlowe (Munich Kammerspiele).
   Trommeln in der Nacht (Deutsches Theater, Berlin).
   The Threepenny Opera (Theater am Schiffbauerdamm, Berlin).
   Die Pioniere von Ingolstadt (Theater am Schiffbauerdamm).
   Aufstieg und Fall der Stadt Mahagonny, opera (Aufricht's Kurfür-stendammtheater, Berlin).
   Mann ist Mann (Staatstheater, Berlin).
   Die Massnahme (Grosses Schauspielhaus, Berlin).
   The Adventures of the Good Soldier Schweik (Piscator's Theater am Nollendorfplatz, Berlin).
   Die Plattköpfe und die Spitzköpfe (Riddersalen, Copenhagen).
   Señora Carrar's Rifles (Copenhagen, Paris).
   Furcht und Elend des Dritten Reiches (Paris).

3. E.g. such mechanical means as very brilliant illumination of the stage (since a half-lit stage plus a completely darkened auditorium makes the spectator less level-headed by preventing him from observing his neighbour and in turn hiding him from his neighbour's eyes) and also *making visible the sources of light.*

MAKING VISIBLE THE SOURCES OF LIGHT

There is a point in showing the lighting apparatus openly, as it is one of the means of preventing an unwanted element of illusion; it scarcely disturbs the necessary concentration. If we light the actors and their performance in such a way that the lights themselves are within the spectator's field of vision we destroy part of his illusion of being present at a spontaneous, transitory, authentic, unrehearsed event. He sees that arrangements have been made to show something; something is being repeated here under special conditions, for instance in a very brilliant light. Displaying the actual lights is meant to be a counter to the old-fashioned theatre's efforts to hide them. No one would expect the lighting to be hidden at a sporting event, a boxing match for instance. Whatever the points of difference between the modern theatre's presentations and those of a sporting promoter, they do not include the same conceal-ment of the sources of light as the old theatre found necessary.

(Brecht: 'Der Bühnenbau des epischen Theaters')

5. Cf. these remarks by Poul Reumert, the best-known Danish actor:

'. . . If I feel I am *dying*, and if I *really* feel it, then so does everybody
else; if I act as though I had a dagger in my hand, and am entirely filled
by the one idea of killing the child, then everybody shudders. . . . The
whole business is a matter of mental activity being communicated by
emotions, or the other way round if you prefer it: a feeling so strong as
to be an obsession, which is translated into thoughts. If it comes off it is
the most infectious thing in the world; anything external is then a
matter of complete indifference. . . .'
And Rapaport, 'The Work of the Actor', *Theater Workshop*, October
1936:

'. . . On the stage the actor is surrounded entirely by fictions. . . . The
actor must be able to regard all this as though it were true, as though he
were convinced that all that surrounds him on the stage is a living
reality and, along with himself, he must convince the audience as well.
This is the central feature of our method of work on the part. . . . Take
any object, a cap for example; lay it on the table or on the floor and try
to regard it as though it were a rat; make believe that it is a rat, and not
a cap. . . . Picture what sort of a rat it is; what size, colour? . . . We thus
commit ourselves to believe quite naïvely that the object before us is
something other than it is and, at the same time, learn to compel the
audience to believe. . . .'

This might be thought to be a course of instruction for conjurers,
but in fact it is a course of acting, supposedly according to Stanislavsky's method. One wonders if a technique that equips an actor to
make the audience see rats where there aren't any can really be all that
suitable for disseminating the truth. Given enough alcohol it doesn't
take acting to persuade almost anybody that he is seeing rats: pink ones.

7. QUOTATION

Standing in a free and direct relationship to it, the actor allows his
character to speak and move; he presents a report. He does not have to
make us forget that the text isn't spontaneous, but has been memorized,
is a fixed quantity; the fact doesn't matter, as we anyway assume that
the report is not about himself but about others. His attitude would be
the same if he were simply speaking from his own memory. [. . .]

8. The epic actor has to accumulate far more material than has been the
case till now. What he has to represent is no longer himself as king,
himself as scholar, himself as gravedigger, etc., but just kings, scholars,
gravediggers, which means that he has to look around him in the world
of reality. Again, he has to learn how to imitate: something that is dis-

couraged in modern acting on the ground that it destroys his individuality.

9. The theatre can create the corresponding A-effect in the performance in a number of ways. The Munich production of *Edward II* for the first time had titles preceding the scenes, announcing the contents. The Berlin production of *The Threepenny Opera* had the titles of the songs projected while they were sung. The Berlin production of *Mann ist Mann* had the actors' figures projected on big screens during the action.

13. Another thing that makes for freedom in the actor's relationship with his audience is that he does not treat it as an undifferentiated mass. He doesn't boil it down to a shapeless dumpling in the stockpot of the emotions. He does not address himself to everybody alike; he allows the existing divisions within the audience to continue, in fact he widens them. He has friends and enemies in the audience; he is friendly to the one group and hostile to the other. He takes sides, not necessarily with his character but if not with it then against it. (At least, that is his basic attitude, though it too must be variable and change according to what the character may say at different stages. There may, however, also be points at which everything is in the balance and the actor must withhold judgment, though this again must be expressly shown in his acting.)

14. If *King Lear* (in Act I, scene 1) tears up a map when he divides his kingdom between his daughters, then the act of division is alienated. Not only does it draw our attention to his kingdom, but by treating the kingdom so plainly as his own private property he throws some light on the basis of the feudal idea of the family. In *Julius Caesar* the tyrant's murder by Brutus is alienated if during one of his monologues accusing Caesar of tyrannical motives he himself maltreats a slave waiting on him. Weigel as *Maria Stuart* suddenly took the crucifix hanging round her neck and used it coquettishly as a fan, to give herself air. (See too Brecht: 'Übungsstücke für Schauspieler' in *Versuche 11*, p. 107.)

17. THE A-EFFECT AS A PROCEDURE IN EVERYDAY LIFE

The achievement of the A-effect constitutes something utterly ordinary, recurrent; it is just a widely-practised way of drawing one's own or someone else's attention to a thing, and it can be seen in education as also in business conferences of one sort or another. The A-effect consists in turning the object of which one is to be made aware, to which one's attention is to be drawn, from something ordinary, familiar, immediately accessible, into something peculiar, striking and unexpected. What is obvious is in a certain sense made incomprehensible, but this is only in order that it may then be made all the easier to comprehend. Before familiarity can turn into awareness the familiar must be stripped of its inconspicuousness; we must give up assuming that the object in question needs no explanation. However frequently recurrent, modest, vulgar it may be it will now be labelled as something unusual.

A common use of the A-effect is when someone says: 'Have you ever really looked carefully at your watch?' The questioner knows that I've looked at it often enough, and now his question deprives me of the sight which I've grown used to and which accordingly has nothing more to say to me. I used to look at it to see the time, and now when he asks me in this importunate way I realize that I have given up seeing the watch itself with an astonished eye; and it is in many ways an astonishing piece of machinery. Similarly it is an alienation effect of the simplest sort if a business discussion starts off with the sentence: 'Have you ever thought what happens to the waste from your factory which is pumped into the river twenty-four hours a day?' This waste wasn't just swept down the river unobserved; it was carefully channelled into the river; men and machines have worked on it; the river has changed colour, the waste has flowed away most conspicuously, but just as waste. It was superfluous to the process of manufacture, and now it is to become material for manufacture; our eye turns to it with interest. The asking of the question has alienated it, and intentionally so. The very simplest sentences that apply in the A-effect are those with 'Not . . . But': (He didn't say 'come in' but 'keep moving'. He was not pleased but amazed). They include an expectation which is justified by experience but, in the event, disappointed. One might have thought that . . . but one oughtn't to have thought it. There was not just one possibility but two; both are introduced, then the second one is alienated, then the first as well. To see one's mother as a man's wife one needs an A-effect; this is provided, for instance, when one acquires a stepfather. If one sees one's teacher hounded by the bailiffs an A-effect occurs: one is jerked out of a relationship in which the teacher seems big into one where he seems small. An alienation of the motor-car takes place if after driving a modern car for a long while we drive an old model T Ford. Suddenly we hear explosions once more; the motor works on the principle of explosion. We start feeling amazed that such a vehicle, indeed any vehicle not drawn by animal-power, can move; in short, we understand cars, by looking at them as something strange, new, as a triumph of engineering and to that extent something unnatural. Nature, which certainly embraces the motor-car, is suddenly imbued with an element of unnaturalness, and from now on this is an indelible part of the concept of nature.

The expression 'in fact' can likewise certify or alienate. (He wasn't in fact at home; he said he would be, but we didn't believe him and had a look; or again, we didn't think it possible for him not to be at home, but it was a fact.) The term 'actually' is just as conducive to alienation. ('I don't actually agree'.) Similarly the Eskimo definition 'A car is a wingless aircraft that crawls along the ground' is a way of alienating the car.

In a sense the alienation effect itself has been alienated by the above explanation; we have taken a common, recurrent, universally-practised operation and tried to draw attention to it by illuminating its peculiarity. But we have achieved the effect only with those people who have truly ('in fact') grasped that it does 'not' result from every representation 'but' from certain ones: only 'actually' is it familiar.

18. ABOUT RATIONAL AND EMOTIONAL POINTS OF VIEW

The rejection of empathy is not the result of a rejection of the emotions, nor does it lead to such. The crude aesthetic thesis that emotions can only be stimulated by means of empathy is wrong. None the less a non-aristotelian dramaturgy has to apply a cautious criticism to the emotions which it aims at and incorporates. Certain artistic tendencies like the provocative behaviour of Futurists and Dadaists and the icing-up of music point to a crisis of the emotions. Already in the closing years of the Weimar Republic the post-war German drama took a decisively rationalistic turn. Fascism's grotesque emphasizing of the emotions, together perhaps with the no less important threat to the rational element in Marxist aesthetics, led us to lay particular stress on the rational. Nevertheless there are many contemporary works of art where one can speak of a decline in emotional effectiveness due to their isolation from reason, or its revival thanks to a stronger rationalist message. This will surprise no one who has not got a completely conventional idea of the emotions.

The emotions always have a quite definite class basis; the form they take at any time is historical, restricted and limited in specific ways. The emotions are in no sense universally human and timeless.

The linking of particular emotions with particular interests is not unduly difficult so long as one simply looks for the interests corresponding to the emotional effects of works of art. Anyone can see the colonial adventures of the Second Empire looming behind Delacroix's paintings and Rimbaud's 'Bateau Ivre'.

If one compares the 'Bateau Ivre' say, with Kipling's 'Ballad of East and West', one can see the difference between French mid-nineteenth century colonialism and British colonialism at the beginning of the twentieth. It is less easy to explain the effect that such poems have on ourselves, as Marx already noticed. Apparently emotions accompanying social progress will long survive in the human mind as emotions linked with interests, and in the case of works of art will do so more strongly than might have been expected, given that in the meantime contrary interests will have made themselves felt. Every step forward means the end of the previous step forward, because that is where it starts and goes on from. At the same time it makes use of this previous step, which in a sense survives in men's consciousness as a step forward, just as it survives in its effects in real life. This involves a most interesting type of generalization, a continual process of abstraction. Whenever the works of art handed down to us allow us to share the emotions of other men, of men of a bygone period, different social classes, etc., we have to conclude that we are partaking in interests which really were universally human. These men now dead represented the interests of classes that gave a lead to progress. It is a very different matter when Fascism today conjures up on the grandest scale emotions which for most of the people who succumb to them are not determined by interest.

19. IS THE CRITICAL ATTITUDE AN INARTISTIC ONE?

An old tradition leads people to treat a critical attitude as a predominantly negative one. Many see the difference between the scientific and artistic attitudes as lying precisely in their attitude to criticism. People cannot conceive of contradiction and detachment as being part of artistic appreciation. Of course such appreciation normally includes a higher level, which appreciates critically, but the criticism here only applies to matters of technique; it is quite a different matter from being required to observe not a representation of the world but the world itself in a critical, contradictory, detached manner.

To introduce this critical attitude into art, the negative element which it doubtless includes must be shown from its positive side: this criticism of the world is active, practical, positive. Criticizing the course of a river means improving it, correcting it. Criticism of society is ultimately revolution; there you have criticism taken to its logical conclusion and playing an active part. A critical attitude of this type is an operative factor of productivity; it is deeply enjoyable as such,

and if we commonly use the term 'arts' for enterprises that improve
people's lives why should art proper remain aloof from arts of this sort?

['Kurze Beschreibung einer neuen Technik der
Schauspielkunst, die einen Verfremdungseffekt
hervorbringt', from *Versuche 11*, 1951, less notes 2,
4, 6, 10, 11, 15, 16 and part of 7]

NOTE: Written, according to a prefatory note, in 1940 but not published at the
time. The concluding notes here omitted are often repetitious (including passages from 'Alienation Effects in Chinese Acting'). The essay on 'Stage design in
the epic theatre' quoted in Note 3 has not been found in Brecht's papers and is
only known from this one reference. The list of plays in Note 1 includes two that
are not by Brecht, and evidently gives those productions that seemed important to
him at the time; it omits several of his plays and gets the name of *Die Rundköpfe
und die Spitzköpfe* wrong. It is interesting to compare it with a diary note of
30 January 1941:
'Six [*sic*] completed plays which have not been produced in a theatre. Johanna,
Furcht und Elend, Galileo, Courage, Puntila.
Six plays performed: Baal, Edward, Mann ist Mann, Threepenny Opera, Die
Rundköpfe und die Spitzköpfe, Die Mutter.
Omitted because uncongenial: Trommeln, Dickicht.'
Neither list is anything like complete, and the differences between the two
may give some idea of Brecht's ruthless and ever-changing judgment of his own
work.
The 'practice scenes for actors' referred to at the end of Note 14 are new
scenes to go with *Hamlet, Romeo and Juliet*, etc., showing the characters in a
slightly different light; they are published in *Versuche 11*. One was performed in
the George Tabori/Lotte Lenya programme *Brecht on Brecht*. There is an unpublished note by Brecht (Archive 154/56) outlining what again seems to be the
programme for an actors' course, where these are included:
Repertoire of the School
1. Bible scene
2. Shakespeare studies
   (a) Hamlet
   (b) Romeo and Juliet
3. Opening and first scene of AUS NICHTS WIRD NICHTS
   [unfinished play by Brecht]
4. A dog went into the kitchen
5. DIE MUTTER, scene 5

32 · Two Essays on Unprofessional Acting

The first thing that strikes one about a proletarian actor is the simplicity of his playing. What I mean by a proletarian actor is neither an actor of the bourgeois theatre who has proletarian origins nor a bourgeois actor performing for the proletariat, but a proletarian who has not gone through a bourgeois acting school and does not belong to a professional association. What I call simplicity of playing seems to me to be the alpha and the omega of proletarian acting.

Let me at once admit that I do not by any means find simple acting *ipso facto* good or prefer it to anything less simple. I am not automatically moved by the enthusiasm of untrained or inadequately trained people who none the less feel passionately about art, nor have I any use for the snobbery that makes a few persons with jaded palates prefer 'plain wholemeal bread' to any delicacy.

The actors of the small working-class theatres that are to be found in all those chief cities of Europe, Asia and America which have not been struck down by Fascism are by no means dilettantes, and their acting is not wholemeal. It is simple, but only in one specific respect.

Small working-class theatres are always very poor; they cannot afford to spend much on a production. By daytime the actors are working. Those who are out of work have almost as much to do every day as the rest, since hunting for a job is a job in itself. Certainly they are no less exhausted in the evening when they arrive at rehearsal. The way these people act does to some extent betray their lack of surplus energy. A certain absence of assurance at the same time takes the shine off their acting. Great individual emotions, displaying different personalities' varying psychological make-up, the 'rich inner life' in general: such things aren't shown by working-class theatres. To that extent the acting is simple, i.e. poor.

And yet there is another kind of simplicity to be found in their acting, a kind that does not result from a lack of origins but from a specific outlook and a specific concern. We speak of simplicity when complicated problems are so mastered as to make them easier to deal with and less difficult to grasp. A great number of seemingly self-contradictory facts, a vast and discouraging tangle, is often set in order by science in such a way that a relatively simple truth emerges. This kind of simplicity does not involve poverty. Yet it is this that one finds in the playing of the best proletarian actors, whenever it is a question of portraying men's social life together.

Small working-class theatres often shed a surprising light on the complex and baffling relationships between the people of our time. Where wars come from, and who fights them and who pays for them; what kind of destruction results from men's oppressiveness towards other men; what the efforts of the many are directed to; what the easy life of the few comes from; whose knowledge serves whom; who is hurt by whose actions: all this is shown by the small and struggling theatres of the workers. I am not speaking just of the plays but of those who perform them best and with the liveliest concern.

A little more money, and the room shown on the stage would be a room; a little speech training, and the actors' speech would be that of 'educated people'; a little public acclaim, and the performance would gain in forceful-ness; more money for eating and leisure, and the actors would cease to be tired. Cannot these things be provided? It is much less easy to provide what is missing in wealthy bourgeois theatres. How can war possibly be war on their stages? How can they show what the efforts of the many are directed to and what the easy life of the few comes from? How can they find out the great simple truths about men's life together and put them across? Once it can overcome poverty the small working-class theatre stands some chance of overcoming the simplicity which is the hallmark poverty gives to its per-formances; but the wealthy bourgeois theatre stands no chance of achieving the simplicity that comes from searching after truth.

So what about the great individual emotions, the variations in different personalities' psychological make-up, the rich inner life? Yes, what about this rich inner life which for many intellectuals is merely a poor substitute for a rich outer life? The answer is that art can have nothing to do with it so long as it remains a substitute. The great individual emotions will appear in art simply as distorted, unnatural speech and overheated, constricted temperament; variations in psychological make-up merely as unhealthy and exaggerated exceptions, so long as individuality remains the privilege of a minority which owns not only 'personality' but other, more material things.

True art becomes poor with the masses and grows rich with the masses.

(b) IS IT WORTH SPEAKING ABOUT THE AMATEUR THEATRE?

Anybody who seriously sets out to study the art of the theatre and its social function will do well to pay some attention to the many forms of theatrical activity that can be found outside the great institutions: i.e. the rudi-mentary, distorted, spontaneous efforts of the amateurs. Even if the ama-teurs were only what the professionals take them to be – members of the audience getting up on stage – they would still be interesting enough. Sweden is among the countries particularly well off for amateur theatres. The vast distances in this country, which is virtually a continent on its own, make it difficult to provide visits by professional companies from the capital. People in the provinces accordingly make their own theatre.

There are nearly a thousand active theatrical groups in the Swedish amateur theatrical movement, and they put on at least two thousand shows a year to an audience of at least half a million. A movement like this is of great cultural importance in a country of six million inhabitants.

It is often said that amateur theatrical performances are on a low artistic and intellectual level. We won't go into that here. There is also another school of thought which holds that some performances at least give evidence of considerable natural talent and some groups show a genuine concern with perfection. It has, however, become so usual to look down on the amateur theatre that one wonders how it would be if its level were really so bad. Would it no longer count? The answer is plainly no.

For it mustn't be imagined that there is no point in discussing amateur efforts in the arts if nothing of benefit to the arts results. A bad stage performance is not just one which, by contrast with a good one, makes no impression. The impression made may not be good, but an impression is made none the less: a bad one. In the arts, if nowhere else, the principle that 'if it doesn't do much good at least it can't do any harm' is quite mistaken. Good art stimulates sensitivity to art. Bad art damages it; it doesn't leave it untouched.

Most people have no clear idea of art's consequences, whether for good or for bad. They suppose that a spectator who is not inwardly gripped by art, because it is not good enough, is not affected at all. Quite apart from the fact that one can be gripped by bad art as easily as by good, even if one *isn't* gripped something happens to one.

Good or bad, a play always includes an image of the world. Good or bad, the actors show how people behave under given circumstances. A jealous man behaves in such-and-such a way, one gathers, or this and that action are the result of jealousy. A rich man is subject to these particular passions, an old man experiences these particular feelings, a country woman acts in this particular way, etc., etc. Furthermore the spectator is encouraged to draw certain conclusions about how the world works. If he behaves in such-and-such a way, he hears, he must reckon with this and that result. He is brought to share certain feelings of the persons appearing on the stage and thereby to approve them as universally human feelings, only natural, to be taken for granted. Since films resemble plays in this respect but are more widely known, perhaps a film can serve to illustrate what is meant.

In the film *Gunga Din*, based on a short story by Kipling, I saw British occupation forces fighting a native population. An Indian tribe – this term itself implies something wild and uncivilized, as against the word 'people' – attacked a body of British troops stationed in India. The Indians were primitive creatures, either comic or wicked: comic when loyal to the British and wicked when hostile. The British soldiers were honest, good-humoured chaps and when they used their fists on the mob and 'knocked some sense' into them the audience laughed. One of the Indians betrayed his compatriots to the British, sacrificed his life so that his fellow-countrymen should be defeated, and earned the audience's heartfelt applause.

My heart was touched too: I felt like applauding, and laughed in all the right places. Despite the fact that I knew all the time that there was something wrong, that the Indians are not primitive and uncultured people but have a magnificent age-old culture, and that this Gunga Din could also be seen in a very different light, e.g. as a traitor to his people. I was amused and touched because this utterly distorted account was an artistic success and considerable resources in talent and ingenuity had been applied in making it.

Obviously artistic appreciation of this sort is not without effects. It weakens the good instincts and strengthens the bad, it contradicts true experience and spreads misconceptions, in short it perverts our picture of the world. There is no play and no theatrical performance which does not in some way or other affect the dispositions and conceptions of the audience. Art is never without consequences, and indeed that says something for it.

A good deal of attention has been paid to the theatre's – even the supposedly unpolitical theatre's – political influence: its effect on the formation of political judgments, on political moods and emotions. Neither the socialist thinker nor the parson in his pulpit would deny that our morals are affected by it. It matters how love, marriage, work and death are treated on the stage, what kind of ideals are set up and propagated for lovers, for men struggling for their existence and so on. In this exceedingly serious sphere the stage is virtually functioning as a fashion show, parading not only the latest dresses but the latest ways of behaving: not only what is being worn but what is being done.

Perhaps the most illuminating, though not the most vital point is the theatre's influence on the formation of taste. How does one express oneself beautifully? What is the best way of grouping? What is beauty anyway?

What constitutes light-hearted behaviour? What is laudable deception? In countless detailed ways the stage affects the taste of the audience gazing up at it, for better or for worse. For taste plays a decisive part even in realistic art, nowhere more so. Even the representation of ugliness needs to be guided by it. The groupings on the stage, the passage of the characters across it, the scale of colours, the control of sound and of vocal cadences: all this is a question of taste.

So political, moral and aesthetic influences all radiate from the theatre: good when it is good, bad when it is bad.

One easily forgets that human education proceeds along highly theatrical lines. In a quite theatrical manner the child is taught how to behave; logical arguments only come later. When such-and-such occurs, it is told (or sees), one must laugh. It joins in when there is laughter, without knowing why; if asked why it is laughing it is wholly confused. In the same way it joins in shedding tears, not only weeping because the grown-ups do so but also feeling genuine sorrow. This can be seen at funerals, whose meaning escapes children entirely. These are theatrical events which form the character. The human being copies gestures, miming, tones of voice. And weeping arises from sorrow, but sorrow also arises from weeping.

It is no different with grown-ups. Their education never finishes. Only the dead are beyond being altered by their fellow-men. Think this over, and you will realize how important the theatre is for the forming of character. You will see what it means that thousands should act to hundreds of thousands. One can't just shrug off so many people's concern with art.

And art itself is not unaffected by the way in which it is practised on the most casual, carefree, naïve level. The theatre is so to speak the most human and universal art of all, the one most commonly practised, i.e. practised not just on the stage but also in everyday life. The theatre of a given people or a given time must be judged as a whole, as a living organism which isn't healthy unless it is healthy in every limb. That is another reason why it is worth speaking about the amateur theatre.

['Einiges über proletarische Schauspieler' and 'Lohnt es sich, vom Amateurtheater zu reden?' *Schriften zum Theater* 4, pp. 59–68]

NOTE: Both essays are published from the typescripts. Their references to Fascism and to Sweden show that they date from Brecht's exile, the second of them probably from 1940. Brecht was then virtually cut off from the professional theatre, and his work being performed only by amateurs. Even before 1933 he had written the Lehrstücke primarily for non-professional performers; his first acquaintance with 'proletarian actors' and singers being evidently due to productions of *Die Massnahme* and *Die Mutter*. In exile he came into contact notably with the German semi-amateur groups in Paris who gave the premières of *Furcht und Elend des Dritten Reiches* and *Señora Carrar's Rifles* (1938 and 1937 respectively), with the New York Theater Union, Unity Theatre in London, the Copenhagen Revolutionary Theatre under Dagmar Andreassen and other Scandinavian amateur companies. Throughout the Hitler period, moreover, his songs and sketches featured in the programmes of German exiled groups in many countries.

33 · Notes on the Folk Play

The 'Volksstück' or folk play is normally a crude and humble kind of theatre which academic critics pass over in silence or treat with condescension. In the second case they prefer it to be what it is, just as some régimes prefer their 'Volk' crude and humble. It is a mixture of earthy humour and sentimentality, homespun morality and cheap sex. The wicked get punished and the good get married off; the industrious get left legacies and the idle get left in the lurch. The technique of the people who write these plays is more or less international; it hardly ever varies. To act in them all that is needed is a capacity for speaking unnaturally and a smoothly conceited manner on the stage. A good helping of superficial slickness is enough.

The big cities moved with the times, progressing from the folk play to the revue. Revue is to the folk play as a song-hit to a folksong, though the folk play lacked the folksong's nobility. More recently the revue has been taken up as a literary form. Wangenheim of Germany, Abell of Denmark, Blitzstein of the USA and Auden of England have written interesting plays in the form of revues, plays that are neither crude nor humble. Their plays have something of the poetry of the old folk play but absolutely nothing of its naïvety. They avoid its conventional situations and schematized characters, though on closer inspection they are even more romantic. Their situations are grotesque and at bottom they hardly have characters, barely even parts for the actors. The linear story has been thrown on the scrap heap, the story itself as well as its line, for the new plays have no story, hardly even a connecting thread. Their performance demands virtuosity – they cannot be played by amateurs – but it is the virtuosity of the cabaret.

It seems futile to hope to revive the old folk play. Not only it is utterly bogged down but, more important, it never really flourished. Against that, the literary revue has never managed to become 'popular'. It is too full of cheap titbits. None the less it has proved the existence of certain needs, even though it cannot satisfy them. It can in fact be assumed that there is a need for naïve but not primitive, poetic but not romantic, realistic but not ephemerally political theatre. What might a new folk play of this sort look like? With regard to the story the literary revue gives some useful hints. As already mentioned, it does without any unified and continuous story and presents 'numbers', that is to say loosely-linked sketches. This is a form which revives the 'Pranks and Adventures' of the old popular epics, though admittedly in a form difficult to recognize. The sketches are not bound by narration, and they have few epic elements, just as Low's caricatures have little that is epic by comparison with Hogarth's. They are wittier, more concentrated on a single point. The new kind of folk play could draw conclusions from the more autonomous achievements of the literary revue, but it needs to provide more epic substance and to be more realistic.

The literary revue also gives pointers where poetry is concerned. In particular those plays which Auden wrote with Isherwood contain sections of great poetic beauty. He uses choruses and very fine poems, and the events themselves are also sometimes elevated. It is all more or less symbolic, however; he even reintroduces allegory. If one compares him with Aristophanes – which Auden wouldn't mind – one sees the markedly subjective character of this poetry and symbolism; so that the new folk play ought to learn from the poetry but provide greater objectivity. The poetry ought perhaps to be more in the actual situations instead of being expressed by the characters reacting to them.

It is most important to find a style of presentation which is both artistic and natural. Given the Babylonian confusion of styles prevailing on the European stage this is extremely difficult. The stage at present has two styles with which one can reckon, although they are pretty well entangled with each other. The 'elevated' style of presentation that was worked out for great poetic masterpieces and can still be used, e.g. for Ibsen's early plays, is still available, if in a slightly battered condition. The second style available – the naturalistic – supplemented rather than succeeded it; the two ways of acting went on existing side by side like sail and steam. The elevated style used to be kept exclusively for unrealistic plays, while a realistic play got on more or less 'without style'. Stylized theatre and elevated theatre meant the same thing. But as naturalism became feebler it made all sorts of compromises, so that today even in realistic plays we find a peculiar mixture of the casual and the declamatory. Nothing can be done with a cocktail like this. All that has been provided by the elevated style is the unnaturalness and artificiality, the schematism and pompousness into whose depths this style tumbled before naturalism took over. And all that survives here of the great period of naturalism is the accidental, shapeless, unimaginative element which was part of naturalism even at its best. Thus new paths must be found. In what direction? The fusion of the two styles of acting – romantic-classical and naturalistic – to form a romantic-naturalistic cocktail was a marriage of weakness. Two tottering rivals propped each other up for fear of falling over for good. The mixture took place almost unconsciously, by mutual concessions, silent relinquishing of principles, in short by corruption. But if this synthesis had been consciously and forcefully carried out it really would have been the right solution. The contrast of art and nature can be made a fruitful one if the work of art brings it to a head, but without smoothing it out. We saw art creating its own nature, its own world, a world of art, one which had and wished to have very little indeed to do with the real world; and we saw art just exhausting itself in the effort to copy the real world, and sacrificing its imagination almost completely in the process. We need an art that masters nature; we need an artistic representation of reality, and (also) a natural art.

A theatre's cultural standard is decided partly by its degree of success in overcoming the contrast between 'noble' (elevated, stylized) and realistic ('keyhole') acting. It is often supposed that realistic acting is 'by nature' slightly 'ignoble' and 'noble' acting correspondingly unrealistic. The idea here is that because fishwives are not noble nothing noble can emerge from their life-like representation. There is some fear that even queens may appear not quite noble if realistically portrayed. This is a bundle of fallacies. The fact is that when an actor has to represent crudity, meanness and ugliness, whether the subject be a fishwife or a queen, he simply cannot get along without delicacy, a sense of fairness and a feeling for the beautiful. A truly cultured theatre never has to buy its realism at the cost of sacrificing artistic beauty. Reality may lack beauty, but that by no means disqualifies it for a stylized stage. Just its lack of beauty may be the chief subject of the representation – in a comedy such base human characteristics as avarice, swank, stupidity, ignorance, disputatiousness; in a serious play the de-humanized social setting. Whitewashing is in itself something unquestionably ignoble, love of truth unquestionably noble. Art is in a position to represent the ugly man's ugliness in a beautiful manner, the base man's baseness in a noble manner, for the artist can also show ungraciousness graciously and meekness with power. There is no reason why the subject matter of a comedy portraying 'life as it is' should not be ennobled. The theatre has at its command delicate colours, agreeable and significant grouping, original gests – in short, *style* –; it has humour, imagination and wisdom with which to overcome ugliness.

These things have to be said because our theatres are not naturally disposed to waste anything so superior as style on plays whose form and content is that of a folk play. They might perhaps respond to the demand for a cleaner style if they were dealing with a type of play whose outward appearance was already quite distinct from the naturalistic problem play: the verse play, for instance. They might admit without prompting that the verse play's attitude to the 'problem' and its treatment of the psychological aspects were different. It is harder for a play in prose, and popular prose at that, which has neither much of a 'problem' nor any great psychological complications. The whole category of folk plays is not recognized as a literary category. The ballad and the Elizabethan 'history' are literary categories, but both the Moritat from which the former and the beergarden Guignol from which the latter evolved need to be performed with 'style' whether one agrees to accept them as literary or not. It is admittedly harder to recognize discrimination when judgment has been exercised on a new range of material that has so far been regarded with the merest indifference. [*A number of details from Brecht's play* Puntila *are then gone into.*]

It may seem unsuitable that a single small folk play should be the occasion for such far-reaching commentary, for the conjuring up of such vast phantoms and finally for a demand for an entirely new art of theatrical representation. Yet, like it or not, this demand has got to be made; our whole repertoire calls for a new kind of art which is quite indispensable for the performance of the great masterpieces of the past and has to be developed if new masterpieces are to arise. All that the foregoing is intended to do is to remind people that the demand for a new realistic art applies to the new folk play too. The folk play is a type of work that has long been treated with contempt and left to amateurs and hacks. It is time it was infected with the high ideals to which its very name commits it.

['Anmerkungen zum Volksstück' from *Versuche 10*, 1950, omitting detailed references to *Puntila* in the last paragraph but one]

NOTE: Brecht wrote this essay in Finland in connection with his 'folk –' or more or less lowbrow play *Puntila*, which he wrote in collaboration with the Finnish writer Hella Wuolijoki during the first three weeks of September 1940.

Gustav von Wangenheim ran a left-wing company called 'Truppe 1931'; his didactic play *Da liegt der Hund begraben* was staged at the Theater am Schiffbauerdamm in 1932; he is now working in East Germany. Kjeld Abell, originally a stage designer, wrote *The Melody that got Lost*, which was produced at the Riddersalen Theatre in Copenhagen in 1936. Marc Blitzstein's *The Cradle will Rock* (dedicated to Brecht) was staged by Orson Welles with the Mercury Theatre, New York, on 5 December 1937. Auden's two plays with Isherwood were published in 1935 and 1936, and were produced by Rupert Doone with the (London) Group Theatre.

In the summer of 1941 Brecht left Finland shortly before the entry of the German troops, crossed the USSR and the Pacific Ocean, and settled at Santa Monica outside Los Angeles.

34 · Alienation Effects in the Narrative Pictures of the Elder Brueghel

Anyone making a profound study of Brueghel's pictorial contrasts must realize that he deals in contradictions. In *The Fall of Icarus* the catastrophe breaks into the idyll in such a way that it is clearly set apart from it and valuable insights into the idyll can be gained. He doesn't allow the catastrophe to alter the idyll; the latter rather remains unaltered and survives undestroyed, merely disturbed.

In the great war painting *Dulle Griet* it isn't war's atmosphere of terror that inspires the artist to paint the instigator, the Fury of War, as helpless and handicapped, and to give her the features of a servant. The terror that he creates in this way is something deeper. Whenever an Alpine peak is set down in a Flemish landscape or old Asiatic costumes confront modern European ones, then the one denounces the other and sets off its oddness, while at the same time we get landscape as such, people all over the place. Such pictures don't just give off an atmosphere but a variety of atmospheres. Even though Brueghel manages to balance his contrasts he never merges them into one another, nor does he practise the separation of comic and tragic; his tragedy contains a comic element and his comedy a tragic one.

The Fall of Icarus. Tiny scale of this legendary event (you have to hunt for the victim). The characters turn their backs on the incident. Lovely picture of the concentration needed for ploughing. The man fishing in the right foreground, and his particular relationship to the water. The setting of the sun, which many people find surprising, presumably means that the fall was a long one. How otherwise can it be shown that Icarus flew too high? Daedalus passed from sight long ago. Contemporary Flemings in an ancient Mediterranean landscape. Special beauty and gaiety of the landscape during the frightful event.

River Landscape with the Parable of the Sower. Flemish landscape with a range of Alps. The peasant is sowing on a hillside among brambles. Pigeons are immediately picking up the seeds. They seem to be holding a formal council of war. The width of the world.

Christ Carrying the Cross. Execution as a popular festivity. The Spanish horsemen in red tunics as FOREIGN TROOPS: a thread of scarlet to indicate direction and movement and distract us from the execution. On the extreme left, the common people at work, the least interested. In the left background, people running, frightened of arriving too late. On the right they are already waiting in a circle round the place of execution. The scene in the left foreground – somebody being arrested – excites more attention than does Christ's collapse. Mary less concerned with Jesus than with her own sorrow. Note the woman on her left, the mourner in the rich and carefully-draped dress. The world is beautiful and seductive.

The Conversion of Saul. The fall was from a horse: i.e. the conversion of a better-class person. The passage of the Alps by the Duke of Alba's Spanish army is amusingly alienated by the idea of conversion. Carefully chosen and arbitrarily distributed colours underline the painter's interest.

The Archangel Michael. The beauty of the world (landscape) and the hideousness of its inhabitants (the Devil). The devil wears earth pigments as protective colouring. The earth is his domain. Seemingly the angel hasn't so much overcome him as discovered him (no evidence of struggle). The angel armed and protected, the devil without weapons or armour. The devil's expression tragic, meditative; that of the angel shows sorrow and disgust. He is on the point of cutting off the head like a surgeon. Size of the figures indicated by the smallness of the trees behind, which are very big but smaller than the figures.

Christ Driving the Money-changers from the Temple. Coupling of this with Christ's carring the cross, when the money-changers were expelling him in turn. The first incident big, the second small. Heathen temple architecture with Christian church symbols and a German city in the left background. Jesus in oriental dress among contemporary Flemish. The miracle-worker in the courtyard, left. The mother chastising her child next door. The man in the pillory (criminals are not unknown here either). Time – the twelfth hour.

Dulle Griet. The Fury defending her pathetic household goods with the sword. The world at the end of its tether. Little cruelty, much hypersensitivity.

The Tower of Babel. The tower has been put up askew. It includes portions of cliff, between which one can see the artificiality of the stonework.

Delivery of the building materials is a very laborious business; the effort is obviously wasted; a new plan seems to be being put into execution higher up, cutting down the scale of the original enterprise. Powerful oppression prevails, the attitude of the men bringing up the building materials is extremely servile, the builder is guarded by armed men.

['Verfremdungseffekte in den erzählenden Bildern des älteren Brueghel', from *Bildende Kunst*, Berlin and Dresden, 1957, No. 4]

NOTE: The date of these notes is uncertain, but it seems possible that they were inspired by Brecht's meeting with the Viennese art historian Gustav Glück, author of *Brueghels Gemälde* and *Das grosse Brueghel-Buch*, which Helene Weigel recalls giving him in Denmark about 1934. In the 1940s the Glücks were also living at Santa Monica where, says Frau Weigel, 'Brecht was very pleased that he met the old man. We saw him quite often.' Not all the details mentioned by Brecht are visible in the reproductions in the two books, so that Glück may well have discussed the pictures with him and shown him clearer photographs.

W. H. Auden's book *Another Time*, where the poem 'Musée des Beaux Arts' also comments

In Brueghel's *Icarus*, for instance: how everything turns away
Quite leisurely from the disaster . . .

was published in June 1940. Brueghel's peasant scenes (possibly referred to on p. 135) were no doubt in Brecht's mind when he was writing *The Caucasian Chalk Circle* in the winter of 1943–4, and a further reference to the painter will be found below in connection with the Hollywood production of *Galileo*. The wedding scene in the one play and the carnival scene in the other are both, as staged under Brecht's supervision, very close to the spirit of the pictures.

There is a detailed critique of Brecht's notes by the art historian Wolfgang Hütt in *Wissenschaftliche Zeitschrift der Martin-Luther-Universität Halle-Wittenberg*, 1957–8, p. 281.

35 · A Little Private Tuition for my Friend Max Gorelik

1. The modern playwright's (or scene designer's) relations with his audience are far more complicated than a tradesman's with his customers. But even the customer isn't always right; he by no means represents a final unalterable phenomenon that has been fully explored. Certain habits and appetites can be induced in him artificially; sometimes it is just a matter of establishing their presence. The farmer was not aware throughout the centuries of his need or potential need for a Ford car. The rapid social and economic development of our period alters the audience swiftly and radic-

ally, demanding and facilitating ever new modes of thought, feeling and behaviour. And a new class is standing, *Hannibal ante portas*, outside the doors of the theatre.

2. The sharpening of the class struggle has engendered such conflicts of interest in our audience that it is no longer in a position to react to art spontaneously and unanimously. In consequence the artist cannot take spontaneous success as a valid criterion of his work. Nor can he blindly admit the oppressed classes as a court of first instance, for their taste and their instincts are oppressed as well.

3. In times such as these the artist is driven to do what pleases himself, assuming hopefully that he represents the perfect spectator. He needn't land up in an ivory tower so long as he is really concerned to take part in the struggles of the oppressed, to find out their interests and represent them and develop his art on their behalf. But even an ivory tower is a better place to sit in nowadays than a Hollywood villa.

4. It leads to a lot of confusion when people hope to put across certain truths by wrapping them up and coating them with sugar. This is much the same as trying to raise the drug traffic to a higher moral plane by introducing the truth to its victims; they cannot recognize it in the first place and are certainly incapable of remembering it once they have sobered up.

5. Hollywood's and Broadway's methods of manufacturing certain excitements and emotions may possibly be artistic, but their only use is to offset the fearful boredom induced in any audience by the endless repetition of falsehoods and stupidities. This technique was developed and is used in order to stimulate interest in things and ideas that are not in the interest of the audience.

6. The theatre of our parasitic bourgeoisie has a quite specific effect on the nerves, which can in no way be treated as equivalent to the artistic experience of a more vital period. It 'conjures up' the illusion that it is reflecting real-life incidents with a view to achieving more or less primitive shock effects or hazily defined sentimental moods which in fact are to be consumed as substitutes for the missing spiritual experiences of a crippled and cataleptic audience. One only has to take a brief look to see that every one of these results can also be achieved by utterly distorted reflections of real life. Many artists have indeed come to believe that this up-to-date 'artistic experience' can *only* be the product of such distorted reflections.

7. Against that it has to be remembered that one can feel a natural interest in certain incidents between people quite independently of the artistic sphere. This natural interest can be made use of by art. There is also such a thing as a spontaneous interest in art itself; that is, in the

capacity to reflect real life and to do so in a fantastic, personal, individual way, that of the artist in question. Here we have an autonomous excitement that doesn't have to be manufactured, concerning what happens in reality and how the artist expresses it.

8. The conventional theatre can only be defended by using plainly reactionary phrases like 'the theatre never changes' and 'the play's the thing'. By such means the notion of drama is restricted to the parasitic bourgeoisie and its rotten plays. Jove's thunderbolts in the tiny hands of Louis B. Mayer. Take the element of conflict in Elizabethan plays, complex, shifting, largely impersonal, never soluble, and then see what has been made of it today, whether in contemporary plays or in contemporary renderings of the Elizabethans. Compare the part played by empathy then and now. What a contradictory, complicated and intermittent operation it was in Shakespeare's theatre! What they offer us nowadays as the 'eternal laws of the theatre' are the exceedingly present-day laws decreed by L. B. Mayer and the Theater Guild.

9. A certain amount of confusion about the non-aristotelian drama was due to the identification of 'scientific drama' with the 'drama of a scientific age'. The boundaries between art and science are not absolutely immutable; art's tasks can be taken over by science and science's by art, and yet the epic theatre still remains a theatre. That is to say that the theatre remains theatre even while becoming epic.

10. It is only the opponents of the new drama, the champions of the 'eternal laws of the theatre', who suppose that in renouncing the empathy process the modern theatre is renouncing the emotions. All the modern theatre is doing is to discard an outworn, decrepit, subjective sphere of the emotions and pave the way for the new, manifold, socially productive emotions of a new age.

11. The modern theatre mustn't be judged by its success in satisfying the audience's habits but by its success in transforming them. It needs to be questioned not about its degree of conformity with the 'eternal laws of the theatre' but about its ability to master the rules governing the great social processes of our age; not about whether it manages to interest the spectator in buying a ticket – i.e. in the theatre itself – but about whether it manages to interest him in the world.

['Kleines Privatissimum für meinen Freund Max Gorelik.' *Schriften zum Theater 3*, pp. 258–63]

NOTE: The manuscript is dated 'S.M.', i.e. Santa Monica, 'June 1944', and Brecht handed a copy to Mordecai Gorelik, who writes that he recognized that he wasn't the object of the attack but 'felt then, as I still do, that it was a bit much'.

Bert's thinking, at that time, was aggressively anti-bourgeois, and formed a closed system whose structure was threatened by any effective criticism. I gave him some bad moments, especially when I failed to share his disdain for suspense and climax in drama. As the climax to one such discussion of climax he threatened to throw me out of the window. . . . It was characteristic of him that he would brood for weeks or months over any rent in his thought-fabric until he could knit it back into unity. Later on, when I pointed out to him that his own writing contained suspense and climax, he remarked, airily, 'Is *that* what you mean? That's so elementary that I take it for granted!'

A year after his work on the New York *Die Mutter* Mr Gorelik – Max is a nickname – had come to Europe on a Guggenheim fellowship to get material for his book *New Theatres for Old* (French, New York 1940; Dobson, London 1947), whose plan he discussed in Denmark with Brecht. On returning to America he published an annotated version of some of *The Threepenny Opera* notes which formed the first statement of Brecht's ideas to appear in America (*Theater Workshop*, New York, No. 3, April–July 1937). This was strongly attacked by John Howard Lawson, who referred (in No. 4 of the same magazine) to 'the "new" ideas of Brecht' as being 'discredited and thoroughly un-Marxist' and called Gorelik's presentation of them 'meretricious.'

This was no doubt what Brecht was thinking of in the 'Short List of the most Frequent, Common and Boring Misconceptions about the Epic Theatre' (*Schriften zum Theater 3*, pp. 69–72) which seems to be his only other statement designed for American readers, apart from private letters:

1. It is an over-intellectual, clever-clever abstract theory which has nothing to do with real life.

(In fact it arose from and is associated with many years of practical activity. The plays from which it derives were performed in many German cities and one of them, *The Threepenny Opera*, in almost every major city in the world. Quotations from it served as headlines to leading articles or were used in speeches by famous lawyers. A few plays were banned by the police; one of them got the chief German play award, the Kleist Prize; the theory was studied in university seminars, etc. They were acted by working-class groups and by stars; there was a special theatre, the Theater am Schiffbauerdamm, with a company of actors such as Weigel, Neher, Lorre, etc., who developed these principles. Piscator's two theatres developed some of them too.)

2. One ought to write plays, not devise theories. Anything else is un-Marxist.

(Primitive confusion of theory and ideology. Often based proudly on quotations from Marx and Engels which are themselves of a theoretical kind. Lenin referred to this kind of thing in another context as 'creeping empiricism'.)

3. The epic theatre is against all emotions. But reason and emotion can't be divided.

(The epic theatre isn't against the emotions; it tries to examine them, and is not satisfied just to stimulate them. It is the orthodox theatre which sins by dividing reason and emotion, in that it virtually rules out the former. As soon as one makes the slightest move to introduce a modicum of reason into theatrical practice its protagonists scream that one is trying to abolish the emotions.)

4. Brecht's ideas aren't new. Usually expressed thus: Brecht's 'new' ideas.

(This is mostly said by people who aren't attacking these ideas because they are old and they themselves have newer ones, but because they favour the old ideas and are interested in making others seem equally old. In fact the epic theatre's supporters are always trying to find precedents in theatrical history for some of their principles; they do as much as they can to get rid of the element of novelty which might give these a somewhat fashionable flavour. The principles of the epic theatre haven't much to do with early nineteenth century German philosophical aesthetics; all the same, as Marx repeatedly insisted, this aesthetics (Kant and Hegel) stands head and shoulders above the aesthetic opinions of many supposed Marxists, who in fact have neither knowledge nor understanding of it, or for that matter of Marx's own teaching.)

5. We Americans (French, Danes, Swiss, etc.) must derive our aesthetics from our own American (French, Danish, Swiss, etc.) plays.

(Swiss play-writing doesn't exist; French existed once; American and Danish play-writing strike the European as completely European. In Germany the epic theatre has long been termed 'un-German'; the National Socialists dismiss it as purely decadent. Against that, capitalism is an extraordinarily international phenomenon and has seemingly led to an extraordinary similarity of conditions in different countries. On the question of learning from other people's mistakes cf. Lenin's Infantile Disorder.)

36 · Building up a Part: Laughton's Galileo

In describing Laughton's *Galileo* the play's author is setting out not so much to try and immortalize one of those fleeting works of art that actors create, as to pay tribute to the pains a great actor is prepared to take over a fleeting work of this sort. This is no longer at all common. It is not just that the under-rehearsing in our hopelessly commercialized theatre is to blame for lifeless and stereotyped portraits – give the average actor more time, and he would hardly do better. Nor is it simply that this century has very few outstanding individualists with rich characteristics and rounded contours—if that were all, the same care could be devoted to portraying the 'little' man. Above all it is that we seem to have lost any understanding and appreciation of what we may call a *theatrical conception*: what Garrick did, when as Hamlet he met his father's ghost; Sorel, when as Phèdre she knew that she was going to die; Bassermann, when as Philip he listened to Posa. It is a question of inventiveness.

The spectator could isolate and detach such theatrical conceptions, but they combined to form a single rich texture. Odd insights into men's nature, glimpses of their particular way of living together, were brought about by the ingenious contrivance of the actors.

With works of art even more than with philosophical systems it is impossible to find out how they are made. Those who make them work hard to give the impression that everything just happens, as it were of its own accord, as though an image were forming in a plain inert mirror. Of course this is a swindle, and apparently the idea is that if it comes off it will increase the spectator's pleasure. In fact it does not. What the spectator, anyway the experienced spectator, enjoys about art is the making of art, the active creative element. In art we view nature herself as if she were an artist.

The ensuing account deals with this aspect, with the process of manufacture rather than with the result. It is less a matter of the artist's temperament than of the notions of reality which he has *and communicates*; less a matter of his vitality than of the observations which underlie his portraits and can be derived from them. This means neglecting much that seemed to us to be 'inimitable' in Laughton's achievement, and going on rather to what can be learnt from it. For we cannot create talent; we can only perhaps set it tasks.

It is unnecessary here to examine how the artists of the past used to astonish their public. Asked why he acted, L. answered: 'Because people don't know what they are like, and I think I can show them.' His collaboration in the rewriting of the play showed that he had all sorts of ideas which were begging to be disseminated, about how people *really* live together, about the motive forces that need to be taken into account here. L.'s attitude seemed to the author to be that of a realistic artist of our time. For whereas in relatively stationary ('quiet') periods artists may find it possible to merge wholly with their public and to be a faithful 'embodiment' of the general conception, our profoundly unsettled time forces them to take special measures to penetrate to the truth. Our society will not admit of its own accord what makes it move. It can even be said to exist purely through the secrecy with which it surrounds itself. What attracted L. about *Galileo* was not only one or two formal points but also the sheer substance; he thought this might become what he called a *contribution*. And so great was his anxiety to show things as they really are that despite all his indifference (indeed timidity) in political matters he suggested and even demanded that not a few of the play's points should be made sharper, on the simple ground that such passages seemed 'somehow weak' to him, by which he meant that they did not do justice to things as they are.

We usually met in L.'s big house above the Pacific, as the dictionaries of synonyms were too big to cart about. He had continual and inexhaustibly patient recourse to these tomes, and used in addition to fish out the most varied literary texts in order to examine this or that gest, or some particular mode of speech: Aesop, the Bible, Molière, Shakespeare. In my house he gave readings of Shakespeare's works to which he would devote perhaps a fortnight's preparation. In this way he read *The Tempest* and *King Lear*, simply for himself and one or two guests who happened to have dropped in. After that we would briefly discuss what seemed relevant, an 'aria' perhaps, or an effective scene opening. These were exercises, and he would pursue them in various directions, assimilating them in the rest of his work. If he had to give a reading on the radio he would get me to hammer out the syncopated rhythms of Whitman's poems (which he found somewhat strange) on a table with my fists, and once he hired a studio where we recorded half a dozen different acts telling the story of the Creation, in which he was an African planter telling the negroes how he had created the world, or an English butler ascribing it to His Lordship. We needed such broadly ramified studies, because he spoke no German whatever and we had to decide the gest of each piece of dialogue by my acting it all in bad English or even in German and his then acting it back in proper English in a variety of ways until I could say: that's it. The result he would write down sentence by sentence in longhand. Some sentences, indeed many, he carried around for days, changing them continually. This system of performance-and-repetition had one immense advantage in that psychological discussions were almost entirely avoided. Even the most fundamental gests, such as Galileo's way of observing, or his showmanship, or his craze for pleasure, were established in three dimensions by actual performance. Our first concern throughout was for the smallest fragments, for sentences, even for exclamations – each treated separately, each needing to be given the simplest, freshly fitted form, giving so much away, hiding so much or leaving it open. More radical attacks on the structure of entire scenes or of the work itself were meant to help the story to move and to bring out fairly general conclusions about people's attitude to the great physicist. But this reluctance to tinker with the psychological aspect remained with L. all through our long period of collaboration, even when a rough draft of the play was ready and he was giving various readings in order to test reactions, and even during the rehearsals.

The awkward circumstance that one translator knew no German and the other scarcely any English compelled us, as can be seen, from the outset to use acting as our means of translation. We were forced to do what better equipped translators should do too: to translate gests. For language is theatrical in so far as it primarily expresses the mutual attitude of the speakers. (For the 'arias', as has been described, we brought in the author's own gest, by observing Shakespeare in his lyric passages, or the writers of the Bible.) In a most striking and occasionally brutal way L. showed his lack of interest in the 'book', to an extent the author could not always share. What we were making was just a text; the performance was all that counted. Impossible to lure him to translate passages which the author was willing to cut for the proposed performance but wanted to keep in the book. The theatrical occasion was what mattered, the text was only there to make it possible; it would be expended in the production, would go off like gun-powder in a firework. Although L.'s theatrical experience had been in a London which had become thoroughly indifferent to the theatre, the old Elizabethan London still lived in him, the London where theatre was such a passion that it could swallow immortal works of art greedily and bare-facedly as so many 'texts'. These works which have survived the centuries were in fact like improvisations thrown off for an all-important moment. Printing them at all was a matter of little interest, and probably only took place so that the spectators, in other words those who were present at the actual event, the performance, might have a souvenir of their enjoyment. And the theatre seems in those days to have been so potent that the cuts and interpolations made at rehearsal can have done little harm to the text.

We used to work in L.'s small library, in the mornings. But often L. would come and meet me in the garden, running barefoot in shirt and trousers over the damp grass, and would show me some changes in his flowerbeds; for his garden always occupied him, providing many problems and subtle-ties. The gaiety and the beautiful proportions of this world of flowers over-lapped in a most pleasant way into our work. For quite a while our work embraced everything we could lay our hands on. If we discussed gardening it was only a diversion from one of the scenes in *Galileo;* if we combed a New York museum for technical drawings by Leonardo to use as background pictures in the performance we would be diverted to Hokusai's graphic work. L., I could see, would allow such material just to brush against him. The parcels of books, or photocopies from books, which he persistently ordered, never turned him into a bookworm. He obstinately sought for the external: not for physics but for the physicist's behaviour. It was a matter of putting together a bit of theatre, something slight and superficial. As the material piled up, L. became set on the idea of getting a good draughtsman to produce entertaining sketches in the manner of Caspar Neher, to expose the anatomy of the action. 'Before you amuse others you have to amuse yourself,' he said.

For this no trouble was too great. As soon as L. heard of Caspar Neher's delicate stage sketches, which allow the actors to group themselves according to a great artist's compositions and to take up attitudes that are both precise and realistic, he asked an excellent draughtsman from the Walt Disney Studios to make similar sketches. They did not turn out very successfully; L. used them, but with caution.

What pains he took over the costumes; not only his own, but those of all the actors! And how much time we spent on the casting of the many parts!

First we had to look through works on costume and also old pictures showing costumes in order to find costumes that were free of any element of fancy dress. We sighed with relief when we found a small sixteenth-century panel that showed long trousers. Then we had to distinguish the classes. There the elder Brueghel was of great service. Finally we had to work out the colour scheme. Each scene had to have its basic tone: the first, e.g., a delicate morning one of white, yellow and grey. But the entire sequence of scenes had to have its development in terms of colour. In the first scene a deep and distinguished blue made its entrance with Ludovico Marsili, and this deep blue remained, set apart, in the second scene with the upper bourgeoisie in their grey-green coats made of felt and leather. Galileo's social ascent could be followed by means of colour. The silver and pearl-grey of the fourth (court-) scene led into a nocturne in brown and black (where Galileo is jeered at by the monks of the Collegium Romanum), then on to the eighth, the cardinal's ball, with delicate and fantastic individual masks (ladies and gentlemen) moving among the cardinals' crimson figures. That was a burst of colour, but it still had to be fully unleashed, and this occurred in the ninth scene, the carnival. After the nobility and the cardinals the poor people too had their masked ball. Then came the descent into dull and sombre colours. The difficulty of such a plan of course lies in the fact that the costumes and their wearers wander through several scenes; they have always to fit in, and to help build up the colour scheme of the scenes that follow.

We filled the parts mainly with young actors. The speeches presented certain problems. The American stage shuns speeches except in (maybe because of) its frightful Shakespearean productions. Speeches just mean a break in the story, and, as commonly delivered, that is what they are. L. worked with the young actors in a masterly and conscientious manner, and the author was impressed by the freedom which he gave them, by the way in which he avoided anything Laughtonish and simply taught them the

structure. To those actors who were too easily influenced by his own personality he read passages from Shakespeare, without rehearsing the actual text
at all; to none did he read the text itself. The actors were incidentally asked
on no account to prove their suitability for the part by putting something
'impressive' into it.

[*Brecht then repeats numbers 1–8 of the last section of the Notes on the play,
and says that they were jointly agreed.*]

The performance took place in a small theatre in Beverly Hills, and L.'s
chief worry was the prevailing heat. He asked that trucks full of ice should
be parked against the theatre walls, and fans be set in motion 'so that the
audience can think'.

> [From *Galilei – Aufbau einer Rolle*, East Berlin,
> 1956/8. 'Vorwort' to the Laughton section, omitting
> eight paragraphs at the end which duplicate the
> notes to the play.]

NOTE: In conversation Brecht later referred to *Galileo* as 'ein zweijähriger
Spass' – a piece of fun that lasted two years. He finished rewriting the play in
December 1945; the production took place in the Coronet Theater, Los Angeles,
in August 1947, and was repeated in December in New York. In neither city
did it have any great critical or commercial success. Brecht himself returned to
Europe before the New York performance.

Joseph Losey directed, with settings by Robert Davison and music by Eisler
(who was also living in Hollywood at the time). Besides Laughton, the cast
included Frances Heflin as Virginia and Hugo Haas as Barberini. T. Edward
Hambleton was the producer (in the American sense), and the draughtsman here
referred to was John Hubley, later one of the leading lights in UPA. It was not
the first production of the play, which had been given in Zurich in its earlier
version in 1943, with Leonard Steckel as Galileo.

The notes to the play are published in *Brecht: Plays 1*, London, 1960.

37 · 'Der Messingkauf': an editorial note

Many readers of Brecht's work will have noticed his references to 'Der Messingkauf', notably in the poems published in *Theaterarbeit* (Dresdner-Verlag, Dresden 1952), which have appeared in English under the title 'Poems on the Theatre'. 'Der Messingkauf' (or 'Buying Brass') was never completed or properly put into shape by Brecht, and because it evidently came to serve him as a kind of classificatory title much like 'Über eine nicht-aristotelische Dramatik' had done earlier – as a label that could be stuck on a wide variety of theoretical notes and fragments – it has remained something of a problem. In fact it was meant to be one of his most substantial works, running even in its incomplete form to over 200 handwritten and typescript pages, of which a loosely-reconstructed version is to form *Schriften zum Theater 5*.

The plan dates back to about 1937. The main drafts (Brecht-Archive Nos. 124–7) evidently follow after *Furcht und Elend des Dritten Reiches* and seem to coincide with Brecht's work on *Galileo* (whose Dialogues suggested the form, according to a diary note of 12 February 1939), on *Mother Courage* (whose scene titles are quoted on p. 125/10) and perhaps also on the *Flüchtlingsgespräche*, with which they have some affinities of style. *Versuche 11* (1951, p. 108) refers to it as 'a four-sided conversation about a new way of making theatre', and in the original plan it was to be just this, absorbing the themes of such essays as 'The Street Scene' and 'Alienation Effects in Chinese Acting' together with much new material into a lively dialogue. 'As we discuss the theatre,' says one of the speakers, 'we can sit here and feel that we are conducting our conversation in front of an audience: in other words that we ourselves are performing a kind of playlet. And now and again we can stage a small experiment or two, if it helps to clarify matters.'

Werner Hecht takes this to mean that the work was designed to be playable with various *ad lib.* insertions, and the Berliner Ensemble have made up a stage version on this assumption.

It is not clear how the poems were to be worked in, or at what point Brecht decided to include them under the 'Messingkauf' label. Three of the seven 'Poems from the Messingkauf' published in *Versuche 15* were written independently of, and perhaps even prior to the original plan. The other four were written in 1950 specially for *Theaterarbeit*, together with the essay 'Stage Design for the Epic Theatre' which appears on p. 230; they are classed together in the typescript (Brecht-Archive No. 62) as 'The Playwright's Wishes. Seventeen further poems are printed in *Gedichte 4* as 'Poems belonging to the Messingkauf', and five of these are linked to each other, though not to the main dialogue, by patches of prose. In *Versuche 11* the 'Practice Scenes for Actors' (see p. 147 above) are also labelled as part of the Messingkauf, though that need not mean that they were conceived as such.

Most of the work on the dialogue was done between 1937 and 1940, though Brecht evidently planned to add to it while in the United States; thus a pencilled note (127/14) shows him meaning to work in a reference to Laughton, and other fragments may also possibly date from then. The cryptic title derives from the analogy with a man who buys a brass instrument for the metal it is made of rather than for the music it makes. The theatre, in other words, is being cross-examined about its content, from a hard-headed practical point of view.

The dialogue is divided into four 'nights'. An early version sets the scene as 'A big theatre after the performance. A philosopher has come to talk with the theatre people. An actress invited him. The theatre people are disgruntled. They took part in the campaign for a theatre of the scientific age. But science has hardly gained, while the theatre has in many ways suffered . . .' (124/02). Another draft beginning runs thus:

THE FIRST NIGHT

> A stage on which a stagehand is slowly dismantling the set. An actor, a *Dramaturg* and a philosopher are sitting on chairs or bits of the set. The *Dramaturg* reaches for a small basket put there by the stagehand, and takes out bottles which he then uncorks. The actor pours the wine into glasses and hands it round.
>
> THE ACTOR: All this dust makes it thirsty work sitting on a stage. I advise you all to take a good swig . . . (126/13).

The characters are the Philosopher, the Actor, the *Dramaturg*, the Actress and the Worker, Stagehand or Electrician; how they were to be reduced to four is not clear, though neither Actress nor Electrician has much to say. 'The Philosopher wishes to apply the theatre ruthlessly to his own ends. It must furnish accurate images of incidents between people, and allow the spectator to adopt a standpoint. The Actor wishes to express himself. Story and characters serve his purpose. . . . The *Dramaturg* puts himself at the Philosopher's disposal, and promises to apply his knowledge and abilities to the conversion of the theatre into the thaëter of the Philosopher. He hopes the theatre will get a new lease of life. The Electrician represents the new audience. He is a worker and dissatisfied with the world.' (124/07.)

'The Philosopher is welcomed to the the theatre/the theatre's business is good/the Philosopher's business not so good . . .' – so the scheme for the first night begins. At different times Brecht noted a variety of other possible topics for it: the relation between film and theatre, 'literarization', montage, naturalism, commitment. The most coherent of the proposed sequences however runs on thus:

> unfortunate circumstances better not mentioned as they have 'nothing to do with the case'/what the Philosopher finds interesting about the theatre/ the theatre shows reality/no reality no theatre/proposal by the Philosopher, who wants to hire the theatre for his own purposes/but the audience comes to the theatre to get away from reality/it's a playground for idlers/buying brass/the Philosopher salutes the theatre (126/12).

Subjects dealt with on the second night include 'the emotion racket', science, and the differences between the artistic and the philosophical character; possibly also the hero, Brueghel's painting, 'lightness' and the alienation effect. This culminates in the 'foundation of the thaëter' (that is to say, the standing on its head of the traditional notion of the theatre in order to meet the Philosopher's demands, the Philosopher being quite plainly a Marxist – a philosopher as defined on p. 72). A discussion of Piscator's theatre is also supposed to fit in here.

The third night covers such points as experimental theatre, the Street Scene, the smokers' theatre, the element of variation and near-improvisation in Shakespeare, and Brecht's own *Furcht und Elend des Dritten Reiches*. The fullest outline of the fourth and last night runs:

> reconversion of the thaëter into a theatre/comedy/fairground narrative/the A-effect in Chinese acting/cheerful criticism/teachers/the Philosopher's empty hands/Weigel descends into fame/an auditorium of statesmen (125/02).

What seems like a sketch for the ending opens with the Actor exclaiming: 'I can't stand all that talk about art being the handmaiden of society. There sits society, fat and powerful. Art isn't a part of her; it just belongs to her; it's simply her skivvy. Are we all supposed to be a lot of servants? Can't we all be masters? Can't art become a mistress? Let's get rid of domestic service altogether, in art just as much as anywhere else!'

PHILOSOPHER: Bravo!
DRAMATURG: What d'you mean, bravo? You've ruined everything you've said by that piece of spontaneous applause. All anybody has to do is tell you he's oppressed, and you're on his side at once.

PHILOSOPHER: I hope I am. I see what he's getting at now. He's worried we're going to turn him into a civil servant or a master of ceremonies or a revivalist preacher operating by 'artistic means'. Cheer up; that's not the plan. The art of acting needs to be treated simply as an elementary human utterance which contains its own purpose. That's where it differs from the art of war, whose purpose is external to itself. The art of acting is one of society's elementary capacities; it is based on a direct social asset, one of humanity's pleasures in society; it is like language itself; it's really a language of its own. I propose we rise to our feet to make this tribute stick in our memory.

All rise.

PHILOSOPHER: And now I propose that we should take advantage of the fact that we've risen to our feet, and go and relieve ourselves.

ACTOR: O God, you've wrecked the whole thing. I protest.

PHILOSOPHER: Why? Once again I'm obeying an instinct, bowing to it, respecting it, and at the same time seeing that the ceremony comes to a suitably banal conclusion.

'There is a pause', says the typescript (124/83), but alas, the next page seems to be missing.

The actual body of the dialogue, as we have it, takes the form of fragments, of anything from a few lines to two or three pages in length, which are allotted to the various 'nights' more or less in accordance with Brecht's scheme. It is like a collection of pieces of different shapes and sizes, quite disjointed as they stand, but intended eventually to be sorted out and mounted into a patchwork. They do not on the whole include the subjects already dealt with in essays (e.g. 'Chinese Acting' and 'The Street Scene') but instead concentrate on new arguments. Thus, in a section on Shakespeare:

ACTOR: From your account it sounds as if Shakespeare added a fresh scene every day.

DRAMATURG: That's it. I mean, they were experimenting. They were experimenting just as Galileo was at that time experimenting in Florence and Bacon in London. And so it is as well to produce the plays in a spirit of experiment.

ACTOR: People think that's sacrilege.

DRAMATURG: If it weren't for sacrilege the plays wouldn't exist. (124/75.)

Or, on addressing the audience directly:

WORKER: I'm for realistic acting.

PHILOSOPHER: But it's also a reality that you are sitting in a theatre, and not with your eye glued to a keyhole. How can it be realistic to try and gloss that over? We want to demolish the fourth wall: I herewith announce our

22. Alexander Granach, 1933.

23. *Mother* (*Die Mutter*), final scene in the Theatre Union's production, New York, 1935.

24. Chinese actor, Mei Lan-fang, with Eisenstein (right), Moscow, 1935.

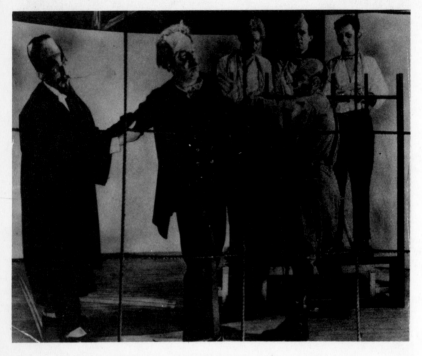

25. *Die Rundköpfe und die Spitzköpfe*, Copenhagen, 1936.

26. Okhlopkhov's production of Pogodin's *The Aristocrats* in the Moscow Realistic Theatre, 1937.

27. *Señora Carrar's Rifles*, Paris, 1937, with Helene Weigel (right).

28. Film of *Gunga Din*, directed by George Stevens, 1938.

29. Brueghel's *Dulle Griet*, Mayer van den Berg Museum, Antwerp.

30. Laughton's *Galileo*, Hollywood, 1947: scene with the little monk.

joint operation. In future please don't be bashful; just show us that you've arranged everything in the way best calculated to help us understand.

ACTOR: That's official, is it, that from now on we can look down at you and even talk to you?

PHILOSOPHER: Of course. Any time it furthers the demonstration.

ACTOR (*mutters*): So its back to asides, to 'Honoured Sirs, behold before you King Herod', and to the girls showing off their legs to the officers in the boxes . . .

PHILOSOPHER (*mutters*): The hardest advance of all: backwards to common sense. (127/47.)

Or a new qualification of Brecht's view of empathy:

ACTOR: Does getting rid of empathy mean getting rid of every emotional element?

PHILOSOPHER: No, no. Neither the public nor the actor must be stopped from taking part emotionally; the representation of emotions must not be hampered, nor must the actor's use of emotions be frustrated. Only one out of many possible sources of emotion needs to be left unused, or at least treated as a subsidiary source – empathy. (125/21.)

Or a point that Brecht had forgotten to emphasize earlier: 'A theatre that can't be laughed in is a theatre to laugh at. Humourless people are ridiculous.' (127/42.)

Not the least interesting thing here is the discussion of Brecht's own experience of the theatre. Though both the Philosopher and the *Dramaturg* seem at times to be voicing his views, in this connection he is spoken of impersonally as 'The Augsburger' or, a subsequent amendment, 'The Playwright'.

The Augsburger's theatre was very small. It performed very few plays. It trained very few actors. The chief actresses were Weigel, Neher and Lenya. The chief actors were Homolka, Lorre and Lingen. The singer Busch likewise belonged to this theatre, but he seldom appeared on the stage. The chief scene designer was Caspar Neher, no relation to the actress. The musicians were Weill and Eisler. (125/11.)

'The Augsburger', says the *Dramaturg*,

rejected the audience's demand that the actor should be wholly absorbed in his part. His actors weren't waiters who must serve up the meat and have their private, personal feelings treated as gross importunities. They were servants neither of the writer nor of the audience. His actors weren't officials of a political movement, and they weren't high priests of art. Their job as political human beings was to use art or anything else to further their social cause. On his stage there were private jokes, improvisations and extemporizations such as would have been unthinkable in the old theatre. (124/58.)

It was only 'an unfortunate fact that his objections to empathy in art were taken as objections to feeling in art'. (124/60.)

'Did the Augsburger say anything about his audience?' asks the Actor.

PHILOSOPHER: Yes. This:
>The other day I met my audience.
>In a dusty street
>He gripped a pneumatic drill in his fists.
>For a second
>He looked up. Rapidly I set up my theatre
>Between the houses. He
>Looked expectant.
>
>In the pub
>I met him again. He was standing at the bar.
>Grimy with sweat, he was drinking. In his fist
>A thick sandwich. Rapidly I set up my theatre. He
>Looked astonished.
>
>Today
>I brought it off again. Outside the station
>With brass bands and rifle butts I saw him
>Being herded off to war.
>In the midst of the crowd
>I set up my theatre. Over his shoulder
>He looked back
>And nodded. (124/85.)

A section designed for the fourth night, 'Weigel's descent into fame', is a moving tribute by Brecht not just to his wife's acting, but to her willingness to throw up a brilliant career to take part in little-advertised political performances, then in exile to team up with very mixed companies of amateurs. There is also the passage on 'Leichtigkeit' (meaning both lightness and ease) which includes two of the 'Poems belonging to the Messingkauf' of *Gedichte 4*. Who is addressing whom is not clear, but it is Brecht's own voice:

> When your work is complete, it must look light, easy. The ease must recall effort; it is effort conquered or effort victorious. From the outset of your work you must adopt the attitude that aims at achieving ease. You mustn't leave out the difficulties, but must collect them and make them come easy through your work. For the only worthwhile kind of ease is that which is a victory of effort.
>
>> Observe the ease
>> With which the mighty
>> River tears down its banks!
>> The earthquake
>> Shakes the ground with relaxed hand.

The dreadful fire
Cheerfully reaches for the many-housed city
And devours it in comfort:
A practised consumer.

There is an attitude of beginning which favours the achievement of ease. It can be learned. You realize that mastery consists in having learned how to learn. If one wants to exert one's full powers one has to be economical with them. One should do nothing that one can't do, nor do anything yet that one can't yet do. One has to divide up one's task so that one masters the individual parts with ease, for undue strain makes the achievement of ease impossible.

O joy of beginning! O early morning!
First grass, when none remembers
What green means! O first page of the book
Long awaited, the surprise of it! Read it
Slowly; all too soon
The unread part will grow thin! And the first spray of water
On a sweaty face! The clean
Cool shirt! O beginning of love! Glance that strays away!
O beginning of work! To pour oil
Into the cold engine! First handling and first humming
Of the motor as it starts! And first puff
Of smoke filling the lungs! And you too
New idea! (127/03-04.)

All this is just raw material, and to Brecht raw material was always expendable, to be ruthlessly rewritten and pruned. How this last passage, for instance, would ever have been fitted into the dialogue, or whether it was really meant to be, is quite impossible to say. Generally speaking the foregoing is nothing but a rough indication of the subjects covered by 'Der Messingkauf' in the confused and fragmentary state in which Brecht left it, and also (let us hope) of the liveliness of tone which seems to run right through.

Nobody knows why he never finished it. He evidently had the plan still in mind during his stay in the United States, and he no doubt worked on it, though he seems to have written very few theoretical notes or essays while there, partly perhaps because there were not the magazines in which to publish them, partly because he needed first to earn money by work on film treatments and other more or less time-wasting pursuits. That he never entirely lost sight of the idea is evident from his adding the six 'Playwright's Wishes' when he returned to Berlin after the war. The dialogue proper however remained a vast but dishevelled sequence of scraps, and on arriving in Europe in November 1947 he chose to recast all his views on the theatre in a rather more closely-argued form.

Part 3
1947-1948
(Zurich)

38 · A Short Organum for the Theatre

[Sections marked † are those which Brecht subsequently considered modifying by the series of appendices on p. 276ff.]

PROLOGUE

The following sets out to define an aesthetic drawn from a particular kind of theatrical performance which has been worked out in practice over the past few decades. In the theoretical statements, excursions, technical indications occasionally published in the form of notes to the writer's plays, aesthetics have only been touched on casually and with comparative lack of interest. There you saw a particular species of theatre extending or contracting its social functions, perfecting or sifting its artistic methods and establishing or maintaining its aesthetics – if the question arose – by rejecting or converting to its own use the dominant conventions of morality or taste according to its tactical needs. This theatre justified its inclination to social commitment by pointing to the social commitment in universally accepted works of art, which only fail to strike the eye because it was the accepted commitment. As for the products of our own time, it held that their lack of any worthwhile content was a sign of decadence: it accused these entertainment emporiums of having degenerated into branches of the bourgeois narcotics business. The stage's inaccurate representations of our social life, including those classed as so-called Naturalism, led it to call for scientifically exact representations; the tasteless rehashing of empty visual or spiritual palliatives, for the noble logic of the multiplication table. The cult of beauty, conducted with hostility towards learning and contempt for the useful, was dismissed by it as itself contemptible, especially as nothing beautiful resulted. The battle was for a theatre fit for the scientific age, and where its planners found it too hard to borrow or steal from the armoury of aesthetic concepts enough weapons to defend themselves against the aesthetics of the Press they simply threatened 'to transform the means of enjoyment into an instrument of instruction, and to convert certain amusement establishments into organs of mass communication' ('Notes to the opera *Mahagonny*' – [see No. 13]): i.e. to emigrate from the realm of the merely enjoyable. Aesthetics, that heirloom of a by now depraved and parasitic class, was in such a lamentable state that a theatre would certainly have gained both in reputation and in elbowroom if it had rechristened itself thaëter. And yet what we achieved in the way of theatre for a scientific age was not science but theatre, and the accumulated innovations worked out during the Nazi period and the war – when practical demonstration was impossible – compel some attempt to set this species of theatre in its aesthetic background, or anyhow to sketch for it the outlines of a conceivable aesthetic. To explain the theory of theatrical alienation except within an aesthetic framework would be impossibly awkward.

Today one could go so far as to compile an aesthetics of the exact sciences. Galileo spoke of the elegance of certain formulae and the point of an experiment; Einstein suggests that the sense of beauty has a part to play in the making of scientific discoveries; while the atomic physicist R. Oppenheimer praises the scientific attitude, which 'has its own kind of beauty and seems to suit mankind's position on earth'.

Let us therefore cause general dismay by revoking our decision to emigrate from the realm of the merely enjoyable, and even more general dismay by announcing our decision to take up lodging there. Let us treat the theatre as a place of entertainment, as is proper in an aesthetic discussion, and try to discover which type of entertainment suits us best.

I

'Theatre' consists in this: in making live representations of reported or invented happenings between human beings and doing so with a view to entertainment. At any rate that is what we shall mean when we speak of theatre, whether old or new.

2

To extend this definition we might add happenings between humans and gods, but as we are only seeking to establish the minimum we can leave such matters aside. Even if we did accept such an extension we should still have to say that the 'theatre' set-up's broadest function was to give pleasure. It is the noblest function that we have found for 'theatre'.

3†

From the first it has been the theatre's business to entertain people, as it also has of all the other arts. It is this business which always gives it its particular dignity; it needs no other passport than fun, but this it has got to have. We should not by any means be giving it a higher status if we were to turn it e.g. into a purveyor of morality; it would on the contrary run the risk of being debased, and this would occur at once if it failed to make its moral lesson enjoyable, and enjoyable to the senses at that: a principle, admittedly, by which morality can only gain. Not even instruction can be demanded of it: at any rate, no more utilitarian lesson than how to move pleasurably, whether in the physical or in the spiritual sphere. The theatre must in fact remain something entirely superfluous, though this indeed means that it is the superfluous for which we live. Nothing needs less justification than pleasure.

4†

Thus what the ancients, following Aristotle, demanded of tragedy is nothing higher or lower than that it should entertain people. Theatre may be said to be derived from ritual, but that is only to say that it becomes theatre once the two have separated; what it brought over from the mysteries was not its former ritual function, but purely and simply the pleasure which accompanied this. And the catharsis of which Aristotle writes – cleansing by fear and pity, or from fear and pity – is a purification which is performed not only in a pleasurable way, but precisely for the purpose of pleasure. To ask or to accept more of the theatre is to set one's own mark too low.

5

Even when people speak of higher and lower degrees of pleasure, art stares impassively back at them; for it wishes to fly high and low and to be left in peace, so long as it can give pleasure to people.

6

Yet there are weaker (simple) and stronger (complex) pleasures which the theatre can create. The last-named, which are what we are dealing with in great drama, attain their climaxes rather as cohabitation does through love: they are more intricate, richer in communication, more contradictory and more productive of results.

7

And different periods' pleasures varied naturally according to the system under which people lived in society at the time. The Greek demos [literally: the demos of the Greek circus] ruled by tyrants had to be entertained differently from the feudal court of Louis XIV. The theatre was required to deliver different representations of men's life together: not just representations of a different life, but also representations of a different sort.

8

According to the sort of entertainment which was possible and necessary under the given conditions of men's life together the characters had to be given varying proportions, the situations to be constructed according to varying points of view. Stories have to be narrated in various ways, so that these particular Greeks may be able to amuse themselves with the inevitability of divine laws where ignorance never mitigates the punishment; these French with the graceful self-discipline demanded of the great ones of this earth by a courtly code of duty; the Englishmen of the Elizabethan age with the self-awareness of the new individual personality which was then uncontrollably bursting out.

9

And we must always remember that the pleasure given by representations of such different sorts hardly ever depended on the representation's likeness to the thing portrayed. Incorrectness, or considerable improbability even, was hardly or not at all disturbing, so long as the incorrectness had a certain consistency and the improbability remained of a constant kind. All that mattered was the illusion of compelling momentum in the story told, and this was created by all sorts of poetic and theatrical means. Even today we are happy to overlook such inaccuracies if we can get something out of the spiritual purifications of Sophocles or the sacrificial acts of Racine or the unbridled frenzies of Shakespeare, by trying to grasp the immense or splendid feelings of the principal characters in these stories.

10

For of all the many sorts of representation of happenings between humans which the theatre has made since ancient times, and which have given entertainment despite their incorrectness and improbability, there are even today an astonishing number that also give entertainment to us.

11

In establishing the extent to which we can be satisfied by representations from so many different periods – something that can hardly have been possible to the children of those vigorous periods themselves – are we not at the same time creating the suspicion that we have failed to discover the special pleasures, the proper entertainment of our own time?

12†

And our enjoyment of the theatre must have become weaker than that of the ancients, even if our way of living together is still sufficiently like theirs for it to be felt at all. We grasp the old works by a comparatively new method – empathy – on which they rely little. Thus the greater part of our enjoyment is drawn from other sources than those which our predecessors were able to exploit so fully. We are left safely dependent on beauty of language, on elegance of narration, on passages which stimulate our own private imaginations: in short, on the incidentals of the old works. These are precisely the poetical and theatrical means which hide the imprecisions of the story. Our theatres no longer have either the capacity or the wish to tell these stories, even the relatively recent ones of the great Shakespeare, at all clearly: i.e. to make the connection of events credible. And according to Aristotle – and we agree there – narrative is the soul of drama. We are more and more disturbed to see how crudely and carelessly men's life together is represented, and that not only in old works but also in contemporary ones constructed according to the old recipes. Our whole way of appreciation is starting to get out of date.

13

It is the inaccurate way in which happenings between human beings are represented that restricts our pleasure in the theatre. The reason: we and our forebears have a different relationship to what is being shown.

14

For when we look about us for an entertainment whose impact is immediate, for a comprehensive and penetrating pleasure such as our theatre could give us by representations of men's life together, we have to think of ourselves as children of a scientific age. Our life as human beings in society – i.e. our life – is determined by the sciences to a quite new extent.

15

A few hundred years ago a handful of people, working in different countries but in correspondence with one another, performed certain experiments by which they hoped to wring from Nature her secrets. Members of a class of craftsmen in the already powerful cities, they transmitted their discoveries to people who made practical use of them, without expecting more from the new sciences than personal profit for themselves.

Crafts which had progressed by methods virtually unchanged during a thousand years now developed hugely; in many places, which became linked by competition, they gathered from all directions great masses of men, and these, adopting new forms of organization, started producing on a giant scale. Soon mankind was showing powers whose extent it would till that time scarcely have dared to dream of.

16

It was as if mankind for the first time now began a conscious and co-ordinated effort to make the planet that was its home fit to live on. Many of the earth's components, such as coal, water, oil, now became treasures. Steam was made to shift vehicles; a few small sparks and the twitching of frogs' legs revealed a natural force which produced light, carried sounds across continents, etc. In all directions man looked about himself with a new vision, to see how he could adapt to his convenience familiar but as yet unexploited objects. His surroundings changed increasingly from decade to decade, then from year to year, then almost from day to day. I who am writing this write it on a machine which at the time of my birth was unknown. I travel in the new vehicles with a rapidity that my grandfather could not imagine; in those days nothing moved so fast. And I rise in the air: a thing that my father was unable to do. With my father I already spoke across the width of a continent, but it was together with my son that I first saw the moving pictures of the explosion at Hiroshima.

17

The new sciences may have made possible this vast alteration and all-important alterability of our surroundings, yet it cannot be said that their spirit determines everything that we do. The reason why the new way of thinking and feeling has not yet penetrated the great mass of men is that the sciences, for all their success in exploiting and dominating nature, have been stopped by the class which they brought to power – the bourgeoisie – from operating in another field where darkness still reigns, namely that of the relations which people have to one another during the exploiting and dominating process. This business on which all alike depended was performed without the new intellectual methods that made it possible ever illuminating the mutual relationships of the people who carried it out. The new approach to nature was not applied to society.

18

In the event people's mutual relations have become harder to disentangle than ever before. The gigantic joint undertaking on which they are engaged seems more and more to split them into two groups; increases in production lead to increases in misery; only a minority gain from the exploitation of nature, and they only do so because they exploit men. What might be progress for all then becomes advancement for a few, and an ever-increasing part of the productive process gets applied to creating means of destruction for mighty wars. During these wars the mothers of every nation, with their children pressed to them, scan the skies in horror for the deadly inventions of science.

19†

The same attitude as men once showed in face of unpredictable natural catastrophes they now adopt towards their own undertakings. The bourgeois class, which owes to science an advancement that it was able, by ensuring that it alone enjoyed the fruits, to convert into domination, knows very well that its rule would come to an end if the scientific eye were turned on its own undertakings. And so that new science which was founded about a hundred years ago and deals with the character of human society was born in the struggle between rulers and ruled. Since then a certain scientific spirit has developed at the bottom, among the new class of workers whose natural element is large-scale production; from down there the great catastrophes are spotted as undertakings by the rulers.

20

But science and art meet on this ground, that both are there to make men's life easier, the one setting out to maintain, the other to entertain us. In the age to come art will create entertainment from that new productivity which can so greatly improve our maintenance, and in itself, if only it is left unshackled, may prove to be the greatest pleasure of them all.

21

If we want now to surrender ourselves to this great passion for producing, what ought our representations of men's life together to look like? What is that productive attitude in face of nature and of society which we children of a scientific age would like to take up pleasurably in our theatre?

22

The attitude is a critical one. Faced with a river, it consists in regulating the river; faced with a fruit tree, in spraying the fruit tree; faced with movement, in constructing vehicles and aeroplanes; faced with society, in turning society upside down. Our representations of human social life are designed for river-dwellers, fruit farmers, builders of vehicles and upturners of society, whom we invite into our theatres and beg not to forget their cheerful occupations while we hand the world over to their minds and hearts, for them to change as they think fit.

23

The theatre can only adopt such a free attitude if it lets itself be carried along by the strongest currents in its society and associates itself with those who are necessarily most impatient to make great alterations there. The bare wish, if nothing else, to evolve an art fit for the times must drive our theatre of the scientific age straight out into the suburbs, where it can stand as it were wide open, at the disposal of those who live hard and produce much, so that they can be fruitfully entertained there with their great problems. They may find it hard to pay for our art, and immediately to grasp the new method of entertainment, and we shall have to learn in many respects what they need and how they need it; but we can be sure of their interest. For these men who seem so far apart from natural science are only apart from it because they are being forcibly kept apart; and before they can get their hands on it they have first to develop and put into effect a new science of society; so that these are the true children of the scientific age, who alone can get the theatre moving if it is to move at all. A theatre which makes productivity its main source of entertainment has also to take it for its theme, and with greater keenness than ever now that man is everywhere hampered by men from self-production: i.e. from maintaining himself, entertaining and being entertained. The theatre has to become geared into reality if it is to be in a position to turn out effective representations of reality, and to be allowed to do so.

24

But this makes it simpler for the theatre to edge as close as possible to the apparatus of education and mass communication. For although we cannot bother it with the raw material of knowledge in all its variety, which would stop it from being enjoyable, it is still free to find enjoyment in teaching and inquiring. It constructs its workable representations of society, which are then in a position to influence society, wholly and entirely as a game: for those who are constructing society it sets out society's experiences, past and present alike, in such a manner that the audience can 'appreciate' the feelings, insights and impulses which are distilled by the wisest, most active and most passionate among us from the events of the day or the century. They must be entertained with the wisdom that comes from the solution of problems, with the anger that is a practical expression of sympathy with the underdog, with the respect due to those who respect humanity, or rather whatever is kind to humanity; in short, with whatever delights those who are producing something.

25

And this also means that the theatre can let its spectators enjoy the particular ethic of their age, which springs from productivity. A theatre which converts the critical approach – i.e. our great productive method – into pleasure finds nothing in the ethical field which it must do and a great deal that it can. Even the wholly anti-social can be a source of enjoyment to society so long as it is presented forcefully and on the grand scale. It then often proves to have considerable powers of understanding and other un-usually valuable capacities, applied admittedly to a destructive end. Even the bursting flood of a vast catastrophe can be appreciated in all its majesty by society, if society knows how to master it; then we make it our own.

26

For such an operation as this we can hardly accept the theatre as we see it before us. Let us go into one of these houses and observe the effect which it has on the spectators. Looking about us, we see somewhat motionless figures in a peculiar condition: they seem strenuously to be tensing all their muscles, except where these are flabby and exhausted. They scarcely com-municate with each other; their relations are those of a lot of sleepers, though of such as dream restlessly because, as is popularly said of those who have nightmares, they are lying on their backs. True, their eyes are open, but they stare rather than see, just as they listen rather than hear. They look at the stage as if in a trance: an expression which comes from the Middle Ages, the days of witches and priests. Seeing and hearing are activities, and can be pleasant ones, but these people seem relieved of activity and like men to whom something is being done. This detached state, where they seem to be given over to vague but profound sensations, grows deeper the better the work of the actors, and so we, as we do not ap-prove of this situation, should like them to be as bad as possible.

27

As for the world portrayed there, the world from which slices are cut in order to produce these moods and movements of the emotions, its appear-ance is such, produced from such slight and wretched stuff as a few pieces of cardboard, a little miming, a bit of text, that one has to admire the theatre folk who, with so feeble a reflection of the real world, can move the feelings of their audience so much more strongly than does the world itself.

28

In any case we should excuse these theatre folk, for the pleasures which they sell for money and fame could not be induced by an exacter representation of the world, nor could their inexact renderings be presented in a less magical way. Their capacity to represent people can be seen at work in various instances; it is especially the rogues and the minor figures who reveal their knowledge of humanity and differ one from the other, but the central figures have to be kept general, so that it is easier for the onlooker to identify himself with them, and at all costs each trait of character must be drawn from the narrow field within which everyone can say at once: that is how it is.

For the spectator wants to be put in possession of quite definite sensations, just as a child does when it climbs on to one of the horses on a roundabout: the sensation of pride that it can ride, and has a horse; the pleasure of being carried, and whirled past other children; the adventurous daydreams in which it pursues others or is pursued, etc. In leading the child to experience all this the degree to which its wooden seat resembles a horse counts little, nor does it matter that the ride is confined to a small circle. The one important point for the spectators in these houses is that they should be able to swap a contradictory world for a consistent one, one that they scarcely know for one of which they can dream.

29

That is the sort of theatre which we face in our operations, and so far it has been fully able to transmute our optimistic friends, whom we have called the children of the scientific era, into a cowed, credulous, hypnotized mass.

30

True, for about half a century they have been able to see rather more faithful representations of human social life, as well as individual figures who were in revolt against certain social evils or even against the structure of society as a whole. They felt interested enough to put up with a temporary and exceptional restriction of language, plot and spiritual scope; for the fresh wind of the scientific spirit nearly withered the charms to which they had grown used. The sacrifice was not especially worth while. The greater subtlety of the representations subtracted from one pleasure without satisfying another. The field of human relationships came within our view, but not within our grasp. Our feelings, having been aroused in the old (magic) way, were bound themselves to remain unaltered.

31

For always and everywhere theatres were the amusement centres of a class which restricted the scientific spirit to the natural field, not daring to let it loose on the field of human relationships. The tiny proletarian section of the public, reinforced to a negligible and uncertain extent by renegade intellectuals, likewise still needed the old kind of entertainment, as a relief from its predetermined way of life.

32

So let us march ahead! Away with all obstacles! Since we seem to have landed in a battle, let us fight! Have we not seen how disbelief can move mountains? Is it not enough that we should have found that something is being kept from us? Before one thing and another there hangs a curtain: let us draw it up!

33

The theatre as we know it shows the structure of society (represented on the stage) as incapable of being influenced by society (in the auditorium). Oedipus, who offended against certain principles underlying the society of his time, is executed: the gods see to that; they are beyond criticism. Shakespeare's great solitary figures, bearing on their breast the star of their fate, carry through with irresistible force their futile and deadly outbursts; they prepare their own downfall; life, not death, becomes obscene as they collapse; the catastrophe is beyond criticism. Human sacrifices all round! Barbaric delights! We know that the barbarians have their art. Let us create another.

34

How much longer are our souls, leaving our 'mere' bodies under cover of the darkness, to plunge into those dreamlike figures up on the stage, there to take part in the crescendos and climaxes which 'normal' life denies us? What kind of release is it at the end of all these plays (which is a happy end only for the conventions of the period – suitable measures, the restoration of order –), when we experience the dreamlike executioner's axe which cuts short such crescendos as so many excesses? We slink into *Oedipus*; for taboos still exist and ignorance is no excuse before the law. Into *Othello*; for jealously still causes us trouble and everything depends on possession. Into *Wallenstein*; for we need to be free for the competitive struggle and to observe the rules, or it would peter out. This deadweight of old habits is also needed for plays like *Ghosts* and *The Weavers*, although there the social structure, in the shape of a 'setting', presents itself as more open to question. The feelings, insights and impulses of the chief characters are forced on us, and so we learn nothing more about society than we can get from the 'setting'.

35

We need a type of theatre which not only releases the feelings, insights and impulses possible within the particular historical field of human relations in which the action takes place, but employs and encourages those thoughts and feelings which help transform the field itself.

36

The field has to be defined in historically relative terms. In other words we must drop our habit of taking the different social structures of past periods, then stripping them of everything that makes them different; so that they all look more or less like our own, which then acquires from this process a certain air of having been there all along, in other words of permanence pure and simple. Instead we must leave them their distinguishing marks and keep their impermanence always before our eyes, so that our own period can be seen to be impermanent too. (It is of course futile to make use of fancy colours and folklore for this, such as our theatres apply precisely in order to emphasize the similarities in human behaviour at different times. We shall indicate the theatrical methods below.)

37

If we ensure that our characters on the stage are moved by social impulses and that these differ according to the period, then we make it harder for our spectator to identify himself with them. He cannot simply feel: that's how I would act, but at most can say: if I had lived under those circumstances. And if we play works dealing with our own time as though they were historical, then perhaps the circumstances under which he himself acts will strike him as equally odd; and this is where the critical attitude begins.

38

The 'historical conditions' must of course not be imagined (nor will they be so constructed) as mysterious Powers (in the background); on the contrary, they are created and maintained by men (and will in due course be altered by them): it is the actions taking place before us that allow us to see what they are.

39

If a character responds in a manner historically in keeping with his period, and would respond otherwise in other periods, does that mean that he is not simply 'Everyman'? It is true that a man will respond differently according to his circumstances and his class; if he were living at another time, or in his youth, or on the darker side of life, he would infallibly give a different response, though one still determined by the same factors and like anyone else's response in that situation at that time. So should we not ask if there are any further differences of response? Where is the man himself, the living, unmistakeable man, who is not quite identical with those identified with him? It is clear that his stage image must bring him to light, and this will come about if this particular contradiction is recreated in the image. The image that gives historical definition will retain something of the rough sketching which indicates traces of other movements and features all around the fully-worked-out figure. Or imagine a man standing in a valley and making a speech in which he occasionally changes his views or simply utters sentences which contradict one another, so that the accompanying echo forces them into confrontation.

40

Such images certainly demand a way of acting which will leave the spectator's intellect free and highly mobile. He has again and again to make what one might call hypothetical adjustments to our structure, by mentally switching off the motive forces of our society or by substituting others for them: a process which leads real conduct to acquire an element of 'unnaturalness', thus allowing the real motive forces to be shorn of their naturalness and become capable of manipulation.

41

It is the same as when an irrigation expert looks at a river together with its former bed and various hypothetical courses which it might have followed if there had been a different tilt to the plateau or a different volume of water. And while he in his mind is looking at a new river, the socialist in his is hearing new kinds of talk from the labourers who work by it. And similarly in the theatre our spectator should find that the incidents set among such labourers are also accompanied by echoes and by traces of sketching.

42

The kind of acting which was tried out at the Schiffbauerdamm Theater in Berlin between the First and Second World Wars, with the object of producing such images, is based on the 'alienation effect' (A-effect). A representation that alienates is one which allows us to recognize its subject, but at the same time makes it seem unfamiliar. The classical and medieval theatre alienated its characters by making them wear human or animal masks; the Asiatic theatre even today uses musical and pantomimic A-effects. Such devices were certainly a barrier to empathy, and yet this technique owed more, not less, to hypnotic suggestion than do those by which empathy is achieved. The social aims of these old devices were entirely different from our own.

43

The old A-effects quite remove the object represented from the spectator's grasp, turning it into something that cannot be altered; the new are not odd in themselves, though the unscientific eye stamps anything strange as odd. The new alienations are only designed to free socially-conditioned phenomena from that stamp of familiarity which protects them against our grasp today.

44

For it seems impossible to alter what has long not been altered. We are always coming on things that are too obvious for us to bother to understand them. What men experience among themselves they think of as 'the' human experience. A child, living in a world of old men, learns how things work there. He knows the run of things before he can walk. If anyone is bold enough to want something further, he only wants to have it as an exception. Even if he realizes that the arrangements made for him by 'Providence' are only what has been provided by society he is bound to see society, that vast collection of beings like himself, as a whole that is greater than the sum of its parts and therefore not in any way to be influenced. Moreover, he would be used to things that could not be influenced; and who mistrusts what he is used to? To transform himself from general passive acceptance to a corresponding state of suspicious inquiry he would need to develop that detached eye with which the great Galileo observed a swinging chandelier. He was amazed by this pendulum motion, as if he had not expected it and could not understand its occurring, and this enabled him to come on the rules by which it was governed. Here is the outlook, disconcerting but fruitful, which the theatre must provoke with its representations of human social life. It must amaze its public, and this can be achieved by a technique of alienating the familiar.

45†

This technique allows the theatre to make use in its representations of the new social scientific method known as dialectical materialism. In order to unearth society's laws of motion this method treats social situations as processes, and traces out all their inconsistencies. It regards nothing as existing except in so far as it changes, in other words is in disharmony with itself. This also goes for those human feelings, opinions and attitudes through which at any time the form of men's life together finds its expression.

46

Our own period, which is transforming nature in so many and different ways, takes pleasure in understanding things so that we can interfere. There is a great deal to man, we say; so a great deal can be made out of him. He does not have to stay the way he is now, nor does he have to be seen only as he is now, but also as he might become. We must not start with him; we must start on him. This means, however, that I must not simply set myself in his place, but must set myself facing him, to represent us all. That is why the theatre must alienate what it shows.

47

In order to produce A-effects the actor has to discard whatever means he has learnt of getting the audience to identify itself with the characters which he plays. Aiming not to put his audience into a trance, he must not go into a trance himself. His muscles must remain loose, for a turn of the head, e.g. with tautened neck muscles, will 'magically' lead the spectators' eyes and even their heads to turn with it, and this can only detract from any speculation or reaction which the gesture may bring about. His way of speaking has to be free from parsonical sing-song and from all those cadences which lull the spectator so that the sense gets lost. Even if he plays a man possessed he must not seem to be possessed himself, for how is the spectator to discover what possessed him if he does?

48

At no moment must he go so far as to be wholly transformed into the character played. The verdict: 'he didn't act Lear, he was Lear' would be an annihilating blow to him. He has just to show the character, or rather he has to do more than just get into it; this does not mean that if he is playing passionate parts he must himself remain cold. It is only that his feelings must not at bottom be those of the character, so that the audience's may not at bottom be those of the character either. The audience must have complete freedom here.

49

This principle – that the actor appears on the stage in a double role, as Laughton and as Galileo; that the showman Laughton does not disappear in the Galileo whom he is showing; from which this way of acting gets its name of 'epic' – comes to mean simply that the tangible, matter-of-fact process is no longer hidden behind a veil; that Laughton is actually there, standing on the stage and showing us what he imagines Galileo to have been. Of course the audience would not forget Laughton if he attempted the full change of personality, in that they would admire him for it; but they would in that case miss his own opinions and sensations, which would have been completely swallowed up by the character. He would have taken its opinions and sensations and made them his own, so that a single homogeneous pattern would emerge, which he would then make ours. In order to prevent this abuse the actor must also put some artistry into the act of showing. An illustration may help: we find a gesture which expresses one-half of his attitude – that of showing – if we make him smoke a cigar and then imagine him laying it down now and again in order to show us some further characteristic attitude of the figure in the play. If we then subtract any element of hurry from the image and do not read slackness into its refusal to be taut we shall have an actor who is fully capable of leaving us to our thoughts, or to his own.

50

There needs to be yet a further change in the actor's communication of these images, and it too makes the process more 'matter-on-fact'. Just as the actor no longer has to persuade the audience that it is the author's character and not himself that is standing on the stage, so also he need not pretend that the events taking place on the stage have never been rehearsed, and are now happening for the first and only time. Schiller's distinction is no longer valid: that the rhapsodist has to treat his material as wholly in the past: the mime his, as wholly here and now.[1] It should be apparent all through his performance that 'even at the start and in the middle he knows how it ends' and he must 'thus maintain a calm independence throughout'. He narrates the story of his character by vivid portrayal, always knowing more than it does and treating its 'now' and 'here' not as a pretence made possible by the rules of the game but as something to be distinguished from yesterday and some other place, so as to make visible the knotting-together of the events.

[1] Letter to Goethe, 26.12.1797 [quoted on p. 210].

51

This matters particularly in the portrayal of large-scale events or ones where the outside world is abruptly changed, as in wars and revolutions. The spectator can then have the whole situation and the whole course of events set before him. He can for instance hear a woman speaking and imagine her speaking differently, let us say in a few weeks' time, or other women speaking differently at that moment but in another place. This would be possible if the actress were to play as though the woman had lived through the entire period and were now, out of her memory and her knowledge of what happened next, recalling those utterances of hers which were important at the time; for what is important here is what became important. To alienate an individual in this way, as being 'this particular individual' and 'this particular individual at this particular moment', is only possible if there are no illusions that the player is identical with the character and the performance with the actual event.

52

We shall find that this has meant scrapping yet another illusion: that everyone behaves like the character concerned. 'I am doing this' has become 'I did this', and now 'he did this' has got to become 'he did this, when he might have done something else'. It is too great a simplification if we make the actions fit the character and the character fit the actions: the inconsistencies which are to be found in the actions and characters of real people cannot be shown like this. The laws of motion of a society are not to be demonstrated by 'perfect examples', for 'imperfection' (inconsistency) is an essential part of motion and of the thing moved. It is only necessary – but absolutely necessary – that there should be something approaching experimental conditions, i.e. that a counter-experiment should now and then be conceivable. Altogether this is a way of treating society as if all its actions were performed as experiments.

53†

Even if empathy, or self-identification with the character, can be usefully indulged in at rehearsals (something to be avoided in a performance) it has to be treated just as one of a number of methods of observation. It helps when rehearsing, for even though the contemporary theatre has applied it in an indiscriminate way it has none the less led to subtle delineation of personality. But it is the crudest form of empathy when the actor simply asks: what should I be like if this or that were to happen to me? what would it look like if I were to say this and do that? – instead of asking: have I ever heard somebody saying this and doing that? in order to piece together all sorts of elements with which to construct a new character such as would allow the story to have taken place – and a good deal else. The coherence of the character is in fact shown by the way in which its individual qualities contradict one another.

54

Observation is a major part of acting. The actor observes his fellow-men with all his nerves and muscles in an act of imitation which is at the same time a process of the mind. For pure imitation would only bring out what had been observed; and this is not enough, because the original says what it has to say with too subdued a voice. To achieve a character rather than a caricature, the actor looks at people as though they were playing him their actions, in other words as though they were advising him to give their actions careful consideration.

55†

Without opinions and objectives one can represent nothing at all. Without knowledge one can show nothing; how could one know what would be worth knowing? Unless the actor is satisfied to be a parrot or a monkey he must master our period's knowledge of human social life by himself joining in the war of the classes. Some people may feel this to be degrading, because they rank art, once the money side has been settled, as one of the highest things; but mankind's highest decisions are in fact fought out on earth, not in the heavens; in the 'external' world, not inside people's heads. Nobody can stand above the warring classes, for nobody can stand above the human race. Society cannot share a common communication system so long as it is split into warring classes. Thus for art to be 'un-political' means only to ally itself with the 'ruling' group.

56

So the choice of viewpoint is also a major element of the actor's art, and it has to be decided outside the theatre. Like the transformation of nature, that of society is a liberating act; and it is the joys of liberation which the theatre of a scientific age has got to convey.

57

Let us go on to examine how, for instance, this viewpoint affects the actor's interpretation of his part. It then becomes important that he should not 'catch on' too quickly. Even if he straightway establishes the most natural cadences for his part, the least awkward way of speaking it, he still cannot regard its actual pronouncement as being ideally natural, but must think twice and take his own general opinions into account, then consider various other conceivable pronouncements; in short, take up the attitude of a man who just wonders. This is not only to prevent him from 'fixing' a particular character prematurely, so that it has to be stuffed out with after-thoughts because he has not waited to register all the other pronouncements, and especially those of the other characters; but also and principally in order to build into the character that element of 'Not – But' on which so much depends if society, in the shape of the audience, is to be able to look at what takes place in such a way as to be able to affect it. Each actor, moreover, instead of concentrating on what suits him and calling it 'human nature', must go above all for what does not suit him, is not his speciality. And along with his part he must commit to memory his first reactions, reserves, criticisms, shocks, so that they are not destroyed by being 'swallowed up' in the final version but are preserved and perceptible; for character and all must not grow on the audience so much as strike it.

58

And the learning process must be co-ordinated so that the actor learns as the other actors are learning and develops his character as they are developing theirs. For the smallest social unit is not the single person but two people. In life too we develop one another.

59

Here we can learn something from our own theatres' deplorable habit of letting the dominant actor, the star, 'come to the front' by getting all the other actors to work for him: he makes his character terrible or wise by forcing his partners to make theirs terrified or attentive. Even if only to secure this advantage for all, and thus to help the story, the actors should sometimes swap roles with their partners during rehearsal, so that the characters can get what they need from one another. But it is also good for the actors when they see their characters copied or portrayed in another form. If the part is played by somebody of the opposite sex the sex of the character will be more clearly brought out; if it is played by a comedian, whether comically or tragically, it will gain fresh aspects. By helping to develop the parts that correspond to his own, or at any rate standing in for their players, the actor strengthens the all-decisive social standpoint from which he has to present his character. The master is only the sort of master his servant lets him be, etc.

60

A mass of operations to develop the character are carried out when it is introduced among the other characters of the play, and the actor will have to memorize what he himself has anticipated in this connection from his reading of the text. But now he finds out much more about himself from the treatment which he gets at the hands of the characters in the play.

61

The realm of attitudes adopted by the characters towards one another is what we call the realm of gest. Physical attitude, tone of voice and facial expression are all determined by a social gest: the characters are cursing, flattering, instructing one another, and so on. The attitudes which people adopt towards one another include even those attitudes which would appear to be quite private, such as the utterances of physical pain in an illness, or of religious faith. These expressions of a gest are usually highly complicated and contradictory, so that they cannot be rendered by any single word and the actor must take care that in giving his image the necessary emphasis he does not lose anything, but emphasizes the entire complex.

62

The actor masters his character by paying critical attention to its manifold utterances, as also to those of his counterparts and of all the other characters involved.

63

Let us get down to the problem of gestic content by running through the opening scenes of a fairly modern play, my own *Life of Galileo*. Since we wish at the same time to find out what light the different utterances cast on one another we will assume that it is not our first introduction to the play. It begins with the man of forty-six having his morning wash, broken by occasional browsing in books and by a lesson on the solar system for Andrea Sarti, a small boy. To play this, surely you have got to know that we shall be ending with the man of seventy-eight having his supper, just after he has said good-bye for ever to the same pupil? He is then more terribly altered than this passage of time could possibly have brought about. He wolfs his food with unrestrained greed, no other idea in his head; he has rid himself of his educational mission in shameful circumstances, as though it were a burden: he, who once drank his morning milk without a care, greedy to teach the boy. But does he really drink it without care? Isn't the pleasure of drinking and washing one with the pleasure which he takes in the new ideas? Don't forget: he thinks out of self-indulgence. . . . Is that good or bad? I would advise you to represent it as good, since on this point you will find nothing in the whole play to harm society, and more especially because you yourself are, I hope, a gallant child of the scientific age. But take careful note: many horrible things will happen in this connection. The fact that the man who here acclaims the new age will be forced at the end to beg this age to disown him as contemptible, even to dispossess him; all this will be relevant. As for the lesson, you may like to decide whether the man's heart is so full that his mouth is overflowing, so that he has to talk to anybody about it, even a child, or whether the child has first to draw the knowledge out of him, by knowing him and showing interest. Again, there may be two of them who cannot restrain themselves, the one from asking, the other from giving the answer: a bond of this sort would be interesting, for one day it is going to be rudely snapped. Of course you will want the demonstration of the earth's rotation round the sun to be conducted quickly, since it is given for nothing, and now the wealthy unknown pupil appears, lending the scholar's time a monetary value. He shows no interest, but he has to be served; Galileo lacks resources, and so he will stand between the wealthy pupil and the intelligent one, and sigh as he makes his choice. There is little that he can teach his new student, so he learns from him instead; he hears of the telescope which has been invented in Holland: in his own way he gets something out of the disturbance of his morning's work. The Rector of the university arrives. Galileo's application for an increase in salary has been turned down; the university is reluctant to pay so much for the theories of physics as for those of theology; it wishes him, who after all is operating on a generally-accepted low level of scholarship, to produce something useful here and now. You will see from the way in which he offers his thesis that he is used to being refused and corrected. The Rector reminds him that the Republic guarantees freedom of research even if she doesn't pay; he replies that he cannot make much of this freedom if he lacks the leisure which good payment permits. Here you should not find his impatience too peremptory, or his poverty will not be given due weight. For shortly after that you find him having ideas which need some explanation: the prophet of a new age of scientific truth considers how he can swindle some money out of the Republic by offering her the telescope as his own invention. All he sees in the new invention, you will be surprised to hear, is a few scudi, and he examines it simply with a view to annexing it himself. But if you move on to the second scene you will find that while he is selling the invention to the Venetian Signoria with a speech that disgraces him by its falsehoods he has already almost forgotten the money, because he has realized that the instrument has not only military but astronomical significance. The article which he has been blackmailed – let us call it that – into producing proves to have great qualities for the very research which he had to break off in order to produce it. If during the ceremony, as he complacently accepts the undeserved honours paid him, he outlines to his learned friend the marvellous discoveries in view – don't overlook the theatrical way in which he does this – you will find in him a far more profound excitement than the thought of monetary gain called forth. Perhaps, looked at in this way, his charlatanry does not mean much, but it still shows how determined this man is to take the easy course, and to apply his reason in a base as well as a noble manner. A more significant test awaits him, and does not every capitulation bring the next one nearer?

64

Splitting such material into one gest after another, the actor masters his character by first mastering the 'story'. It is only after walking all round the entire episode that he can, as it were by a single leap, seize and fix his character, complete with all its individual features. Once he has done his best to let himself be amazed by the inconsistencies in its various attitudes, knowing that he will in turn have to make them amaze the audience, then the story as a whole gives him a chance to pull the inconsistencies together; for the story, being a limited episode, has a specific sense, i.e. only gratifies a specific fraction of all the interests that could arise.

65

Everything hangs on the 'story'; it is the heart of the theatrical performance. For it is what happens *between* people that provides them with all the material that they can discuss, criticize, alter. Even if the particular person represented by the actor has ultimately to fit into more than just the one episode, it is mainly because the episode will be all the more striking if it reaches fulfilment in a particular person. The 'story' is the theatre's great operation, the complete fitting together of all the gestic incidents, embracing the communications and impulses that must now go to make up the audience's entertainment.

66

Each single incident has its basic gest: *Richard Gloster courts his victim's widow. The child's true mother is found by means of a chalk circle. God has a bet with the Devil for Dr Faustus's soul. Woyzeck buys a cheap knife in order to do his wife in*, etc. The grouping of the characters on the stage and the movements of the groups must be such that the necessary beauty is attained above all by the elegance with which the material conveying that gest is set out and laid bare to the understanding of the audience.

67

As we cannot invite the audience to fling itself into the story as if it were a river and let itself be carried vaguely hither and thither, the individual episodes have to be knotted together in such a way that the knots are easily noticed. The episodes must not succeed one another indistinguishably but must give us a chance to interpose our judgment. (If it were above all the obscurity of the original interrelations that interested us, then just this circumstance would have to be sufficiently alienated.) The parts of the story have to be carefully set off one against another by giving each its own structure as a play within the play. To this end it is best to agree to use titles like those in the preceding paragraph. The titles must include the social point, saying at the same time something about the kind of portrayal wanted, i.e. should copy the tone of a chronicle or a ballad or a newspaper or a morality. For instance, a simple way of alienating something is that normally applied to customs and moral principles. A visit, the treatment of an enemy, a lovers' meeting, agreements about politics or business, can be portrayed as if they were simply illustrations of general principles valid for the place in question. Shown thus, the particular and unrepeatable incident acquires a disconcerting look, because it appears as something general, something that has become a principle. As soon as we ask whether in fact it should have become such, or what about it should have done so, we are alienating the incident. The poetic approach to history can be studied in the so-called panoramas at sideshows in fairs. As alienation likewise means a kind of fame certain incidents can just be represented as famous, as though they had for a long while been common knowledge and care must be taken not to offer the least obstacle to their further transmission. In short: there are many conceivable ways of telling a story, some of them known and some still to be discovered.

68

What needs to be alienated, and how this is to be done, depends on the exposition demanded by the entire episode; and this is where the theatre has to speak up decisively for the interests of its own time. Let us take as an example of such exposition the old play *Hamlet*. Given the dark and bloody period in which I am writing – the criminal ruling classes, the widespread doubt in the power of reason, continually being misused – I think that I can read the story thus: It is an age of warriors. Hamlet's father, king of Denmark, slew the king of Norway in a successful war of spoliation. While the latter's son Fortinbras is arming for a fresh war the Danish king is likewise slain: by his own brother. The slain king's brothers, now themselves kings, avert war by arranging that the Norwegian troops shall cross Danish soil to launch a predatory war against Poland. But at this point the young Hamlet is summoned by his warrior father's ghost to avenge the crime committed against him. After at first being reluctant to answer one bloody deed by another, and even preparing to go into exile, he meets young Fortinbras at the coast as he is marching with his troops to Poland. Overcome by this warrior-like example, he turns back and in a piece of barbaric butchery slaughters his uncle, his mother and himself, leaving Denmark to the Norwegian. These events show the young man, already somewhat stout, making the most ineffective use of the new approach to Reason which he has picked up at the university of Wittenberg. In the feudal business to which he returns it simply hampers him. Faced with irrational practices, his reason is utterly unpractical. He falls a tragic victim to the discrepancy between such reasoning and such action. This way of reading the play, which can be read in more than one way, might in my view interest our audience.

69

Whether or no literature presents them as successes, each step forward, every emancipation from nature that is scored in the field of production and leads to a transformation of society, all those explorations in some new direction which mankind has embarked on in order to improve its lot, give us a sense of confidence and triumph and lead us to take pleasure in the possibilities of change in all things. Galileo expresses this when he says: 'It is my view that the earth is most noble and wonderful, seeing the great number and variety of changes and generations which incessantly take place on it.'

70

The exposition of the story and its communication by suitable means of alienation constitute the main business of the theatre. Not everything depends on the actor, even though nothing may be done without taking him into account. The 'story' is set out, brought forward and shown by the theatre as a whole, by actors, stage designers, mask-makers, costumiers, composers and choreographers. They unite their various arts for the joint operation, without of course sacrificing their independence in the process.

71

It emphasizes the general gest of showing, which always underlies that which is being shown, when the audience is musically addressed by means of songs. Because of this the actors ought not to 'drop into' song, but should clearly mark it off from the rest of the text; and this is best reinforced by a few theatrical methods such as changing the lighting or inserting a title. For its part, the music must strongly resist the smooth incorporation which is generally expected of it and turns it into an unthinking slavey. Music does not 'accompany' except in the form of comment. It cannot simply 'express itself' by discharging the emotions with which the incidents of the play have filled it. Thus Eisler, e.g. helped admirably in the knotting of the incidents when in the carnival scene of *Galileo* he set the masked procession of the guilds to a triumphant and threatening music which showed what a revolutionary twist the lower orders had given to the scholar's astronomical theories. Similarly in *The Caucasian Chalk Circle* the singer, by using a chilly and unemotional way of singing to describe the servant-girl's rescue of the child as it is mimed on the stage, makes evident the terror of a period in which motherly instincts can become a suicidal weakness. Thus music can make its point in a number of ways and with full independence, and can react in its own manner to the subjects dealt with; at the same time it can also quite simply help to lend variety to the entertainment.

72

Just as the composer wins back his freedom by no longer having to create atmosphere so that the audience may be helped to lose itself unreservedly in the events on the stage, so also the stage designer gets considerable freedom as soon as he no longer has to give the illusion of a room or a locality when he is building his sets. It is enough for him to give hints, though these must make statements of greater historical or social interest than does the real setting. At the Jewish Theatre in Moscow *King Lear* was alienated by a structure that recalled a medieval tabernacle; Neher set *Galileo* in front of projections of maps, documents and Renaissance works of art; for *Haitang erwacht* at the Piscator-Theater Heartfield used a background of reversible flags bearing inscriptions, to mark changes in the political situation of which the persons on the stage were sometimes unaware.

73

For choreography too there are once again tasks of a realistic kind. It is a relatively recent error to suppose that it has nothing to do with the repre-

sentation of 'people as they really are'. If art reflects life it does so with
special mirrors. Art does not become unrealistic by changing the proportions but by changing them in such a way that if the audience took its
representations as a practical guide to insights and impulses it would go
astray in real life. It is of course essential that stylization should not remove
the natural element but should heighten it. Anyhow, a theatre where everything depends on the gest cannot do without choreography. Elegant movement and graceful grouping, for a start, can alienate, and inventive miming
greatly helps the story.

74

So let us invite all the sister arts of the drama, not in order to create an
'integrated work of art' in which they all offer themselves up and are lost,
but so that together with the drama they may further the common task in
their different ways; and their relations with one another consist in this:
that they lead to mutual alienation.

75

And here once again let us recall that their task is to entertain the
children of the scientific age, and to do so with sensuousness and humour.
This is something that we Germans cannot tell ourselves too often, for with
us everything easily slips into the insubstantial and unapproachable,
and we begin to talk of *Weltanschauung* when the world in question has
already dissolved. Even materialism is little more than an idea with us.
Sexual pleasure with us turns into marital obligations, the pleasures of art
subserve general culture, and by learning we mean not an enjoyable process
of finding out, but the forcible shoving of our nose into something. Our
activity has none of the pleasure of exploration, and if we want to make an
impression we do not say how much fun we have got out of something but
how much effort it has cost us.

76

One more thing: the delivery to the audience of what has been built up
in the rehearsals. Here it is essential that the actual playing should be
infused with the gest of handing over a finished article. What now comes
before the spectator is the most frequently repeated of what has not been
rejected, and so the finished representations have to be delivered with the
eyes fully open, so that they may be received with the eyes open too.

That is to say, our representations must take second place to what is represented, men's life together in society; and the pleasure felt in their perfection must be converted into the higher pleasure felt when the rules emerging from this life in society are treated as imperfect and provisional. In this way the theatre leaves its spectators productively disposed even after the spectacle is over. Let us hope that their theatre may allow them to enjoy as entertainment that terrible and never-ending labour which should ensure their maintenance, together with the terror of their unceasing transformation. Let them here produce their own lives in the simplest way; for the simplest way of living is in art.

['Kleines Organon für das Theater', from *Sinn und Form* Sonderheft Bertolt Brecht, Potsdam, 1949]

NOTE: The Short Organum was written in Switzerland in 1948, while Brecht was staying outside Zurich. 'More or less finished with Organum – short condensation of the Messingkauf', says a diary note of 18 August. But if the 'Messingkauf' was derived from Galileo the new work seems to relate both formally and stylistically to the *Novum Organum* of Francis Bacon, the other great Renaissance scientist whose name occurs a number of times in Brecht's writings. (On this point, see Dr Reinhold Grimm's essay in the symposium *Das Ärgernis Brecht*, Basilius Presse, Basle 1961, where he suggests that Bacon's book attracted Brecht because it was directed against the *Organum* of Aristotle, Aristotle being of course not only the implied enemy of the non-aristotelian drama but also the ideological villain of *Galileo*.)

When the Short Organum was reprinted in 1953 in *Versuche 12* a covering note called it 'a description of a theatre of the scientific age'. Later Brecht wrote a number of appendices to it and linked it to his last collection of notes, 'Die Dialektik auf dem Theater', which he derived from the short reference to dialectical materialism in paragraph 45. Failing completion of 'Der Messingkauf', the 'Short Organum' became (and remained) Brecht's most important theoretical work.

For Professor Eric Bentley's expostulation with Brecht about his odd reading of *Hamlet* in paragraph 68, and Brecht's reply, see *Playwrights on Playwriting*, edited by Toby Cole (Hill and Wang, New York, 1960), pp. 100–101.

Part 4
1948-1956
(Berlin)

39 · Masterful Treatment of a Model

(Foreword to *Antigone*)

Thanks to its total moral and material collapse our harrowed and harrowing country has no doubt acquired a vague appetite for novelty; moreover where the arts are concerned it is apparently being encouraged from various quarters to test out new ideas. But since there seems to be a good deal of confusion as to what is new and what is old, while fear that the old will return has become mixed with fear that the new will step in; and since the conquered are always being told in general terms that they must get rid of all moral and intellectual traces of Nazism, artists would be well advised not to rely blindly on the assurance that new ideas are welcome. Yet art can only find its feet by going ahead, and it needs to do so in company with the advanced part of the population and not away from them. Together with them it must stop waiting for others to act, and go on to act itself; it must find some starting point in the general ruin.

It is not going to be at all easy for art to regain control of its technical equipment and extend it in new directions. The rapid decline of artistic methods under the Nazis seems to have taken place almost unnoticed. The damage done to theatre buildings is far more conspicuous than that done to the standard of performance. This is partly because the former took place with the fall of the Nazi régime, but the latter during its rise. Even today people will speak of the 'brilliant' technique of the Goering-style theatre, as if such a technique could be taken over without bothering what direction its brilliance took. A technique which served to hide the causality at work in society can hardly be used to show it up. And it is high time for a theatre for inquisitive people.

Bourgeois society, with its anarchic system of production, only becomes aware of its own laws of motion in a crisis: as Marx said, it is the roof falling in on its head that gives it its first introduction to the law of gravity. But mere catastrophe is a bad teacher. One learns hunger and thirst from it, but seldom hunger for truth and thirst for knowledge. No amount of illness will turn a sick man into a physician; neither the distant view nor close inspection makes an eye-witness into an expert. If the theatre is capable of showing the truth, then it must also be capable of making the sight of it a pleasure. How then can such a theatre be created? The difficulty about ruins is that the house has gone, but the site isn't there either. And the architects' plans, it seems, never get lost. This means that reconstruction brings back the old dens of iniquity and centres of disease. Fevered life claims to be particularly vital life; none steps so firmly as the consumptive who has lost all feeling in the soles of his feet. Yet the tricky thing about art is that however hopeless its affairs may seem, it has to conduct them with complete ease.

Thus it may not be easy to create progressive art in the period of reconstruction. And this should be a challenge.

2

The Antigone story was picked for the present theatrical operation as providing a certain topicality of subject matter and posing some interesting formal questions. So far as the subject's political aspect went, the present-day analogies emerged astonishingly powerfully as a result of the rationalization process, but on the whole they were a handicap; the great character of the resister in the old play does not represent the German resistance fighters who necessarily seem most important to us. It was not the occasion for a poetic tribute to them; and this is all the more pity because so little is now done to preserve their memory and so much to make people forget it. Not everyone will necessarily realize that they are not the subject in this case, but only he who does so will be able to summon the measure of strangeness needed if the really remarkable element in this Antigone play – the role of force in the collapse of the head of the state – is to be observed with profit. Even the prologue could only contribute by posing a point of actuality and outlining the subjective problem. The Antigone story then unrolls the whole chain of incidents objectively, on the unfamiliar level of the rulers. This possibility of objectively presenting a major state operation was due precisely to the fact (fatal in another respect) that the old play was historically so remote as to tempt nobody to identify himself with its principal figure. Here too its elements of epic form were a help, and provided something of interest to our theatre on their own account. Greek dramaturgy uses certain forms of alienation, notably interventions by the chorus, to try and rescue some of that freedom of calculation which Schiller is uncertain how to ensure.[1] However, there can be no question of using the Antigone story as a means or pretext for 'conjuring up the spirit of antiquity'; philological interests cannot be taken into account. Even if we felt

---

[1] A dramatic plot will move before my eyes; an epic seems to stand still while I move round it. In my view this is a significant distinction. If a circumstance moves before my eyes, then I am bound strictly to what is present to the senses; my imagination loses all freedom; I feel a continual restlessness develop and persist in me; I have to stick to the subject; any reflection or looking back is forbidden me, for I am drawn by an outside force. But if I move round a circumstance which cannot get away from me, then my pace can be irregular; I can linger or hurry according to my own subjective needs, can take a step backwards or leap ahead, and so forth.
Schiller-Goethe correspondence, 26 December 1797

obliged to do something for a work like *Antigone* we could only do so by
letting the play do something for us.

3

As it is not so much a new school of playwriting as a new way of performance being tried out on an old play, our new adaptation cannot be
handed over in the usual way to theatres to do what they like with. An
obligatory model production has been worked out, which can be grasped
from a collection of photographs accompanied by explanatory instructions.
Such a model of course will stand or fall according to the ease with which it
can be imitated and varied. Possibly the whole, or certain parts, may give
no impression of life when reproduced; in that case the whole or the parts
in question must be discarded. A model cannot depend on cadences whose
charm is due to particular voices or on gestures and movements whose
beauty springs from particular physical characteristics; that sort of thing
cannot serve as a model, for it is not exemplary so much as inimitable. If
something is to be usefully copied it must first be put forward for copying.
What is actually achieved when the model is put to use can then be a mixture of the inimitable and the exemplary.

The idea of making use of models is a clear challenge to the artists of a
period that applauds nothing but what is 'original', 'incomparable', 'never
been seen before', and encourages all that is 'unique'. They may realize
quite well that a model is not a blueprint, and yet find that their way of
going to work gives them no help in the use of models. It is hard enough
for them to hurry up and forget the examples of their youth; and now they
have learnt to create everything bearing on their parts themselves, entirely
from within the resources of the self. What, they will ask, is in any way
creative about the use of models? The answer is that today's division of
labour has transformed creation in many important spheres. The act of
creation has become a collective creative process, a continuum of a dialectical sort in which the original invention, taken on its own, has lost much
of its importance. The initial invention of a model truly need not count for
all that much, for the actor who uses it immediately makes his own personal
contribution. He is free to invent variations on the model, that is to say
such variations as will make the image of reality which he has to give truer
and richer in its implications, or more satisfying artistically. The choreographic figures (positions, movements, groupings, etc.[1]) can be treated

---

[1] Neher's sketches served as the basis for the grouping and the masks, so that the inventors of
the model were themselves already, as it were, working to pattern.

either slavishly or masterfully; that is, masterfully in so far as reality penetrates them freely. If the variations are undertaken in the right way they too take on the qualities of a model; the learner becomes the teacher and the model itself changes.

For the model is not set up in order to fix the style of performance; quite the contrary. The emphasis is on development: changes are to be provoked and to be made perceptible; sporadic and anarchic acts of creation are to be replaced by creative processes whose changes progress by steps or leaps.[1] The model was worked out in a dozen and a half rehearsals at the municipal theatre in Chur, and must be regarded as by definition incomplete. The very fact that its shortcomings cry out for improvement should stimulate theatres to use it.

4

Neher's stage for 'Antigone'. Long benches, on which the actors can sit and wait for their cue, stand in front of a semicircle of screens covered in red-coloured rush matting. In the middle of these screens a gap is left, where the record turntable stands and is visibly operated; through this the actors can go off when their part is done. The acting area is bounded by four posts, from which horses' skulls hang suspended. In the left foreground is a board for props, with bacchic masks on sticks, Creon's laurel wreath made of copper, the millet bowl and the wire jar for Antigone and a stool for Tiresias. Subsequently Creon's sword is hung up here by one of the elders. On the right is a framework with a sheet of iron on which an elder beats with his fist during the choral song 'Geist der Freude, der du von den Wässern'. For the prologue a white wall is lowered on wires. There are a door and a cupboard in it. A kitchen table and two chairs stand in front of it; a sack lies in the right foreground. At the beginning a board with the time and the place on it is lowered above the wall. There is no curtain.

The reason why the actors sit openly on the stage and only adopt the attitudes proper to their parts once they enter the (very brilliantly lit) acting area is that the audience must not be able to think that it has been transported to the scene of the story, but must be invited to take part in the delivery of an ancient poem, irrespective how it has been restored.

There were two plans for the stage. The first was that the actors' benches should as it were represent the scene of the old poem. The screen behind

---

[1] The first attempt to use models of epic theatre was made by R. Berlau in Copenhagen. For Dagmar Andreassen's performances of *Die Mutter* and *Señora Carrar's Rifles* she used photographs of previous productions. Andreassen's Vlassova and Carrar were completely different from the figures created by Helene Weigel, who had created something that could at the same time be imitated and altered.

them consisted of ox blood-coloured canvases reminiscent of sails and tents, and the posts with horses' skulls stood in between. The acting area was simply to be brilliantly lit and marked out by little flags. This would have represented a visible separation of the original poem and its secularized version. We became more and more dissatisfied with this plan, until we eventually decided to situate the new part of the story also between the barbaric war emblems. As a third possibility one could cut the prologue and replace the screens behind the benches by a board showing bomb damage in a modern city.

Costumes and props. The men's costumes were made of undyed sackcloth, the women's of cotton. Creon's and Hamon's costumes had inserts of red leather. Antigone's and Ismene's were grey. Particular care was taken over the props; good craftsmen worked on them. This was not so that the audience or the actors should imagine that they were real, but simply so as to provide the audience and the actors with beautiful objects.

5

As for the style of presentation, we agree with Aristotle in holding that the story is the kernel of the tragedy, even if we disagree about the purpose for which it should be performed. The story ought not just to be a jumping-off point for all kinds of excursions into soul-probing or elsewhere, but ought to contain everything and be the object of all our attentions, so that once it has been told the whole thing is concluded. The grouping and movement of the characters has to narrate the story, which is a chain of incidents, and this is the actor's sole task. The stylization by which his acting becomes art must not in the process destroy naturalness, but has on the contrary to heighten it. Obtrusive temperament or speech of outstanding clarity are to be discouraged. Stylization means a general elaboration of what is natural, and its object is to show the audience, as being a part of society, what is important for society in the story. Thus the so-called 'poet's own world' must not be treated as arbitrary, cut off and 'obeying its own logic'; instead whatever it contains of the real world must be brought out and made effective. The 'poet's words' are only sacred in so far as they are true; the theatre is the handmaiden not of the poet but of society.

6

To keep the performance subordinate to the story, *bridge verses* were given to the actors at rehearsals, for them to deliver with the attitude of a narrator. Before stepping into the acting area for the first time Helene Weigel said (and in subsequent rehearsals heard the prompter saying):

'So then Antigone went, the daughter of Oedipus, gathering
  Dust in her pottery bowl, to cover the dead Polyneikes
  Whom the tyrant had thrown to the crows and the dogs in his anger.'
The actress playing Ismene, before entering, said:
'And her sister Ismene came upon her as she did this.'
Before Verse 1 Weigel said:
'Bitterly then she wept, bewailing the fate of her brother.'
And so on. Each speech or action that is introduced by such verses comes
to seem like their realization in practice, and the actor is prevented from
transforming himself completely into the character: he is showing some-
thing. [. . .]

More makeup than usual was used for the faces, and this too was meant
to tell a story: in the case of the elders, for instance, the ravages left on the
face by the habit of commanding, and so forth. As the photographs show,
this did not entirely come off.

The tempo of the performance was very fast.

7

The present model is to some extent made difficult to study by the fact
that it contains much that is provisional and unintentional; this has to be
located and cut out. It includes the entire field of mime on which all the
actors apart from Weigel as it were depend for their living. This is a field
that brings one up against the almost inextricable tangle of styles of our
period of sell-out, which exhibits plays of every period and every country
and invents the most disparate styles for them, without having any style of
its own. Of course such efforts are a failure, and in a single performance
one may find both the resonant pathos and the quaintness which would ruin
a play by Aeschylus or Gozzi respectively; quite plainly the actors have
completely different aims in view. This unhappy state of things is also
bound to affect the proper sphere of the model, that of attitudes and groupings. Generally speaking it is the grouping to which most care has been
devoted. Economy in the moves of the groups and figures was intended to
ensure that these movements had meaning. The separate constellations,
even the distances between them, have a dramatic significance, and at certain moments a single movement of one of the actors' hands may be able
to transform a situation. It was also hoped that the inventions of the producers and the actors would be clearly visible as theatrical ideas; this is a
field where all standards have been lost, so that no one can any longer
distinguish great from small.

Here as in other respects the perusal of pictures and notes was chiefly meant to induce that elementary and distinctive approach which must break into the bursting confusion of our perfected, conclusive and generalized attitude towards the making of art.

If the whole experiment is not to be dismissed as unimportant, irrespective whether it is thought to have been properly carried out, then nobody must be put off by the fear that it might mean the sacrifice of all our experience to date. The theatre is simple enough when it is not complicated. And dancing often reaches its climax when someone dances out of line. Working with models need not be pursued with greater seriousness than is needed for any kind of playing. It may reasonably be considered to have something in common with the 'Well-Tempered Clavichord'.

[From *Antigonemodell 1948*, West Berlin, 1949.]

NOTE: *Antigone*, based on Hölderlin's translation of Sophocles, with a new prologue set in Berlin at the end of the war, was produced in February 1948 at Chur in Switzerland, while Brecht was living outside Zurich. In three ways it was his first return to pre-1933 conditions. It was his first job as director in a professional German-language theatre, his first collaboration with Neher (who had never gone into exile), and his wife's first part of any kind for ten years.

From now on Brecht, who had been introduced to photography mainly by his Danish collaborator Rut'. Berlau, took to making 'model books' (some of which have been published), of any production which he wished to establish as standard.

40 · From the Mother Courage Model

MODELS

After the great war life still goes on in our ruined cities, but it is a different life, the life of different or differently composed circles, guided or handicapped by a new environment whose newness consists in its degree of destruction. Where the great piles of rubble lie, the costly foundations lie too, the drainage system and the gas and electricity network. Even the large building that has remained intact will have been sympathetically affected by the damage and confusion around it, and may sometimes act as a barrier to planning. Temporary structures have to be built, and the danger is that they will remain. All this is reflected in art, for our way of thinking is part of our way of living. Where the theatre is concerned we put forward models to fill the gap. They at once run into strong resistance from all supporters of the old ways, of the routine that masquerades as experience and the conventionality that calls itself creative freedom. And they are not helped by those who take them up without having learnt how to use them. Meant to simplify matters, they are not simple to handle. They are intended not to render thought unnecessary but to provoke it: not as a substitute for artistic creation but as its stimulus.

To start with one has to imagine that the printed text's conclusions about certain events – in this case, Mother Courage's adventures and set-backs – have been to some extent filled in; it has now been established that when the woman's dead son was brought to her she was sitting beside her dumb daughter, and so forth: the sort of conclusion which an artist painting some historic incident can arrive at by cross-examining eye-witnesses. He can make use of them to change particular details as for one reason or another he may think advisable. Until a high standard has been achieved in the lively and intelligent copying of models (and in setting them up) it would be wrong to copy too much. Such things as the Cook's makeup or Courage's costume should not be imitated. The model must not be pressed too far.

Pictures and descriptions of a performance are not enough. One does not learn much by reading that a character moves in a particular direction after a given sentence, even if the tone of speech, the way of walking and a con-vincing reason can all be supplied (which is very difficult). The persons available for the imitation are quite different from those in the pattern; with them it would never have come about. Anyone who deserves the name of artist is unique; he represents generalities in a special way. He can neither be perfectly imitated nor give a perfect imitation. Nor is it anyway so important for artists to imitate art as to imitate life. The use of models is a particular kind of art, and just so much can be learnt from it. The aim must be neither to copy the pattern exactly nor to break away from it at once.

In studying what follows – a number of explanations and discoveries emerging from the rehearsal of a play – what matters is that seeing how certain problems are solved should lead one to see the problems themselves.

[A paragraph then discusses the relation of photographs to the actual performance, from the point of view of light and shade, etc.]

MUSIC

Paul Dessau's music for *Mother Courage* is not meant to be particularly easy; like the stage set, it left something to be supplied by the audience; it was up to them to link voice and melody aurally. Art is no Land of Cock-aigne. In order to make the transition to the musical part, to let music get its word in, we lowered a musical emblem from the flies whenever a song came which did not arise directly out of the action, or arose from it but none the less remained clearly apart. This consisted of a trumpet, a drum, a flag and electric globes that lit up: a slight and delicate thing, pleasant to look at, even if scene nine found it shot to pieces. Some people thought it a pure frivolity, an unrealistic element. But one ought not to disapprove too much of frivolity in the theatre so long as it is kept within bounds. Nor on the other hand was it purely unrealistic, in that it lifted the music above the reality of the action; it served us as a visible sign of the shift to another artistic level – that of music – and gave the right impression of musical insertions instead of leading people to think quite wrongly that the songs sprang from the action. Those who take exception to this are quite simply against anything intermittent, inorganic, pieced-together, and this is primarily because they are against any breaking of the illusion. What they ought to have objected to was not the tangible symbol of music but the manner of fitting the musical items into the play: i.e., as insertions.

The musicians were placed so that they could be seen, in one of the stage boxes, and thanks to this their performances became little concerts, independent contributions made at suitable points in the play. The box communicated with the stage, so a musician or two could occasionally go backstage for trumpet calls or when music occurred as part of the action.

We began with the overture. It was slightly thin, as it was performed by four players only; all the same it was a reasonably ceremonious preparation for the confusions of war.

STAGE DESIGN

For the production which we are describing, at the Deutsches Theater in Berlin, we used the famous scheme devised by Teo Otto for the Zurich Schauspielhaus during the war. There was a permanent framework of huge screens, making use of such materials as were available in the military encampments of the seventeenth century: tenting, wooden posts lashed together with ropes, etc. Structures like the parsonage and the peasants' cottage were introduced three-dimensionally, using realistic building methods and materials, but in the form of an artistic indication, giving only as much of the structure as served the acting. Coloured projections were thrown on the cyclorama, and the revolving stage was used to convey travel. We varied the size and position of the screens, and used them only for the camp scenes, so as to distinguish these from the scenes on the road. The Berlin stage designer made his own versions of the structures (in scenes 2, 4, 5, 9, 10, 11), but on the same general lines. We dispensed with the background projections used in Zurich, and suspended the various countries' names above the stage in large black letters. Our lighting was white and even and as brilliant as our equipment allowed. This enabled us to get rid of any remnants of 'atmosphere' such as would have given the incidents a slightly romantic flavour. Nearly all the rest we kept, often down to the smallest details (chopping block, fireplace, etc.), particularly the admirable positionings of the waggon, which meant a lot since these determined from the outset much of the grouping and of the sequence of events.

Extraordinarily little is lost by sacrificing complete freedom of 'artistic creation'. One has to make a start somewhere, with something, and it may as well be with something that has been properly thought out. Freedom comes with the principle of contradiction, which is continually active and vocal in us all.

REALISTIC THEATRE AND ILLUSION

Goethe, writing in 1826, spoke of the 'inadequacy of the English wooden stage' of Shakespeare's day. He says: 'There is no trace here of these aids to naturalness which we have become accustomed to thanks to the improvement in machinery, in the art of perspective and in the wardrobe.' 'Who,' he asks, 'would tolerate such a scheme today? Under those conditions Shakespeare's plays would become highly interesting fairy-tales narrated by a number of players who had tried to create an impression by making up as the characters, coming and going and carrying out the movements required by the story, but left it to the audience to imagine as many paradises and palaces as they liked on the empty stage.'

Since he wrote these words there has been a hundred years' improvement in the mechanical equipment of our theatres; 'aids to naturalness' have led to such emphasis being put on illusion that we newcomers would sooner think of Shakespeare on an empty stage than a Shakespeare who had ceased to stimulate or provoke any use of the imagination.

In Goethe's day this improvement in the mechanics of illusion was hardly thinkable, for the machinery was so imperfect, so much 'in the childhood of its beginnings' that theatre itself was still a reality, and imagination and inventiveness alike could be used to turn nature into art. The various scenes of the action were still theatrical displays in which the stage designer gave an artistic and poetic interpretation of the places concerned.

The bourgeois classical theatre was happily situated half-way along the road to naturalistic illusionism, at a point where the stage machinery provided enough elements of illusion to improve the representation of some aspects of reality, but not so much as to make the audience feel that it was no longer in a theatre – i.e. stopping short of the point where art comes to mean obliterating all the clues that show art to be involved. There was no electricity, so lighting effects were still primitive; if lack of taste decreed that there should be a sunset, lack of proper mechanical resources prevented the worst horrors. The Meiningers' authenticity of costume came later; it was usually handsome if not always beautiful, and it was after all compensated by an inauthentic mode of speech. In short, wherever it failed in the business of deception the theatre still proved to be theatre. Restoring the theatre's reality as theatre is now a precondition for any possibility of arriving at realistic images of human social life. Too much heightening of the illusion in the setting, together with a 'magnetic' way of acting that gives the spectator the illusion of being present at a fleeting, accidental, 'real' event, create such an impression of naturalness that one can no longer interpose one's judgment, imagination or reactions, and must simply conform by sharing in the experience and becoming one of 'nature's' objects. The illusion created by the theatre must be a partial one, in order that it may always be recognized as an illusion. Reality, however complete, has to be altered by being turned into art, so that it can be seen to be alterable and be treated as such.

And this is why we too are inquiring into naturalness: we want to alter the nature of our social life.

ELEMENTS OF ILLUSION?

No doubt the sight of the cyclorama behind a completely empty stage (in the Prologue and in the seventh and last scenes) creates the illusion of a flat landscape with a huge sky. There is no objection to this, for there must be some stirring of poetry in the spectator's soul for such an illusion to come about. Thanks to the ease with which it is created the actors can suggest at the start that here is a wide horizon lying open to the business enterprise of the small family with their canteen, then at the end that the exhausted seeker after happiness is faced by a measureless devastation. And we can always hope that this impression of substance will combine with a formal one: that the spectator will be able to share in the initial void from which everything arises, by seeing the bare empty stage, soon to be inhabited. This, he realizes, is the *tabula rasa* on which the actors have been working for weeks, testing first one detail then another, learning the incidents of the chronicle by portraying them, and portraying them by judging them. And now we are starting, and Courage's waggon comes rolling on to the stage.

If in big matters there is such a thing as a beautiful approximation, in small there is not. What counts in a realistic portrayal is carefully worked out details of costumes and props, for here the audience's imagination can add nothing. Any implements connected with working and eating must have been most lovingly made. Nor can the costumes be as for a folklore festival; they have to show signs of individuality and social class. They are worn longer or shorter, of cheaper or more expensive material, more or less carefully looked after, etc.

The costumes for this production of *Mother Courage* were by Palm.

WHAT IS A PERFORMANCE OF MOTHER COURAGE AND HER CHILDREN PRIMARILY MEANT TO SHOW?

That in wartime big business is not conducted by small people. That war is a continuation of business by other means, making the human virtues fatal even to those who exercise them. That no sacrifice is too great for the struggle against war.

[*Couragemodell 1949*, East Berlin, 1958]

NOTE: *Mother Courage*, which had first been produced by Leopold Lindtberg at the Zurich Schauspielhaus in 1941, was produced by Brecht and Erich Engel at the Deutsches Theater in Berlin on 11 January 1949, with Helene Weigel taking the title part. There is a complete photographic record of this production, as also of various revisions which it later underwent. These 'models' have been used as a basis for many productions elsewhere, including Brecht's own at the Munich Kammerspiele (1950) and the English productions by Theatre Workshop (1955), Unity Theatre (1958) and the Bristol Old Vic (1961).

The published 'model' from which this introduction is taken contains, besides photographs, a number of comments on individual scenes. Three of them seem of particular interest as showing how far Brecht was willing to accept the fact of his play's evident emotional appeal, and how far he felt it to be based on a mis-understanding by audiences and producers. (Together with other extracts from the model they appeared in *Theaterarbeit*, pp. 230, 246 and 244 respectively, in 1952.) In the first, Brecht starts off by describing the opening song and the rumble of Mother Courage's cart on the revolving stage as evidence of the long journey which she has behind her:

We felt that the tradeswoman's voluntary and active participation in the war was made clear enough by showing the great distance which she has travelled to get into it. From a number of press notices, however, and a lot of discussions with members of the audience it appeared that many people see Courage as the representative of the 'little people' who get 'caught up' in the war because 'there's nothing they can do about it', they are 'powerless in the hands of fate', etc. Deep-seated habits lead theatre audiences to pick on the characters' more emotional utterances and forget all the rest. Business deals are accepted with the same boredom as descriptions of landscape in a novel. The 'business atmosphere' is simply the air we breathe and pay no special attention to. In our discussions war was always cropping up in this way as a timeless abstraction, however hard we might try to present it as the sum of everybody's business operations.

Similarly, of Courage's final determination to carry on trading (emphasized by the addition to the text of the new last line 'I must get back into business' after the Munich production of 1950):

In 1938, when the play was written, Courage's inability to learn from the futility of war was prophetic. In 1948, when it was performed in Berlin, the wish was expressed that she ought to come to her senses, at least in the play.

In order that the play's realistic attitude may be of advantage to the audience – so that the audience, in fact, may learn something – our theatres must establish a way of acting which does not aim at the audience's identification with the main character (the heroine).

For example, it sounds from press notices and spectators' reports as if the Zurich première, while attaining a high artistic level, simply presented a picture of war as a natural disaster, an unavoidable blow of fate, and so confirmed the petty-bourgeois spectator's confidence in his own indestructibility, his power of survival. Yet the play always left the equally petty-bourgeois Courage quite free to choose whether or no she should take part. Hence the production must have represented Courage's business activity, her keenness to get her cut, her willingness to take risks, as a 'perfectly natural', 'eternally human' way of behaving, so that she was left without any alternative.

'Experience shows,' adds another note that only appears in *Theaterarbeit* (p. 298–9), 'that many actresses playing Courage find it easier and more congenial to play this final scene simply for its tragedy. This is no service to the playwright. He doesn't want to detract from the tragedy, but there is something that he wants to add: the warning that Courage has learnt *nothing*.'

The one scene which is unquestionably emotional, even in Brecht's own production, is scene 11 where Kattrin beats the drum, and this is discussed under the heading 'The Dramatic Scene':

The scene with the drum particularly stirred the spectators. Some people explained this by saying that it is the most dramatic scene in the play and that the audience liked its theatre dramatic rather than epic. In reality the epic theatre is in a position to portray other occurrences besides excitements, collisions, conspiracies, spiritual torments, etc., but it is at the same time also in a position to portray these. Members of the audience may identify themselves with dumb Kattrin in this scene; they may get into her skin by empathy and enjoy feeling that they themselves have the same latent strength. But they will not have experienced empathy throughout the whole play, hardly in the opening scenes for instance.

Another note of more general importance is the concluding paragraph, 'About the Notes Themselves'. 'It is to be hoped' (says Brecht) 'that the present notes, which set out some of the various explanations and devices that are necessary to a play's performance, do not give an impression of forced solemnity. It just isn't easy always to make an analysis of this sort convey the lightness and insouciance which are essential to the theatre. The arts, together with the element of instruction in them, belong to the realm of amusement.'

This was the production which led to the formation of the Berliner Ensemble. Part of the Ensemble's purpose for Brecht was to establish similar 'model' productions of his other plays. Those which he himself was able to direct were *Puntila*, *Die Mutter*, *Señora Carrar's Rifles* and *The Caucasian Chalk Circle* (*Der Hofmeister*, an adaptation made specially for the company, was in a somewhat different category). He was conducting rehearsals of *Galileo* when he died.

41 · Does Use of the Model Restrict the Artist's Freedom?

(A dialogue with E. A. Winds, former Director of the Wuppertal municipal theatre, W. Germany)

WINDS: When we put *Mother Courage* on here you let us use all the material from the Berlin performance to help plan the production. Your representative Frau Berlau gave full information about your wishes to myself, the producer, the scene designer and the actors. This was backed up by a large number of stage photographs together with explanatory texts and also by your written stage directions. As it's hardly usual in the theatre for an author to influence a production in such a detailed way, and as we in Wuppertal are trying the experiment for the first time in this clear-cut form, it would be interesting to know your reasons for evolving a model production and setting it up as a definitive example for others to work on.

BRECHT: As it stands *Mother Courage* can also be staged in the old way. (In fact our theatre can stage anything – from *Oedipus* to Hauptmann's *Biberpelz*, not because it has an individual style strong enough to melt down the products of so many different authors, but because it lacks any style of its own.) But this would certainly mean doing without the quite specific effects of such a play, and its social function would misfire. The first thing a cab-driver would have said if left alone with the motor-car would have been: What's so new about that? Whereupon he would have harnessed up four pairs of horses to it and driven off. There is no purely theoretical way of approaching the epic theatre; the best thing is practical copying, plus a wish to find out the reasons for groupings, movements and gestures. Probably one needs to have made a copy before one can make one's own model.

By representing humanity and its development in artistic terms literature makes its extraordinary contribution to human self-knowledge. Here the new can be made visible at the first stage of its evolution. This great independent task for art can only fall to a genuinely realistic art. So realism is not a matter for esoteric literary discussion but the basis of art's enormous and proper social significance, and thereby of the artist's social position. Our books, our pictures, our theatres, our films and our music can and must contribute decisively to the solution of the nation's vital problems. Scholarship and art take such a high place in our republic's social arrangements because this is the place befitting the significance of progressive scholarship and realist art. A cultural policy of this sort demands creative co-operation from our intellectuals on a level with its aims. It is directed by a literary, theatrical and cinematographic movement which helps thousands to understand past and present and recognize the future: by those painters, sculptors and musicians in whose art something of the essence of our time can be felt, and whose optimism is a help to thousands.

WINDS: Isn't there a danger that a model production in your sense may lead to a certain loss of freedom in the stage performance derived from it?

BRECHT: One can expect people to complain that the creative artist is losing his freedom – in a period when production is in a state of anarchy. But even in this period there is a continuous thread of development: for instance in science and technology the handing-on of knowledge won, the standard. And the free artists of the theatre are not in fact particularly free when you look closer. They are usually the last to be able to rid themselves of hundred-year old prejudices, conventions, complexes. Above all they are quite ignominiously dependent on 'their' public. They have to 'hold its attention'; to 'grip' it at all costs – i.e. to arrange the early scenes so that it will 'take' the later ones, to give it spiritual massage –; to ascertain its taste and take that as a guide. In short, it is not they who have to be amused by their own activities; they must follow the dictates of others. Essentially our theatres are still in the position of merchants purveying to the public; how can they have much freedom to lose? At most the freedom to choose the way in which the public is to be served.

WINDS: And isn't there a danger that the theory of the 'model' may lead to a certain routine and rigidity, and that the production may amount to no more than just a copy?

BRECHT: We must realize that copying is not so despicable as people think. It isn't 'the easy way out'. It is no disgrace, but an art. Or rather it needs to be developed into an art, to the point where there is no question of routine and rigidity. Let me put forward my own experiences as a copyist: as playwright I have copied the Japanese, Greek and Elizabethan drama; as producer the music-hall comedian Karl Valentin's groupings and Caspar Neher's stage sketches; yet I have never felt my freedom restricted. Give me an intelligent model of *King Lear*, and I will find it fun to carry out. What does it matter whether you find that the text says Courage handed the money for Kattrin's burial to the peasants before leaving, or turn to the model and discover that she counted it into her hand and then put one coin back in her purse? In the text you will in fact find only the former; the latter is shown by Weigel in the model. Why should you register the one and forget the other? After all, we have nothing to offer the theatre but copies of human behaviour. The grouping, and the groups' movements, if they amount to anything, are statements about that.

Our theatre is already unrealistic in that it discards observation. Our actors look into themselves instead of at the world round them. They treat the happenings between human beings on which all depends simply as vehicles for a display of temperament, etc. Producers use plays, even new plays, as a stimulus for their 'personal vision', which is not so much vision as distortion of reality. The sooner we put a stop to this the better. Of course copying as an art has to be learned, just as does the construction of models. In order to be imitated a model has to be imitable. The inimitable must be distinguished from the exemplary. And there is slavish imitation and masterful imitation. Though it is worth noting that the latter involves no less element of resemblance.

To put it practically, it is enough if the grouping followed by the model as a means of telling the story is taken as the starting point for the rehearsals. Quite apart from the fact that not all producers are used to groupings which tell stories, and that they are unfamiliar with the stories of plays of the new sort and somewhat out of tune with them, it is high time that the theatre too evolved a method of working which fits our age, a collective method drawing on all possible experiences. We must work towards an increasingly precise description of reality, and this means, aesthetically speaking, an increasingly delicate and powerful one. This can only come about if we make use of what has already been achieved, without of course stopping there. The changes effected in the model, which must be designed exclusively to give greater precision, differentiation, imaginativeness and charm to the process of representing reality with a view to influencing it, will be the more expressive in that they represent a negation of the data: (this for connoisseurs of dialectics).

WINDS: Your instructions for the staging of *Mother Courage* also speak of epic theatre, or the epic style of acting. Do you mind explaining this to me briefly, as I imagine that not only people connected with the theatre but all who are interested in it would like to know more details, especially as it seems to involve a new formal style?

BRECHT: It isn't at all easy to describe the epic style of acting briefly. Most attempts to do so led to highly misleading vulgarizations. (Giving the impression that it was a matter of suppressing the emotional, individual, dramatic, etc. element.) Fairly detailed accounts can be found in the *Versuche*. I should like to add that this way of acting is in course of development, or more precisely in its infancy, and still needs many people's collaboration.

WINDS: Do you feel that the epic style of acting is relevant only for *Mother Courage*, as being a chronicle play, or is it of practical value for all our contemporary work in the theatre, to be applied also to the classics, the romantics and the dramatists around 1900?

BRECHT: An epic way of acting isn't equally valid for every classical work. It seems to be most easily applicable, i.e. to hold most promise of results, in works like Shakespeare's and in the earliest works of our own classic writers (including *Faust*). It depends on their attitude to their social function: representation of reality with a view to influencing it.

[*Schriften zum Theater*, p. 231. Also *Theaterarbeit*, p. 309]

NOTE: Winds's closing remarks are omitted. This and the following interview both took place in 1949. Photographs of the Wuppertal production based on the *Mother Courage* model can be found on p. 314 of *Theaterarbeit*. Herr Winds is now working as a producer in the State Opera in East Berlin.

Brecht repeats himself in this dialogue, but it should be remembered that he had returned to a country where his work and views were quite unfamiliar; viz. Herr Winds's inquiries about the 'epic theatre' as something new. His hopeful views of East Germany's cultural policy were later somewhat modified, but his apparent approval of 'optimism' in art at this time is interesting, as it was an essential element in Zhdanov's Socialist Realism, as officially encouraged there.

The paradoxical conception of 'dialectics' here makes its first appearance in Brecht's writings.

Karl Valentin, the comedian whose groupings he claims to have copied, was active in Munich in the 1920s. His gramophone records are still available, and there is a photograph of Brecht as a young man performing in one of his shows.

42 · Formal Problems Arising from the Theatre's New Content

(Dialogue with the playwright Friedrich Wolf)

WOLF: In the world of the theatre you and I have long been aiming at the same goal, though from differing standpoints as playwrights. The great and well-deserved success of your *Mother Courage* has made it essential to provide present-day theatre-goers with a general discussion of your approach to play-writing. Obviously it was no accident that you called *Mother Courage* a 'chronicle', which I presume is a variety of your 'epic theatre'. Is this conscious use of the chronicle form meant to re-emphasize that your first concern is to let the facts, the naked facts, speak to the audience? Including, in Aristotle's sense, historically possible facts? Or to put it crudely: objective theatre rather than psychological theatre, even though people are not always influenced by the facts?

BRECHT: The chronicle play *Mother Courage and her Children* – with the term 'chronicle' corresponding roughly to that of 'history' in Elizabethan drama – does not of course represent any kind of attempt to persuade anybody of anything by setting forth bare facts. Facts can very seldom be caught without their clothes on, and, as you rightly say, they are hardly seductive. It is however necessary that chronicles should include a factual element, i.e. should be realistic. Nor does the distinction 'objective theatre rather than psychological theatre' help us much, as it is also possible to produce objective psychological theatre, if one takes primarily psychological material as the main subject for artistic representation, while at the same time aiming to be objective. As for the chronicle in question, I don't believe that it leaves the audience in a state of objectivity (i.e. dispassionately balancing pros and cons). I believe rather – or let's say I hope – that it makes them critical.

WOLF: Your theatre appeals in the first place to the spectator's powers of understanding. You want to set out by arousing the audience to a clear recognition of the relationships in actual and possible situations (social conditions), and so to lead it to correct conclusions and decisions. Are you unwilling to address yourself in the same way directly to the feelings and emotions – to the sense of justice, the urge to freedom, the 'sacred wrath' against the oppressor? I am deliberately putting the question simply: in this spirit, and purely to clarify matters, do you think it better not to offer present-day audiences such an historical chronicle as Schiller's *Götz von Berlichingen* (whose character likewise scarcely undergoes any development, conversion or 'catharsis', but which addresses itself above all to an emotional experience)? Do you feel that the Hitler period with its avalanche of perverted emotions has so discredited such works that we have come to treat them as *a priori* suspicious?

BRECHT: It is not true, though it is sometimes suggested, that epic theatre (which is not simply undramatic theatre, as is also sometimes suggested) proclaims the slogan: 'Reason this side, Emotion (feeling) that.' It by no means renounces emotion, least of all the sense of justice, the urge to freedom, and righteous anger; it is so far from renouncing these that it does not even assume their presence, but tries to arouse or to reinforce them. The 'attitude of criticism' which it tries to awaken in its audience cannot be passionate enough for it.

WOLF: You use your projected subtitles (*Threepenny Opera, Courage*) *before* the individual scenes to explain the plot to the audience in advance. You are thus deliberately renouncing the 'dramatic' elements of 'tension' and 'surprise'. In the same way you renounce the emotional experience. Do you want first at all costs to arouse the spectator's powers of understanding? Does this mean that there is a conscious theatrical sequence: understanding without plot and tension, actor and reactor, development and conversion of the characters? How does your school of play-writing analyse the almost thriller-like elements of dramatic tension in *Hamlet*, in *Othello*, in Schiller's *Kabale und Liebe* (exposition – tying the knot; development – startling solution)?

BRECHT: It is impossible to explain in a few words how this type of theatre creates tension and surprise. The old pattern 'exposition – tying the knot – startling solution' is already disregarded in histories like *King John* or *Götz von Berlichingen*. Of course the characters undergo development and conversion, though not necessarily an 'inner conversion' or a 'development to the point of understanding'. That would in many cases be unrealistic; and in my view a materialist representation involves letting the characters' consciousness be determined by their social existence and not manipulating it for dramatic ends.

WOLF: It is precisely in *Courage* – where in my view you stick most consistently to the epic style – that the audience's reactions showed the story's points of maximum emotion to be the highlights of the performance (dumb Kattrin's signal on the drum, and the whole of that scene; the death of the eldest son; the mother's scene where she curses the war, etc.). And now for my real question, arising from the *content* (which even for you has to determine the form of this marvellously-wrought performance). Once she has realized that war doesn't pay, once she has lost not only her capital but her children, mustn't this Mother Courage finish up – history being what is possible – an entirely different person from what she was at the beginning of the play? Particularly for our present German public, who up to the last minute were always justifying themselves with: 'What could we do about it? War's war. Orders are orders. The cart must roll on.'

My dear Brecht, it is precisely this splendid performance and production, this persuasively good production, that brings me to a fundamental question, fundamental *even from your own point of view*. Both of us are trying to use the medium of the stage to advance and transform humanity; the final objective is man's transformation on the stage and in the spectator's consciousness. Now you may say: 'I use my art to represent conditions just as objectively and forcefully as they are in real life, and so I force the spectator himself to decide between good and evil. You, Wolf, start by putting your finger on the sore point even on the stage; you transfer the decision to the stage, and this is too painful a method for the present day audience to hear. You, an adherent of homoeopathy in medicine, approach the stage like a surgeon; my own way is the opposite one: the audience doesn't notice its treatment, so swallows the medicine.' True enough. And yet I do wish you would give us an equally brilliant production of your admirable *St Joan of the Stockyards*; how the pack would howl if you did! But of course it is useless trying to doctor around with a work of art. With the theatre in a state of babylonian confusion, my questions are simply designed to further our common aim: How can our German theatres show our people what is most urgent? Specifically: how can we shake them out of their fatalistic attitude and arouse them against a new war? And in this sense I think *Courage* would have been even *more* effective if at the end the mother had given her curse on the war some visible expression in the action (as Kattrin did) and drawn the logical conclusions from her change of mind. (I might add that the same Thirty Years' War saw peasants banding together and defending themselves against the soldiery.)

BRECHT: As you quite rightly say, the play in question shows that Courage has learnt nothing from the disasters that befall her. The play was written in 1938, when the writer foresaw a great war; he was not convinced that humanity was necessarily going to learn anything from the tragedy which he expected to strike it. My dear Friedrich Wolf, you will surely be the first to admit that the playwright was being a realist about this. But even if Courage learns nothing else at least the audience can, in my view, learn something by observing her. I quite agree with you that the question of choice of artistic means can only be that of how we playwrights give a social stimulus to our audience (get them moving). To this end we should try out every conceivable artistic method which assists that end, whether it is old or new.

[*Theaterarbeit*, Dresden, 1952, p. 253]

NOTE: Dated 1949. Friedrich Wolf (1888–1953), originally a doctor, was another well-known Communist playwright of a more conventional sort, author of *Professor Mamlock* and *The Sailors of Cattaro*; his son is now one of the leading film directors in East Germany. His criticism of *Mother Courage* is symptomatic of a quite widely-held view there that Brecht's plays were not 'positive' and optimistic enough; they were not relevant to current problems. Brecht's answer is contained in the note following the text of the play.

After *Mother Courage* came the production of *Puntila*, then *Der Hofmeister*, which was newly adapted from J. M. R. Lenz's eighteenth-century original and produced by Brecht and Caspar Neher in April 1950.

A note in *Theaterarbeit* (p. 83) explains this choice of play:
> It was partly because the German theatre's classical repertoire had shrunk alarmingly during this period of collapse and we wanted to restock it with plays, but also so as to cut a path through to Shakespeare (without whom a national theatre is almost impossible) that we thought it wise to go back to the dawn of classicism, to the point where it is still realistic, but at the same time poetical . . .

A note 'On Poetry and Virtuosity', which follows the published version of the text (*Versuche 11*, 1951) and introduces the detailed notes, shows that it may also have been designed as a corrective to productions whose merits were only political, and to the kind of realism which they engendered:
> For some time to come we shall need to speak of a play's poetry and a performance's virtuosity: something that seemed relatively unimportant in the

immediate past. It seemed not only unimportant but misleading, and the reason was not that the poetic element had been sufficiently developed and observed but that reality had been tampered with in its name; people imagined they must find poetry wherever reality stopped short. Falsehood then appeared as inventiveness, inexactitude as generosity, slavery to a prevailing form as mastery of form, and so on. Representations of reality in art had to be tested for their truth to reality; the artist's intentions with regard to reality had to be sounded. And so it came about that we had to speak of a truth as distinct from poetry. Recently, however, we have given up examining works of art from their poetic (artistic) aspect, and got satisfaction from theatrical works that have no sort of poetic appeal and from performances that lack all virtuosity. Such works and performances may have some effect, but it can hardly be a profound one, not even politically. For it is a peculiarity of the theatrical medium that it communicates awareness and impulses in the form of pleasure: the depth of the awareness and the impulse will correspond to the depth of the pleasure.

Some of the East Berlin critics again attacked *Der Hofmeister* as a 'negative' play. Brecht's answer to this is given (anonymously but unmistakeably) on p. 120 of *Theaterarbeit*: 'Satire, as is shown by such works as *Tartuffe*, *Don Quixote*, *The Inspector-General* and *Candide*, generally refrains from opposing an exemplary type of character to the type under attack; the concave mirror that it sets up to exaggerate and emphasize its victims would not spare the positive types from distortion. The positive element in *Der Hofmeister* is its bitter anger against inhuman conditions of unjustified privilege and twisted thinking.'

43 · Stage Design for the Epic Theatre

We often begin rehearsing without any knowledge of the stage designs, and our friend merely prepares small sketches of the episodes to be played (for instance, six people grouped round a working-class woman, who is upbraiding them). Perhaps we then find that in the text there are only five people in all, for our friend is no pedant; but he shows us the essential, and a sketch of this sort is always a small and delicate work of art. Whereabouts on the stage the woman is to sit, and her son and her guests, is something we find out for ourselves, and that is where our friend seats them when he comes to construct the set. Sometimes we get his designs beforehand, and then he helps us with groupings and gestures; not infrequently also with the differentiation of the characters and the way they speak. His set is steeped in the atmosphere of the play, and arouses the actor's ambition to take his place in it.

He reads plays in a masterly fashion. Take just one example. In *Macbeth*,

Act I, scene vi, Duncan and his general Banquo, invited by Macbeth to his castle, praise the castle in the famous lines:

> This guest of summer,
> The temple-haunting martlet does approve,
> By his loved mansionry, that the Heaven's breath
> Smells wooingly here . . .

Neher insisted on having a semi-dilapidated grey keep of striking poverty. The guests' words of praise were merely compliments. He saw the Macbeths as petty Scottish nobility, and neurotically ambitious.

His sets are significant statements about reality. He takes a bold sweep, never letting inessential detail or decoration distract from the statement, which is an artistic and an intellectual one. At the same time everything has beauty, and the essential detail is most lovingly carried out.

With what care he selects a chair, and with what thought he places it! And it all helps the playing. One chair will have short legs, and the height of the accompanying table will also be calculated, so that whoever eats at it has to take up a quite specific attitude, and the conversation of these people as they bend more than usual when eating takes on a particular character, which makes the episode clearer. And how many effects are made possible by his doors of the most diverse heights!

This master knows every craft and is careful to see that even the poorest furniture is executed in an artistic way, for the symptoms of poverty and cheapness have to be prepared with art. So materials like iron, wood, canvas are expertly handled and properly combined, economically or lavishly as the play demands. He goes to the blacksmith's shop to have the swords forged and to the artificial florist's to get tin wreaths cut and woven. Many of the props are museum pieces.

These small objects which he puts in the actors' hands – weapons, instruments, purses, cutlery, etc. – are always authentic and will pass the closest inspection; but when it comes to architecture – i.e. when he builds interiors or exteriors – he is content to give indications, poetic and artistic representations of a hut or a locality which do honour as much to his imagination as to his power of observing. They display a lovely mixture of his own handwriting and that of the playwright. And there is no building of his, no yard or workshop or garden, that does not also bear the fingerprints, as it were, of the people who built it or who lived there. He makes visible the manual skills and knowledge of the builders and the ways of living of the inhabitants.

In his designs our friend always starts with 'the people themselves' and 'what is happening to or through them'. He provides no 'décor', frames and backgrounds, but constructs the space for 'people' to experience something in. Almost all that the stage designer's art consists in he can do standing on his head. Of course Shakespeare's Rome was different from Racine's. He constructs the poets' stage and it glows. If he wants he can achieve a richer effect with a varied structure of different greys and whites than many other artists with the entire palette. He is a great painter. But above all he is an ingenious story-teller. He knows better than anyone that whatever does not further the narrative harms it. Accordingly he is always content to give indications wherever something 'plays no part'. At the same time these indications are stimulating. They arouse the spectator's imagination, which perfect reproduction would numb.

He often makes use of a device which has since become an international commonplace and is generally divorced from its sense. That is the division of the stage, an arrangement by which a room, a yard or a place of work is built up to half height downstage while another environment is projected or painted behind, changing with every scene or remaining throughout the play. This second milieu can be made up of documentary material or a picture or a tapestry. Such an arrangement naturally gives depth to the story while acting as a continual reminder to the audience that the scene designer has built a setting: what he sees is presented differently from the world outside the theatre.

This method, for all its flexibility, is of course only one among the many he uses; his settings are as different from one another as the plays themselves. The basic impression is of very lightly constructed, easily transformed and beautiful pieces of scaffolding, which further the acting and help to tell the evening's story fluently. Add the verve with which he works, the contempt he shows for anything dainty and innocuous, and the gaiety of his constructions, and you have perhaps some indication of the way of working of the greatest stage designer of our day.

['Der Bühnenbau des epischen Theaters.' *Schriften zum Theater*, p. 256]

NOTE: Written in 1951 and included with the 'Messingkauf' items published in *Theaterarbeit*. The designer described is Caspar Neher, who went to school with Brecht in Augsburg, designed most of the settings for his plays before 1933 and worked with him after 1945 on *Antigone*, *Puntila*, the Munich *Mother Courage*, *Der Hofmeister*, *Die Mutter*, and the planned productions of *Galileo*, *Coriolanus* and *Die Tage der Commune*. He died in 1962. Another passage in *Theaterarbeit* (which reproduces a number of his drawings) deals specifically with *Puntila* and says (p. 44):

The realistic theatre has no use for the symbolism of the expressionist and existentialist stage, which expressed general ideas, nor can it turn back to the naturalistic stage with its crude mixture of the relevant and the trivial. Just to copy reality isn't enough; reality needs not only to be recognized but also to be understood. The scenery accordingly must have artistic merit and give evidence of an individual handwriting. Wit and imagination on the stage designer's part are specially welcome in comedy.

A much earlier, undated and unpublished note bears more generally on the same point (Brecht-Archive 331/173):

THE SET

It's more important nowadays for the set to tell the spectator he's in a theatre than to tell him he's in, say, Aulis. The theatre must acquire *qua* theatre the same fascinating reality as a sporting arena during a boxing match. The best thing is to show the machinery, the ropes and the flies.

If the set represents a town it must look like a town that has been built to last precisely two hours. One must conjure up the reality of time.

Everything must be provisional yet polite. A place need only have the credibility of a place glimpsed in a dream.

The set needs to spring from the rehearsal of groupings, so in effect it must be a fellow-actor.

Space needs to be brought to life in the vertical plane. This can be achieved by stairs, though not by covering the stairs with people.

On the time-scale the set must plainly become intensified; it must have its own climax and special round of applause.

The materials of the set must be visible. A play can be performed in pasteboard only, or in pasteboard and wood, or in canvas, and so on; but there mustn't be any faking.

It is interesting to note which of these principles survived into Brecht's later work; stairs, e.g., were remarkably uncommon in his productions.

44 · From a Letter to an Actor

I have been brought to realize that many of my remarks about the theatre are wrongly understood. I realize this above all from those letters and articles which agree with me. I then feel as a mathematician would do if he read: Dear Sir, I am wholly of your opinion that two and two make five. I think that certain remarks are wrongly understood because there were important points which instead of defining I took for granted.

Most of the remarks, if not all, were written as notes to my plays, to allow them to be correctly performed. That gives them a rather dry and practical form, as if a sculptor were writing a matter-of-fact order about the placing of his work: where it should go and on what sort of a base. Those addressed might have expected something about the spirit in which the work was created. They would find it difficult to get that from the order.

For instance the description of virtuosity. Art of course cannot survive without artistry, and it becomes important to describe 'how it's done'. Especially when the arts have undergone a decade and a half of barbarism, as they have here. But it should not for a moment be thought that this is something to be coldbloodedly practised and learned. Not even speech training, which is something that the bulk of actors badly need, can be done coldbloodedly, in a mechanical way.

Thus the actor must be able to speak clearly, and this is not just a matter of vowels and consonants but also (and primarily) a matter of the meaning. Unless he learns at the same time how to bring out the meaning of his lines he will simply be articulating like a machine and destroying the sense with his 'beautiful speaking voice'. And within clarity there are all kinds of degrees and distinctions. Different social classes have different kinds of clarity: a peasant may speak clearly in comparison with a second peasant, but his clarity will not be the same as that of an engineer. This means that actors learning to speak must always take care to see that their voice is pliant and flexible. They must never lose sight of the way people really talk.

There is also the problem of dialect. Here again technique needs to be linked up with more general considerations. Our theatrical language is based on High German, but over the years it has grown very mannered and stilted, and has developed into a quite special sort of High German which is no longer so flexible as High German everyday speech. There is nothing against the use of 'heightened' language on the stage, that is to say against the theatre's evolving its own stage language. But it must always be lively, varied and capable of further evolution. The people speaks dialect. Dialect is the medium of its most intimate expression. How can our actors portray the people and address it unless they go back to their own dialect, and allow its inflections to permeate the High German of the stage? Another example. The actor must learn how to economize his voice: he must not grow hoarse. But he must also be able to portray a man seized by passion who is speaking or shouting hoarsely. So his exercises have to contain an element of acting. We shall get empty, superficial, formalistic, mechanical acting if in our technical training we forget for a moment that it is the actor's duty to portray living people.

This brings me to your question whether acting is not turned into something purely technical and more or less inhuman by my insistence that the actor oughtn't to be completely transformed into the character portrayed but should, as it were, stand alongside it criticizing and approving. In my view this is not the case. Such an impression must be due to my way of writing, which takes too much for granted. To hell with my way of writing. Of course the stage of a realistic theatre must be peopled by live, three-dimensional, self-contradictory people, with all their passions, unconsidered utterances and actions. The stage is not a hothouse or a zoological museum full of stuffed animals. The actor has to be able to create such people (and if you could attend our productions you would see them; and they succeed in being people because of our principles, not in spite of them!).

There is however a complete fusion of the actor with his role which leads to his making the character seem so natural, so impossible to conceive any other way, that the audience has simply to accept it as it stands, with the result that a completely sterile atmosphere of 'tout comprendre c'est tout pardonner' is engendered, as happened most notably under Naturalism.

We who are concerned to change human as well as ordinary nature must find means of 'shedding light on' the human being at that point where he seems capable of being changed by society's intervention. This means a quite new attitude on the part of the actor, for his art has hitherto been based on the assumption that people are what they are, and will remain so whatever it may cost society or themselves: 'indestructibly human', 'you can't change human nature' and so on. Both emotionally and intellectually he needs to decide his attitude to his scene and his part. The change demanded of the actor is not a cold and mechanical operation: art has nothing cold or mechanical about it, and this change is an artistic one. It cannot take place unless he has real contact with his new audience and a passionate concern for human progress.

So our theatre's significant stage groupings are not just an effect or a 'purely aesthetic' phenomenon, conducive to formal beauty. They are a part of a hugely-conceived theatre for the new social order, and they cannot be achieved without deep understanding and passionate support of the new structure of human relations.

I cannot rewrite all the notes to my plays. Please take these lines as a provisional appendix to them, an attempt to catch up on what had been wrongly assumed.

That leaves me with one thing still to explain: the relatively quiet style of acting which sometimes strikes visitors to the Berliner Ensemble. This has nothing to do with forced objectivity, for the actors adopt an attitude to their parts; and nothing to do with mock-rationalism, for reason never flings itself coldbloodedly into the battle; it is simply due to the fact that plays are no longer subjected to red-hot 'temperamental' acting. True art is stimulated by its material. On those occasions when the recipient thinks he is observing coldness it is just that he has encountered the mastery without which it would not be art at all.

['Aus einem Brief an einen Schauspieler.' *Schriften zum Theater*, p. 281. Also *Theaterarbeit*, p. 414]

NOTE: Written 1951. The actor addressed has not been identified. This is perhaps the most important of Brecht's modifications of his extreme theoretical position. The doctrines laid down in the 'Short Organum' were by all accounts neither discussed nor put into practice in the Berliner Ensemble. Regine Lutz, one of its principal actresses from 1949 on, told me in 1957 that she had never read Brecht's theoretical works. See also p. 243 below.

45 · Some of the Things that can be Learnt from Stanislavsky

1. *The feeling for a play's poetry.*
   Even when S.'s theatre had to put on naturalistic plays to satisfy the taste of the time the production endowed them with poetic features; it never descended to mere reportage. Whereas here in Germany even classical plays acquire no kind of splendour.

2. *The sense of responsibility to society.*
   S. showed the actors the social meaning of their craft. Art was not an end in itself to him, but he knew that no end is attained in the theatre except through art.

3. *The stars' ensemble playing.*
   S.'s theatre consisted only of stars, great and small. He proved that individual playing only reaches full effectiveness by means of ensemble playing.

4. *Importance of the broad conception and of details.*
   In the Moscow Art Theatre every play acquired a carefully thought-out shape and a wealth of subtly elaborated detail. The one is useless without the other.

5. *Truthfulness as a duty.*
   S. taught that the actor must have exact knowledge of himself and of the men he sets out to portray. Nothing that is not taken from the actor's

31. *Antigone*, 1948: Caspar Neher's design for the prologue in his and Brecht's production.

32. Antigone (Helene Weigel) and Ismene, left; Creon and the elders. right. Photograph from *Antigonemodell 1948*, the first of the "model" books.

33. Sabine Thalbach in Brecht's production of Erwin Strittmatter's *Katzgraben*, 1953.

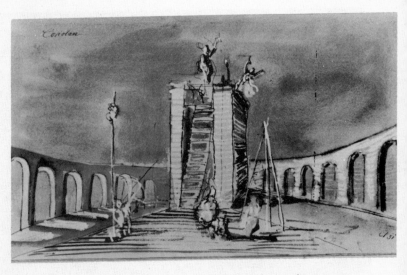

34. Design by Caspar Neher for *Coriolanus*, about 1951.

35. *Mother Courage* model: the opening scene, with Helene Weigel as
Courage.

36. Skating scene from *Der Hofmeister*, 1950, with Hans Gaugler in mid-leap.

37. *Urfaust*, produced by Egon Monk with the Berliner Ensemble, 1953.

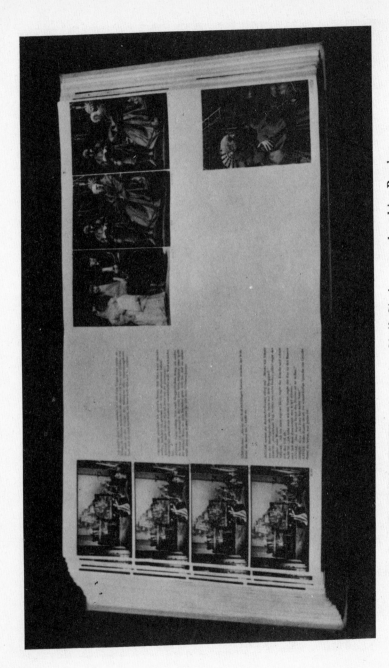

38. Model-book for *The Caucasian Chalk Circle*, as produced by Brecht, 1954.

39. Scene 9 from the Wuppertal production of *Mother Courage*, as based on Brecht's model.

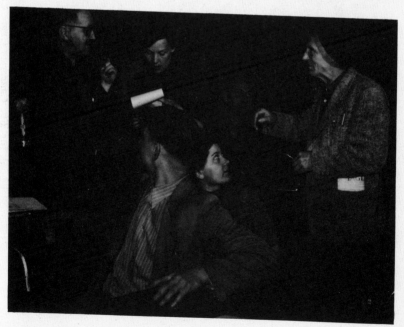

40. Brecht in the 1950's with (front) Bunge, and (left to right) Kilian, Rülicke, Wekwerth; also (extreme right) Ernst Busch.

41. Theater am Schiffbauerdamm, East Berlin, about 1950.

observation, or confirmed by observation, is fit to be observed by the audience.

6. *Unity of naturalness and style.*

In S.'s theatre a splendid naturalness went arm-in-arm with deep significance. As a realist he never hesitated to portray ugliness, but he did so gracefully.

7. *Representation of reality as full of contradictions.*

S. grasped the diversity and complexity of social life and knew how to represent it without getting entangled. All his productions make sense.

8. *The importance of man.*

S. was a convinced humanist, and as such conducted his theatre along the road to socialism.

9. *The significance of art's further development.*

The Moscow Arts Theatre never rested on its laurels. S. invented new artistic methods for every production. From his theatre came such important artists as Vakhtangov, who in turn developed their teacher's art further in complete freedom.

> ['Was unter Anderem vom Theater Stanislawskis gelernt werden kann.' From *Theaterarbeit*, Dresden, 1952, p. 413]

NOTE: There are a number of less-known notes by Brecht on Stanislavsky, which seem to fall into two groups. There are some stimulated by the early stages of the 'Method' in the United States, and by the ideas to which Brecht had apparently been introduced as a result of his first trip there. There are others written after his return to Berlin, at a time when Stanislavsky's virtues were being preached by local critics as part of a general attempt to emulate Soviet cultural standards.

Thus the *Dramaturg* in one of the Messingkauf fragments (Brecht-Archive 124/11) argues that Stanislavsky's productions, kept alive by the Moscow Art Theatre, conserve early twentieth-century class relationships 'as if in a museum'. 'What he cared about was naturalness, and as a result everything in his theatre seemed far too natural for anyone to pause and go into it thoroughly. You don't normally examine your own home or your own feeding habits, do you?' A note of the 1930s (Brecht-Archive 60/26) puts the same point more aggressively: 'The audience's sharp eye frightens him. He shuts it.' By contrast the nine points published in 1952 seem like an effort to take as favourable a view as possible, though there is still a sting in the tail.

The reference to Vakhtangov recalls a note, apparently of the 1930s (*Schriften zum Theater 3*, pp. 213–4), which runs:

The bourgeois theatre has reached its limits.

Progressiveness of Stanislavsky's method. 1. The fact that it's a method.

2. Closer knowledge of man, the private element. 3. Psychological contradictions can be portrayed (end of the moral categories good and evil). 4. Allowance for influence of the environment. 5. Latitude. 6. Naturalness of portrayal.

Vakhtangov's method. 1. Theatre is theatre. 2. The how, not the what. 3. More composition. 4. Greater inventiveness and imagination.

Meyerhold's method. 1. Against the private element. 2. Emphasis on virtuosity. 3. Movement and its mechanics. 4. Abstraction of the environment.

The meeting point=Vakhtangov, who embraces the other two as contradictory elements but is at the same time the freest. By comparison, Meyerhold is strained, Stanislavsky slack: the latter an imitation of real life, the former an abstraction. But when Vakhtangov's actor says 'I'm not laughing, I'm demonstrating laughter', one still doesn't learn anything from his demonstration. Viewed dialectically, Vakhtangov is the Stanislavsky-Meyerhold complex *before* the split rather than its reconciliation later.

Both Meyerhold and Vakhtangov came from Stanislavsky's theatre, though it is notable that in 1952 Brecht prefers not to mention the former at all, despite the fact that the first two points of his method as given here are the same as Brecht's own. (Four years later Brecht was saying privately to the present writer that Meyerhold was 'murdered by that ghastly Stalinism'.) Nevertheless the last of the nine points of 1952 is clearly an appeal not to stick with Stanislavsky. And it may be noted in this connection that a recent Soviet article on Brecht (by B. Singermann in *Teatr*, 1961, No. 1) argued that in his theatre, as in Prokofiev's music and Mayakovsky's poetry, 'left' [or avant-garde] 'art has become classical', and compared the group scenes in *The Caucasian Chalk Circle* with Vakhtangov's famous production of *The Dybbuk*.

Nor are the preceding eight points really the salient features of Stanislavsky's method, but rather the characteristics which he and Brecht had in common. Certainly a conference on Stanislavsky's ideas held shortly afterwards in East Germany led the dominant critics of the day to conclude that the Berliner Ensemble was by no means in step. (See the article 'Für den Sieg des sozialistischen Realismus auf der Bühne' in *Neues Deutschland* for 17 April 1953, quoted by Esslin, p. 161.)

46 · *Theaterarbeit:* an editorial note

The last five items, together with some of the notes from the *Mother Courage* Modellbuch, were printed in the Berliner Ensemble's large illustrated volume *Theaterarbeit* (Dresdner Verlag, Dresden, 1952). This book, edited by Brecht and four other members of the Ensemble, is ostensibly an account of that company's productions of 1949–51: *Puntila, Die Mutter* and *Mother Courage,* and the adaptations of *Der Hofmeister,* Gorki's *Vassa Shelesnova* and Hauptmann's *Biberpelz* and *Roter Hahn* (these last two being telescoped to make a single play). In fact it is an exceedingly mixed bag of essays, notes and fragments by many hands, grouped so as to form a section dealing with each play, a section on the use of models and a final section called 'Handwerkliches' which covers other questions of technique. Sometimes the items are signed (e.g. critical essays by Lukács, Anna Seghers, Paul Rilla, Herbert Ihering and other distinguished East German writers); sometimes they bear initials of members of the Ensemble ('b' for Brecht); sometimes there is nothing to show who they are by. Among those contributed by Brecht himself there is some duplication of poems and notes printed elsewhere in his work, but there is also a good deal that is new. The book is unique in that it tries to show how Brecht's ideas worked out in practice. It fills in many gaps.

It begins with part of a speech delivered by Brecht to an 'all-German' cultural congress at Leipzig in May 1951:

> When Hitler's war was over and we once more started in to make theatre, perhaps the chief difficulty was the failure of artists and public alike to grasp the full extent of the damage done. In the case of factories reduced to rubble and houses without roofs it was easy to see that a special effort was called for, but where the theatre was concerned, even though much more had been destroyed than building operations alone could possibly make good, nobody seemed to demand or to propose more than to carry on, somewhat handicapped by lack of bread and dress circles. Yet the collapse had been disastrous. Brutality and stupidity were triumphant; it was clear that they were all set to survive their heyday.
>
> They spread themselves particularly when it came to reproducing our greatest works of art. This degeneration however passed unnoticed, because it was accompanied by an equally vast degeneration in the capacity to judge.

Brecht then repeats the opening of paragraph two of the introduction to *Antigone,* and goes on:

> When Hitler's war was over and we once more started in to make theatre – theatre in a spirit of progress and experiment, directed towards that trans-

239

formation of society which had become so urgent – those artistic methods which take the theatre so long to develop had been virtually destroyed by the spirit of reaction and shady adventure. Poetry had declined into declamation, art into artificiality; fake profundity and surface glitter were trumps. In lieu of the exemplary we had the symbolic, instead of passion temperament. A whole generation of actors had been selected by false standards and brought up in wrong doctrines.

How were we to organize new productions for a new audience in a theatre that had been debauched in this way – spiritually and technically ruined? How to form the new man who is so urgently needed in this corner of the globe? How to narrate the great stories which indicate the turning points of those social transformations that are so essential? How to show the environment, recently changed from a fixed magnitude into a variable one? How to found a dramaturgy of contradictions and dialectical processes – a dramaturgy, not an objective account? How to induce the new positive critical attitude proper to the new productive audience?

The question implies its own answer. Our tottering theatre could be helped to its feet not by setting it specially easy tasks, but by giving it the toughest jobs possible. Though practically incapable of even the most trivial entertainment it still stood a chance if it tackled problems it had never been set before; inadequate in itself, *qua* theatre, it must strive to alter its surroundings. From now on it could only hope to form its images of the world if it lent a hand in forming the world itself. . . .

Much the same point is made at the start of the section on 'Models' (p. 285), which argues that the arts 'are only too used to making a virtue of their remoteness from reality. So they will have to work hard if they are to contribute anything. It is, however, only by contributing that they can regain their old powers. Nothing but the advance of the workers, and furthering the advance of the workers, can lead to their own advance.' Again, 'The theatre has the noble task of helping in the thorough reshaping of men's life together. A new audience offers it the duty and privilege of demolishing outdated notions about this and providing fresh insights and socialist impulses. It must do so in a manner both beautiful and entertaining. . . .'

So much for Brecht's view of the task, which in terms of his theory perhaps represents nothing very new. What is new, however, is the practical conclusions drawn from his attempts to meet these self-imposed requirements: for instance the account given (unsigned, on p. 256 ff.) of the 'Phases of a Production':

1. *Analysis of the Play*

Find out what socially valuable insights and impulses the play offers. Boil the story down to half a sheet of paper. Then divide it into separate episodes, establishing the nodal points, i.e. the important events that carry the story a stage further. Then examine the relationship of the episodes, their construction.

Think of ways and means to make the story easily narrated and to bring out its social significance.

2. First discussion of the setting

Basic idea of the set. Will a permanent set do the trick? Settings for individual scenes or acts. Creation of stage sketches which supply elements of the story, groupings, individual attitudes of the chief characters.

3. Casting

Preferably not irrevocable. Allow for the actor's need to be given a variety of roles. Avoid theatrical convention wherever it contradicts reality.

4. Reading Rehearsal

The actors read with the least possible expression and characterization, chiefly to acquaint themselves with the play. Distribute the analysis.

5. Positioning Rehearsal

The main episodes are roughly and provisionally translated into positions and movements. Various possibilities are tried out. The actors get a chance to test their own notions. Emphases, attitudes and gestures are roughly indicated. The characters can begin to emerge, though without any attempt at continuity.

6. Set Rehearsal

The experience of the positioning rehearsals is used to transfer the designer's sketches to the stage, so that work on them can start right away; for the sooner the actor can perform in the completed sets the better. From now on everything essential to the acting must be provided in a form fit for use (walls, flats, doors, windows, etc.). Nor should there be any rehearsing without props.

7. Rehearsal of details

Each detail is rehearsed individually, ignoring the final tempo. The actor builds up his character's attitude to the other characters and gets to know what he is like. Once the main episodes are more or less in shape the linking passages are rehearsed with special care.

8. Runs-through

Everything pulled apart during rehearsal of details is now pulled together again. It isn't a matter of tempo but of continuity and balance.

9. Discussion of Costumes and Masks

Once the groupings can be seen as a whole and the characters emerge individually then costumes and masks are discussed and work on them begins. High heels, long skirts, coats, spectacles, beards, etc., have already been tried out experimentally in the early rehearsals.

10. Checking Rehearsals

A check to see whether the play's socially valuable insights and impulses are getting across, whether the story is being fully and elegantly told, and whether the nodal points correspond. It is now a matter of probing, inspecting, polishing.

At this point it is wise to make an additional check of the groupings by taking photographs.

11. *Tempo Rehearsals*
The tempo is now decided. Length of scenes is settled. It is as well to conduct these rehearsals in costume, as this slows matters down.

12. *Dress Rehearsals*

13. *Runs–through*
The play is run through very rapidly without a prompter. Gestures are indicated.

14. *Previews*
To test audience reaction. If possible the audience should be one that encourages discussion, e.g. a factory or student group. Between previews there are correction rehearsals, to apply the lessons learned.

15. *First night*
Without the producer, so that the actors can move without feeling they are being watched.

We have already seen that four of the Messingkauf poems and the 'Playwright's Speech about the Theatre of the Scene-designer Caspar Neher' were apparently written for this volume. There is also another prose note on casting allocated to the Messingkauf but written after the war and only printed here (p. 347); it is called 'The *Dramaturg*'s Speech' (the *Dramaturg* being a permanent play-reader, playwright and literary odd-job man who is part of the staff of every German theatre):

> Parts are allotted wrongly and thoughtlessly. As if all cooks were fat, all peasants phlegmatic, all statesmen stately. As if all who love and are loved were beautiful. As if all good speakers had a fine voice.
>
> Of course there is a lot that has to be taken into account. This Mephisto and this Gretchen will go with this particular Faust. There are actors who are not easy to imagine as a prince; there are all kinds of princes, but at least they have all been brought up to command; and Hamlet is a prince among thousands.
>
> Then actors must be able to develop. Here is a young man who will make a better Troilus once he has played Amtsdiener Mitteldorf [in *Biberpelz und Roter Hahn*]. Here we have an actress who hasn't the lasciviousness needed for Gretchen in the last act: can she get it by playing Cressida (whose situations demand it) or Grusha (whose situations rule it out completely)?
>
> Certainly any actor is better suited by some parts than by others. And yet it may harm him to confine him to one particular type. Only the most gifted are competent to portray characters mutually alike, twins as it were, recognizable as such and yet easily distinguished.

It is pure folly to allot parts according to physical characteristics. 'He has a kingly figure.' Do all kings have to look like Edward VII? 'But he lacks a commanding presence.' Are there so few ways of commanding? 'She seems too respectable for Mother Courage.' Have a look at the fishwives.

Can one go by temperament? One can't. That again would be taking the easy way out.

True, there are gentle people and noisy, violent ones. But it is also true that every man has every variety of temperament. And those varieties which he is repressing may be particularly effective when brought out. Parts moreover which are conceived on a big scale (even small ones) not only show strongly marked features but have room for additions; they are like maps with blank patches. The actor must cultivate all varieties of temperament, for his characters only come to life by means of their own contradictoriness. It is most dangerous to cast a major part on the strength of a single characteristic.

All through *Theaterarbeit* the emphasis is strongly practical. It is no longer a matter of elaborating new ideas but of making a body of ideas work, and as a result it is scarcely surprising when a note (on p. 412) explains the uncertainty of the Ensemble's members as to whether or not there was a special Berliner Ensemble style of acting by saying that, 'This is probably due to the fact that neither Brecht nor any other Berliner Ensemble producer refers to Brecht's theoretical works (notes in the *Versuche*, Short Organum for the Theatre) during rehearsals. In certain plays use is made of one or two practical instructions to be found there, but it is Brecht's view that the theatre is not at present in a state to allow of their full application.'

The contrast between the theoretical and practical approaches is particularly plain if one compares the essay of 1940 on a 'New Technique of Acting' (p. 136 above) with the five notes on acting, unsigned but clearly by Brecht himself, which come towards the end of *Theaterarbeit* (p. 383 ff). Here they are:

If you want to master something difficult, take it easy
Irrespective whether the actor on stage is to get outside or stay inside himself he must know how to take it easy. First he must conquer the setting: that is to say, acquaint himself with it like a blind man acquainting himself with his surroundings. He must divide up his part and modulate it, thoroughly savouring it, until it suits him. He must 'arrange' his movements, whatever they are meant to express, in such a way that he gets fun out of their sweep and rhythm. All these are tasks for the senses, and his training is of a physical kind.

If the actor doesn't take it easy he makes it impossible for the audience to do so.

Control of stage temperament and improvement of stage diction

Before we can arrive at a realistic way of acting we have to combat certain mannerisms that have developed on our stage. For instance, that so-called temperament which is mechanically switched on, quite independent of the meaning of any scene, as soon as the curtain goes up – representing an attempt on the actor's part, which has usually by now become unconscious, to excite the audience by means of his own excitement. It is mostly worked off in artificial or unnecessarily noisy declamation, blanketing the emotions of the personage with the emotions of the actor. There is little chance of hearing any genuine human voice, and one gets the impression that life must be exactly like a theatre instead of the theatre being just like life. Such purely external temperament is needed neither to interest the audience nor to sway it. Then there is so-called stage diction, which has ossified into a mere empty form. Far from helping intelligibility, over-articulated speech hampers it. And High German only comes to life when penetrated by popular dialect. Actors must always watch out to keep language close to everyday life; they must never cease to 'look at the people's mouth'. Only so can they speak verse truly as verse or deliver heightened prose without destroying the character and situation of their part. The pathos of speech and posture that suited Schiller and the Shakespeare performances which we owe to his time is no good for playwrights of our own day, or even for Schiller himself now that it has degenerated into a routine. Great forms only get a new lease of life when they are continually nourished from a continually changing reality.

Taking the tone

Among numerous other items of the actor's technical equipment that seem likely to degenerate is the ability to take one's partner's tone. An actor needs to take the lines served him like a tennis player taking a ball. This is done by catching the tone and passing it on, so that rhythms and cadences develop which run through entire scenes. If this is not done it sounds like the aural equivalent of a group of blind men talking to one another without looking at the person addressed. There is something to be said for replacing the word 'lines' which we use for the various remarks and replies in a part by the word 'rejoinders', as indicating that each remark or reply contains an element of opposition. Even when a reply expresses agreement there is nearly always some modification of what we have just heard, patently due to special interests. Complete agreement, an unqualified 'yes', means removing some doubt on the part of the questioner or else establishing an alliance with him against third parties.

These all-round conflicts between the characters must be built up by the closest teamwork within the ensemble. Teamwork, however, may also become a kind of competition. Failure to take the tone may be evidence just of an unmusical ear, or of incomplete understanding of the sense, but it may also indicate general unsuitability for teamwork. Deliberately sometimes, an actor will perform entirely for himself, beginning each remark afresh and simply annulling the preceding remark by his partner. This sort of actor is also liable to insert those small and deadly gaps into the dialogue, quite tiny hesitations which follow one's partner's remark and cut off the new remark from the rest, emphasizing it, underlining it and giving its speaker a monopoly of the stage.

Common tendencies for actors to guard against

Gravitating to the centre of the stage.

Detaching oneself from groups in order to stand alone.

Getting too close to the person addressed.

Always looking at him.

Always standing parallel to the footlights.

Getting louder when increasing speed.

Playing one thing out of another instead of one thing after another.

Blurring over contradictory traits of character.

Failing to explore the playwright's intentions.

Subordinating one's own experience and observation to what one imagines those intentions to be.

Training new actors

The Berliner Ensemble doesn't believe in cutting new actors off from real life and the live theatre by a monastic wall. Newcomers with talent are taken straightaway after their first stage training. They must however have talent, and finding talent isn't all that easy. It's no good looking for 'stage types', handsome or peculiar-looking personages equipped with the standard actor's outfit, obvious Gretchens, born Mephistos, cinches for Marthe Schwerdtlein. And we must discard the criteria of beauty and character formerly applied by our court theatres in selecting actors and developed by Hollywood (plus UFA) on mass-production lines. The paintings of the great masters show a very different but worthwhile conception of beauty and character. The young – or the not so young, for that matter – ought accordingly to be absorbed at once into the busy life of a working theatre and should appear before an audience as soon as possible. And the audience will provide the most essential part of the education.

The whole book, with its wealth of magnificent photographs, fills in a missing dimension both in the theoretical writings and in the printed plays (much as Weill's, Eisler's and Dessau's gramophone records also do). That Brecht was only too well aware of the theory's lacunae can be seen perhaps from a short unsigned fragment immediately after the introduction (p. 8):

In the theatre people 'act'. One can expect any account of this acting to be reasonably serious, as it matters to society. It should not, however, be thought that it is being treated flippantly if the account and the accompanying technical explanations are not immediately crammed with big words. If this acting is to be artistic it must involve seriousness, fire, jollity, love of truth, inquisitiveness, sense of responsibility. But does one hear real scholars always talking about love of truth or real revolutionaries about feeling for justice? They take that sort of thing for granted.

Something of what Brecht himself had been taking for granted in his theory emerges from this book, and is part of the apparent 'mellowing' of his last years. There is also a glossary of 'technical and foreign terms', giving these definitions:

> *Dialektik*, the study [*Wissenschaft*] of the general laws of motion and development applying to nature, human society and thought. *Episch*, narrating. *Episches Drama* (in Brecht), a narrative drama about the state of society. . . . *Geste*, gesture. *Gestus*, a number of related gestures expressing such different attitudes as politeness, anger and so on. *Grundgestus* (of a scene or play), basic attitude. . . . *Realismus* (in art and literature), the 'reproduction of typical people under typical conditions' (Engels).

Verfremdung, or alienation, is not mentioned.

A certain slowing-down of all the Berliner Ensemble's activity around this time can be inferred from the final statement of 'Preparations for the 1951/2 Season' on page 416:

> The dramaturgical department has started looking through material for Brecht's *Die Tage der Kommune* and *Galileo Galilei* and making preliminary plans for their production. It has begun adapting Shakespeare's *Coriolanus*.
> From the rather small number of scripts for a topical play submitted it appears that their authors (not all of them young) have not broken free from the pattern of naturalistic drama, and at the same time that their political grasp of their material is generally feeble.
> To make a topical play the dramaturgical department is working on reports of trials.
> A one-act play *Bonn im Spiegel* has been compiled from material published in the West German news magazine *Der Spiegel*.
> Material is being collected about a hero of labour of the German Democratic Republic.

For to some extent, certainly, *Theaterarbeit* was also a statement of account, and it is interesting that not one of these preparations should have come to anything. *Galileo* was not staged by the Ensemble for another five years; *Die Tage der Kommune* for ten; *Coriolanus* is only now about to go into rehearsal. The play about Hans Garbe, the hero of labour, was never completed; the play based on trials, if it materialized, is unrecorded; the one-acter has vanished into limbo. The only 'topical play' produced by the Ensemble in Brecht's lifetime was Erwin Strittmatter's *Katzgraben*, the subject of the notes that follow.

47 · Notes on Erwin Strittmatter's Play 'Katzgraben'

Is 'Katzgraben' a play with a message?

I don't see it as one. Wolf's *Cyankali* is a play with a message, and a very good one. It was written during the Weimar Republic, and in it the author demanded the right to abortion for working-class women under capitalism. That was a play with a message. Even Hauptmann's *The Weavers*, which is full of beautiful things, is a play with a message, in my opinion. It is an appeal to the bourgeoisie's humanity, though admittedly a sceptical one. *Katzgraben* however is a historical comedy. The author puts his period on show, and favours the progressive, productive, revolutionary forces. He makes various suggestions as to how the new class should act, but he is out not so much to overcome any particular abuse as to display his new and infectious sense of life. That is why his history is a comedy. He is narrating part of his class's story as a story of surmountable difficulties, corrigible ineptitudes, at which he laughs without ever taking them too lightly. And this is how we must perform the play: we must infect a working-class audience with the urge to alter the world (and supply it with some of the relevant knowledge).

The Positive Hero

X. The view is that the spectator ought to be able to feel himself into a stage character's skin in such a way that he would like to imitate him in real life.

B. Empathy alone may stimulate a wish to imitate the hero, but it can hardly create the capacity. If a feeling is to be an effective one, it must be acquired not merely impulsively but through the understanding. Before a correct attitude can be imitated it must first have been understood that the principle is applicable to situations that are not exactly like those portrayed. It is the theatre's job to present the hero in such a way that he stimulates conscious rather than blind imitation.

X. Isn't that extremely difficult?

B. Yes. It isn't easy to get heroes.

Conversation at Rehearsal

P. How is it that one comes across so many accounts of your theatre (most of them hostile ones) which give no idea at all of what it is really like?

B. My own fault. These accounts, and much of the hostility too, apply not to the theatre that I practise but to the theatre that my critics read into my theoretical essays. I cannot resist sharing my technique and ideas with the reader or spectator; and that has to be paid for.

So far as theory goes I offend against the inflexible rule that the proof of the pudding is in the eating – which happens to be one of my own favourite principles. My theatre (and it can hardly be held against me) is in a naïve sense a philosophical one; that is to say, I am interested in people's attitudes and opinions. My whole theory is much naïver than people think, or than my way of putting it allows them to suppose. Perhaps I can excuse myself by pointing to the case of Albert Einstein, who told the physicist Infeld that ever since boyhood he had merely reflected on the man running after a ray of light and the man shut in a descending lift. And think what complications that led to! I wanted to take the principle that it was not just a matter of interpreting the world but of changing it, and apply that to the theatre. The changes, great or small, that ensued from this intention (which I myself only slowly came to admit) were all changes within the framework of the theatre, so that of course a whole mass of old rules remained wholly unaltered. It was in that little phrase 'of course' that my fault lay. I hardly ever got round to mentioning these still valid rules, and many who read my hints and explanations imagined that I worked to abolish them. If the critics could only look at my theatre as the audience does, without starting out by stressing my theories, then they might well simply see theatre – a theatre, I hope, imbued with imagination, humour and meaning – and only when they began to analyse its effects would they be struck by certain innovations, which they could then find explained in my theoretical writings. I think the root of the trouble was that my plays have to be properly performed if they are to be effective, so that for the sake of (oh dear me!) a non-aristotelian dramaturgy I had to outline (calamity!) an epic theatre.

Emotions

Incidentally, I was not quite right when I said recently that the theatre which we practise contains in itself no element that the audience might find strange. It is truer to say that at any rate our mistakes are different from those of other theatres. Their actors are liable to display too much spurious temperament; ours often show too little of the real thing. Aiming to avoid artificial heat, we fall short in natural warmth. We make no attempt to share the emotions of the characters we portray, but these emotions must none the less be fully and movingly represented, nor must they be treated with coldness but likewise with an emotion of some force: thus, the character's despair with genuine anger on our part, or his anger with genuine despair, as the case may be. If actors in other theatres overplay the moods and outbursts of their characters that does not allow us to underplay them; nor may we overplay the story, which they are apt to underplay.

Formalism and Form

X. In several ways Strittmatter applies a new form in his play. Won't he be accused of formalism?

B. Possibly; you have to understand why. Just as socialism springs from the struggle with capitalism, so a socialist literature springs from the struggle with capitalist. Bourgeois literature, under the impact of the working class's self-organization and increasingly wide successes, is showing symptoms of decline which we call formalistic. The unity of form and content is rapidly breaking up; the question of form becomes a question of style. (Le style, c'est l'oeuvre.) What used to be an organic whole becomes an effect of montage. The construction breaks loose from the subject matter, first of all to put its function in mathematical terms, then breaks loose from function to become an end in itself. Bloated subject matter is crammed into corsets, stringy subject matter stuffed out with padding. The social statement becomes entirely vague. The socialist sector of literature gains strength from fighting against this, and the capitalist sector's collapse is thereby brought nearer.

New content – new form

P. What a lot of people miss in the new theatre is grand passions.

B. They don't realize that they only miss passions that were and are to be found in the old theatre. In the new theatre they can and could find new passions (as well as old) which have developed since or are still developing. Even when they feel these passions within themselves they are not yet able to feel them when they appear on the stage, because the means of expression have changed and are continually changing. We all still recognize jealousy, ambition and greed as passions. But the passion for extracting more fruits from the earth, or the passion for moulding men together into working collectives, passions that dominate Kleinschmidt the new farmer and Steinert the coal-miner [in the play], are even today not so commonly shared and felt.

These new passions lead people into a quite different relationship with their fellows. So their give-and-take follows a different pattern from what we are accustomed to in the theatre. The form of people's give-and-take – and such give-and-take is the basis of the drama – has greatly altered. By the rules of old-fashioned dramaturgy the conflict between the big farmer and the new farmer (for instance) would be brought to a head if, say, the big farmer had one of the new farmer's barns set on fire. Even today this might whip up the audience's interest, but it is not typical. What is typical is to withdraw the horses hired to him, which likewise constitutes a use of force, though it might admittedly seem much less exciting to the audience. When the new farmer fights the big farmer by getting his seed potatoes from the medium farmer that again is an act of conflict in the new style: it too might 'come off' less well than if he married his daughter to the medium farmer's son.

[. . . .]

P. You're again talking of the new audience that needs a new kind of theatre.

B. Yes, I shouldn't do that so often. It is really ourselves rather than the audience whom we should blame when the effects which we intend don't work. But then I must be able to defend certain innovations which we need if we are to 'win the public over'.

P. These innovations oughtn't to take place at the cost of the human element. Or do you feel that the public ought also to give up all claim to full-blooded, universally interesting human characters of a calibre equal to its own?

B. The public doesn't have to give up any of its claims. All I ask of it is to state some new ones. Molière's public laughed at Harpagon, his *Avare*. Usurers and hoarders had come to seem ridiculous in a period when the great merchant was coming in, with his acceptance of risks and his reliance on credit. Our own public could laugh better at Harpagon's stinginess if it saw this represented not as a particular feature, a peculiarity, a 'human failing', but as a kind of occupational disease, as an attitude that has only recently become ridiculous, in short as a social offence. We must be able to portray the human without treating it as 'eternally human'.

P. You are suggesting that the classic Marxist view of human consciousness determined by social being is decisive for the new art of writing plays.

B. Social being that they themselves create. Yes, that is a new way of looking at things, and the old art of play-writing ignored it.

P. But you are always dwelling on the need to learn from the old plays.

B. Not from their technique, which is bound up with an outmoded way of looking at things. What we must learn is precisely the boldness with which previous playwrights would give shape to something that was new for their age. We must study the inventions that allowed them to apply an inherited technique to new purposes. The old must teach us how to make something new.

P. Am I wrong in supposing that certain of our best critics mistrust new forms?

B. No. You are not. There have been some very unhappy experiences with innovations which were not in fact real innovations. In their irresistible and ever faster decline bourgeois play-writing and the bourgeois theatre have tried to camouflage the flavour of an unchanging reactionary social content by wild changes of fashion in external form. These purely formalistic efforts, senseless formal games, have led our best critics to demand closer study of classical plays. And indeed there is much to be learnt from them. The invention of socially significant stories, the art of narrating them dramatically, the creation of interesting persons, the care for language, the putting forward of great ideas and the support of all that leads to social progress.

['Notate zu "Katzgraben",' from *Junge Kunst*, East Berlin, 1958, No. 1]

NOTE: These extracts represent about a quarter of the notes put together after Brecht's death by Wolfgang Pintzka; the rest are omitted because they demand a knowledge of the play. The play itself deals with village politics in contemporary East Germany and was originally written in 1951. Brecht decided to produce it, and started working with Strittmatter in the summer of 1952; the first night was on 17 May 1953. Strittmatter, born in 1912 and probably the most gifted of the writers to come to maturity under the East German régime, was till recently the secretary of the Schriftstellerverband, or Writers' Union. He has written a number of novels.

Play, production and notes are evidence of a considerable effort on Brecht's part to meet the requirements of the official aesthetic policy of the day. The 'positive hero' is the exemplary figure demanded by Socialist Realist doctrine; in these notes Brecht comes to terms in his own way with it and with the anti-'formalist' campaign. 'Conversation at Rehearsal' was separately printed in *Schriften zum Theater* (p. 285); it and 'Emotions' constitute a still further modification of Brecht's theory, due perhaps to middle age, perhaps to critical attacks, perhaps to the everyday problems of running a theatre, or possibly to all three.

From this point on, several of Brecht's theoretical disquisitions took the form of dialogue. It was not usually a literal transcription (like the discussions with Winds and Wolf) but a reconstitution by himself of talks with the younger members of the Ensemble. B. is Brecht and (presumably) P. is Peter Palitzsch, while R. (in the next dialogue) must be Käthe Rülicke and W. Manfred Wekwerth. Palitzsch (now working in Western Germany) and Wekwerth were later jointly responsible, *inter alia*, for the *Mother Courage* film and the Berliner Ensemble's production of *Arturo Ui*.

48 · Study of the First Scene of Shakespeare's 'Coriolanus'

B. How does the play begin?

R. A group of plebeians has armed itself with a view to killing the patrician Caius Marcius, an enemy to the people, who is opposed to lowering the price of corn. They say that the plebeians' sufferance is the patricians' gain.

B. ?

R. Have I left something out?

B. Are Marcius's services mentioned?

R. And disputed.

P. So you think the plebeians aren't all that united? Yet they loudly proclaim their determination.

W. Too loudly. If you proclaim your determination as loudly as that it means that you are or were undetermined, and highly so.

P. In the normal theatre this determination always has something comic about it: it makes the plebeians seem ridiculous, particularly as their weapons are inadequate: clubs, staves. Then they collapse right away, just because the patrician Agrippa makes a fine speech.

B. Not in Shakespeare.

P. But in the bourgeois theatre.

B. Indeed yes.

R. This is awkward. You cast doubt on the plebeians' determination, yet you bar the comic element. Does that mean that you think after all that they won't let themselves be taken in by the patricians' demagogy? So as not to seem more comic still?

B. If they let themselves be taken in I wouldn't find them comic but tragic. That would be a possible scene, for such things happen, but a horrifying one. I don't think you realize how hard it is for the oppressed to become united. Their misery unites them – once they recognize who has caused it. 'Our sufference is a gain to them.' But otherwise their misery is liable to cut them off from one another, for they are forced to snatch the wretched crumbs from each other's mouths. Think how reluctantly men decide to revolt! It's an adventure for them: new paths have to be marked out and followed; moreover the rule of the rulers is always accompanied by that of their ideas. To the masses revolt is the unnatural rather than the natural thing, and however bad the situation from which only revolt can free them they find the idea of it as exhausting as the scientist finds a new view of the universe. This being so it is often the more intelligent people who are opposed to unity and only the most intelligent of all who are also for it.

R. So really the plebeians have not become united at all?

B. On the contrary. Even the Second Citizen joins in. Only neither we nor the audience must be allowed to overlook the contradictions that are bridged over, suppressed, ruled out, now that sheer hunger makes a conflict with the patricians unavoidable.

R. I don't think you can find that in the text, just like that.

B. Quite right. You have got to have read the whole play. You can't begin without having looked at the end. Later in the play this unity of the plebeians will be broken up, so it is best not to take it for granted at the start, but to show it as having come about.

W. How?

B. We'll discuss that. I don't know. For the moment we are making an analysis. Go on.

R. The next thing that happens is that the patrician Agrippa enters, and proves by a parable that the plebeians cannot do without the rule of the patricians.

B. You say 'proves' as if it were in quotes.

R. The parable doesn't convince me.

B. It's a world-famous parable. Oughtn't you to be objective?

R. Yes.

B. Right.

W. The man starts off by suggesting that the dearth has been made by the gods, not the patricians.

P. That was a valid argument in those days, in Rome I mean. Don't the interests of a given work demand that we respect the ideology of a given period?

B. You needn't go into that here. Shakespeare gives the plebeians good arguments to answer back with. And they strongly reject the parable, for that matter.

R. The plebeians complain about the price of corn, the rate of usury, and are against the burden of the war, or at any rate its unjust division.

B. You're reading that into it.

R. I can't find anything against war.

B. There isn't.

R. Marcius comes on and slangs the armed plebeians, whom he would like to see handled with the sword, not with speeches. Agrippa plays the diplomat and says that the plebeians want corn at their own rates. Marcius jeers at them. They don't know what they are talking about, having no access to the Capitol and therefore no insight into the state's affairs. He gets angry at the suggestion that there's grain enough.

P. Speaking as a military man, presumably.

W. In any case as soon as war breaks out he points to the Volscians' corn.

R. During his outburst Marcius announces that the Senate has never granted the plebeians People's Tribunes, and Agrippa finds this strange. Enter Senators, with the officiating Consul Cominius at their head. Marcius is delighted at the idea of fighting the Volscians' leader Aufidius. He is put under Cominius's command.

B. Is he agreeable to that?

R. Yes. But it seems to take the Senators slightly by surprise.

B. Differences of opinion between Marcius and the Senate?

R. Not important ones.

B. We've read the play to the end, though. Marcius is an awkward man.

W. It's interesting, this contempt for the plebeians combined with high regard for a national enemy, the patrician Aufidius. He's very class-conscious.

B. Forgotten something?

R. Yes. Sicinius and Brutus, the new People's Tribunes, came on with the Senators.

B. No doubt you forgot them because they got no welcome or greeting.

R. Altogether the plebeians get very little further attention. A senator tells them sharply to go home. Marcius 'humorously' suggests that they should rather follow him to the Capitol. He treats them as rats, and that is when he refers them to the corn of the Volscians. Then it just says, 'Citizens steal away.'

P. The play makes their revolt come at an unfortunate moment. In the crisis following the enemy's approach the patricians can seize the reins once more.

B. And the granting of People's Tribunes?

P. Was not really necessary.

R. Left alone, the Tribunes hope that the war, instead of leading to Marcius's promotion, will devour him, or make him fall out with the Senate.

P. The end of the scene is a little unsatisfactory.

B. In Shakespeare, you mean?

R. Possibly.

B. We'll note that sense of discomfort. But Shakespeare presumably thinks that war weakens the plebeians' position, and that seems to me splendidly realistic. Lovely stuff.

R. The wealth of events in a single short scene. Compare today's plays, with their poverty of content!

P. The way in which the exposition at the same time gives a rousing send-off to the plot!

R. The language in which the parable is told! The humour!

P. And the fact that it has no effect on the plebeians!

W. The plebeians' native wit! Exchanges like 'Agrippa: Will you undo yourselves? Citizen: We cannot, sir, we are undone already!'

R. The crystal clarity of Marcius's harangue! What an outsize character! And one who emerges as admirable while behaving in a way that I find beneath contempt!

B. And great and small conflicts all thrown on the scene at once: the unrest of the starving plebeians plus the war against their neighbours the Volscians; the plebeians' hatred for Marcius, the people's enemy— plus his patriotism; the creation of the post of People's Tribune – plus Marcius's appointment to a leading role in the war. Well – how much of that do we see in the bourgeois theatre?

W. They usually use the whole scene for an exposition of Marcius's character: the hero. He's shown as a patriot, handicapped by selfish plebeians and a cowardly and weak-kneed Senate. Shakespeare, follow-ing Livy rather than Plutarch, has good reason for showing the Senate 'sad and confused by a double fear – fear of the people and fear of the enemy'. The bourgeois stage identifies itself with the patricians' cause, not the plebeians'. The plebeians are shown as comic and pathetic types (rather than humorous and pathetically treated ones), and Agrippa's remark labelling the Senate's granting of People's Tribunes as strange is used for the light it casts on Agrippa's character rather than to establish a preliminary link between the advance of the Vol-scians and the concessions made to the plebeians. The plebeians' unrest is of course settled at once by the parable of the belly and the members, which is just right for the bourgeoisie's taste, as shown in its relations with the modern proletariat. . . .

R. Although Shakespeare never allows Agrippa to mention that his parable has managed to convince the plebeians, only to say that though they lack discretion (to understand his speech) they are passing cowardly – an accusation, incidentally, that's impossible to understand.

B. We'll note that.

R. Why?

B. It gives rise to discomfort.

R. I must say, the way in which Shakespeare treats the plebeians and their tribunes rather encourages our theatre's habit of letting the hero's hardships be aggravated as far as possible by the 'foolish' behaviour of the people, and so paving the way in anticipatory forgiveness for the later excesses of his 'pride'.

B. All the same Shakespeare does make a factor of the patricians' corn profiteering and their inclination at least to conscript the plebeians for war – Livy makes the patricians say something to the effect that the base plebs always goes astray in peacetime – also the plebeians' unjust indebtedness to the nobles. In such ways Shakespeare doesn't present the revolt as a piece of pure folly.

W. But nor does he do much to bring out Plutarch's interesting phrase: 'Once order had been restored in the city by these means, even the lower classes immediately flocked to the colours and showed the greatest willingness to let the ruling authorities employ them for the war.'

B. All right; if that's so we'll read the phrase with all the more interest: we want to find out as much about the plebeians as we can.

P. 'For here perhaps we have descriptions
   Of famous forebears.'

R. There's another point where Shakespeare refrains from coming down on the aristocratic side. Marcius isn't allowed to make anything of Plutarch's remark that 'The turbulent attitude of the base plebs did not go unobserved by the enemy. He launched an attack and put the country to fire and sword.'

B. Let's close our first analysis at this point. Here is roughly what takes place and what we must bring out in the theatre. The conflict between patricians and plebeians is (at least provisionally) set aside, and that between the Romans and the Volscians becomes all-predominant. The Romans, seeing their city in danger, legalize their differences by appointing plebeian commissars (People's Tribunes). The plebeians have got the Tribunate, but the people's enemy Marcius emerges, *qua* specialist, as leader in war.

*　　*　　*

B. The brief analysis we made yesterday raises one or two very suggestive problems of production.

W. How can one show that there has been opposition to the plebeians uniting, for instance? Just by that questionable emphasis on determination?

R. When I told the story I didn't mention their lack of unity because I took the Second Citizen's remarks as a provocation. He struck me as simply checking on the First Citizen's firmness. But I don't suppose it can be played in this way. It's more that he's still hesitating.

W. He could be given some reason for his lack of warlike spirit. He could be better dressed, more prosperous. When Agrippa makes his speech he could smile at the jokes, and so on. He could be disabled.

R. Weakness?

W. Morally speaking. The burnt child returns to its fire.

B. What about their weapons?

R. They've got to be poorly armed, or they could have got the Tribunate without the Volscians' attacking; but they mustn't be weak, or they could never win the war for Marcius and the war against him.

B. Do they win their war against Marcius?

R. In our theatre, certainly.

P. They can go in rags, but does that mean they have to go raggedly?

B. What's the situation?

R. A sudden popular rising.

B. So presumably their weapons are improvised ones, but they can be good improvisers. It's they who make the army's weapons; who else? They can have got themselves bayonets, butchers' knives on broom-handles, converted fireirons, etc. Their inventiveness can arouse respect, and their arrival can immediately seem threatening.

P. We're talking about the people all the time. What about the hero? He wasn't even the centre of R.'s summary of the content.

R. The first thing shown is a civil war. That's something too interesting to be mere background preparation for the entrance of the hero. Am I supposed to start off: 'One fine morning Caius Marcius went for a stroll in his garden, went to the market place, met the people and quarrelled,' and so on? What bothers me at the moment is how to show Agrippa's speech as ineffective and having an effect.

W. I'm still bothered by P.'s question whether we oughtn't to examine the events with the hero in mind. I certainly think that before the hero's appearance one is entitled to show the field of forces within which he operates.

B. Shakespeare permits that. But haven't we perhaps overloaded it with particular tensions, so that it acquires a weight of its own?

P. And *Coriolanus* is written for us to enjoy the hero!

R. The play is written realistically, and includes sufficient material of a contradictory sort. Marcius fighting the people: that isn't just a plinth for his monument.

B. Judging from the way you've treated the story it seems to me that you've insisted all of you from the first on smacking your lips over the tragedy of a people that has a hero against it. Why not follow this inclination?

P. There may not be much pretext for that in Shakespeare.

B. I doubt it. But we don't have to do the play if we don't enjoy it.

P. Anyway, if we want to keep the hero as the centre of interest we can also play Agrippa's speech as ineffective.

W. As Shakespeare makes it. The plebeians receive it with jeers, pityingly even.

R. Why does Agrippa mention their cowardice – the point I was supposed to note?

P. No evidence for it in Shakespeare.

B. Let me emphasize that no edition of Shakespeare has stage directions, apart from those presumed to have been added later.

P. What's the producer to do?

B. We've got to show Agrippa's (vain) attempt to use ideology, in a purely demagogic way, in order to bring about that union between plebeians and patricians which in reality is effected a little – not very much – later by the outbreak of war. Their real union is due to *force majeure*, thanks to the military power of the Volscians. I've been considering one possibility: I'd suggest having Marcius and his armed men enter rather earlier than is indicated by Agrippa's 'Hail, noble Marcius!' and the stage direction which was probably inserted because of this remark. The plebeians would then see the armed men looming up behind the speaker, and it would be perfectly reasonable for them to show signs of indecision. Agrippa's sudden aggressiveness would also be explained by his own sight of Marcius and the armed men.

W. But you've gone and armed the plebeians better than ever before in theatrical history, and here they are retreating before Marcius's legionaries. . . .

B. The legionaries are better armed still. Anyway they don't retreat. We can strengthen Shakespeare's text here still further. Their few moments' hesitation during the final arguments of the speech is now due to the changed situation arising from the appearance of armed men behind the speaker. And in these few moments we observe that Agrippa's ideology is based on force, on armed force, wielded by Romans.

W. But now there's unrest, and for them to unite there must be something more: war must break out.

R. Marcius can't let fly as he'd like to either. He turns up with armed men, but his hands are tied by the Senate's 'ruth'. They have just granted the mob senatorial representation in the form of the Tribunes. It was a marvellous stroke of Shakespeare's to make it Marcius who announces the setting-up of the Tribunate. How do the plebeians react to that? What is their attitude to their success?

W. Can we amend Shakespeare?

B. I think we can amend Shakespeare if we can amend him. But we agreed to begin only by discussing changes of interpretation so as to prove the usefulness of our analytical method even without adding new text.

W. Could the First Citizen be Sicinius, the man the Senate has just appointed Tribune? He would then have been at the head of the revolt, and would hear of his appointment from Marcius's mouth.

B. That's a major intervention.

W. There wouldn't have to be any change in the text.

B. All the same. A character has a kind of specific weight in the story. Altering it might mean stimulating interest that would be impossible to satisfy later, and so on.

R. The advantage would be that it would allow a playable connection to be established between the revolt and the granting of the Tribunate. And the plebeians could congratulate their Tribune and themselves.

B. But there must be no playing down of the contribution which the Volscians' attack makes to the establishment of the Tribunate; it's the main reason. Now you must start building and take everything into account.

W. The plebeians ought to share Agrippa's astonishment at this concession.

B. I don't want to come to any firm decision. And I'm not sure that that can be acted by pure miming, without any text. Again, if our group of plebeians includes a particular person who probably only represents the semi-plebeian section of Rome, then it will be seen as a part representing the whole. And so on. But I note your astonishment and inquisitiveness as you move around within this play and within these complex events on a particular morning in Rome, where there is much that a sharp eye can pick out. And certainly if you can find clues to these events, then all power to the audience!

W. One can try.

B. Most certainly.

R. And we ought to go through the whole play before deciding anything. You look a bit doubtful, B.

B. Look the other way. How do they take the news that war has broken out?

W. Marcius welcomes it, like Hindenburg did, as a bath of steel.

B. Careful.

R. You mean, this is a war of self-defence.

P. That doesn't necessarily mean the same thing here as usually in our discussions and judgments. These wars led to the unification of Italy.

R. Under Rome.

B. Under democratic Rome.

W. That had got rid of its Coriolanuses.

B. Rome of the People's Tribunes.

P. Here is what Plutarch says about what happened after Marcius's death: 'First the Volscians began to quarrel with the Aequi, their friends and allies, over the question of the supreme command, and violence and death resulted. They had marched out to meet the advancing Romans, but almost completely destroyed one another. As a result the Romans defeated them in a battle. . . .'

R. I.e., Rome without Marcius was weaker, not stronger.

B. Yes, it's just as well not only to have read the play right through before starting to study the beginning, but also to have read the factual accounts of Plutarch and Livy, who were the dramatist's sources. But what I meant by 'careful' was: one can't just condemn wars without going into them any further, and it won't even do to divide them into wars of aggression and wars of defence. The two kinds merge into one another, for one thing. And only a classless society on a high level of production can get along without wars. Anyhow this much seems clear to me: Marcius has got to be shown as a patriot. It takes the most tremendous events – as in the play – to turn him into a deadly enemy of his country.

R. How do the plebeians react to the news of the war?

P. We've got to decide that ourselves; the text gives no clue.

B. And unhappily our own generation is particularly well qualified to judge. The choice is between letting the news come like a thunderbolt that smashes through everyone's defences, or else making something of the fact that it leaves them relatively unmoved. We couldn't possibly leave them unmoved without underlining how strange and perhaps terrible that is.

P. We must make it have tremendous effects, because it so completely alters the situation, if for no other reason.

W. Let's assume then that at first the news is a blow to them all.

R. Even Marcius? His immediate reaction is to say he's delighted.

B. All the same we needn't make him an exception. He can say his famous sentence 'I'm glad on't; then we shall ha' means to vent/Our musty superfluity', once he has recovered.

W. And the plebeians? It won't be easy to exploit Shakespeare's lacuna so as to make them seem speechless. Then there are still other questions. Are they to greet their new Tribunes? Do they get any advice from them? Does their attitude towards Marcius change at all?

B. We shall have to base our solution on the fact that there is no answer to these points; in other words, they have got to be raised. The plebeians must gather round the Tribunes to greet them, but stop short of doing so. The Tribunes must want to lay down a line, but stop short of it. The plebeians must stop short of adopting a new attitude to Marcius. It must all be swallowed up by the new situation. The stage direction that so irritates us, 'Citizens steal away', simply represents the change that has taken place since they came on stage ('Enter a company of mutinous citizens with clubs, staves and other weapons'). The wind has changed, it's no longer a favourable wind for mutinies; a powerful threat affects all alike, and as far as the people goes this threat is simply noted in a purely negative way.

R. You advised us in our analysis to make a note to record our discomfort.

B. And our admiration of Shakespeare's realism. We have no real excuse to lag behind Plutarch, who writes of the base people's 'utmost readiness' for the war. It is a new union of the classes, which has come about in no good way, and we must examine it and reconstitute it on the stage.

W. To start with, the People's Tribunes are included in the new union; they are left hanging useless in mid-air, and they stick out like sore thumbs. How are we to create this visible unity of two classes which have just been fighting one another out of these men and their irreconcilable opponent Marcius, who has suddenly become so vitally needed for Rome as a whole?

B. I don't think we'll get any further by going about it naïvely and waiting for bright ideas. We shall have to go back to the classic method of mastering such complex events. I marked a passage in Mao Tse-tung's essay 'On Contradiction'. What does he say?

R. That in any given process which involves many contradictions there is always a main contradiction that plays the leading, decisive part; the rest are of secondary, subordinate significance. One example he gives is the Chinese Communists' willingness, once the Japanese attacked, to break off their struggle against Chiang Kai-shek's reactionary régime. Another possible example is that when Hitler attacked the USSR even the émigré white Russian generals and bankers were quick to oppose him.

W. Isn't that a bit different?

B. A bit different but also a bit the same thing. But we must push on. We've got a contradictory union of plebeians and patricians, which has got involved in a contradiction with the Volscians next door. The second is the main contradiction. The contradiction between plebeians and patricians, the class struggle, has been put into cold storage by the emergence of the new contradiction, the national war against the Volscians. It hasn't disappeared though. (The People's Tribunes 'stick out like sore thumbs'.) The Tribunate came about as a result of the outbreak of war.

W. But in that case how are we to show the plebeian-patrician contradiction being overshadowed by the main Roman-Volscian contradiction, and how can we do it in such a way as to bring out the disappearance of the new plebeian leadership beneath that of the patricians?

B. That's not the sort of problem that can be solved in cold blood. What's the position? Starving men on one side, armed men on the other. Faces flushed with anger now going red once more. New lamentations will drown the old. The two opposed parties take stock of the weapons they are brandishing against one another. Will these be strong enough to ward off the common danger? It's poetic, what's taking place. How are we going to put it across?

W. We'll mix up the two groups: there must be a general loosening-up, with people going from one side to the other. Perhaps we can use the incident when Marcius knocks into the patrician Lartius on his crutches and says: 'What, art thou stiff? stand'st out?' Plutarch says in connection with the plebeians' revolt: 'Those without any means were taken bodily away and locked up, even though covered with scars from the battles and ordeals suffered in campaigns for the fatherland. They had conquered the enemy, but their creditors had not the least pity for them.' We suggested before that there might be a disabled man of this sort among the plebeians. Under the influence of the naïve patriotism that's so common among ordinary people, and so often shockingly abused, he could come up to Lartius, in spite of his being a member of the class that has so maltreated him. The two war victims could recall their common share in the last war; they could embrace, applauded by all, and hobble off together.

B. At the same time that would be a good way of establishing that it is generally a period of wars.

W. Incidentally, do you feel a disabled man like this could perhaps prevent our group from standing as *pars pro toto*?

B. Not really. He would represent the ex-soldiers. For the rest, I think we could follow up our idea about the weapons. Cominius as Consul and Commander-in-Chief could grin as he tested those home-made weapons designed for civil war and then gave them back to their owners for use in the patriotic one.

P. And what about Marcius and the Tribunes?

B. That's an important point to settle. There mustn't be any kind of fraternization between them. The new-found union isn't complete. It's liable to break at the junction points.

W. Marcius can invite the plebeians condescendingly, and with a certain contempt to follow him to the Capitol, and the Tribunes can encourage the disabled man to accost Titus Lartius, but Marcius and the Tribunes don't look at each other, they turn their backs on one another.

R. In other words both sides are shown as patriots, but the conflict between them remains plain.

B. And it must also be made clear that Marcius is in charge. War is still his business – especially his – much more than the plebeians'.

R. Looking at the play's development and being alert to contradictions and their exact nature has certainly helped us in this section of the story. What about the character of the hero, which is also something that must be sketched out, and in precisely this section of the story?

B. It's one of those parts which should not be built up from his first appearance but from a later one. I would say a battle-scene for Coriolanus, if it hadn't become so hard for us Germans to represent great wartime achievements after two world wars.

P. You want Marcius to be Busch, the great people's actor who is a fighter himself. Is that because you need someone who won't make the hero too likeable?

B. Not too likeable, and likeable enough. If we want to generate appreciation of his tragedy we must put Busch's mind and personality at the hero's disposal. He'll lend his own value to the hero, and he'll be able to understand him, both the greatness and the cost of him.

P. You know what Busch feels. He says he's no bruiser, nor an aristocratic figure.

B. He's wrong about aristocratic figures, I think. And he doesn't need physical force to inspire fear in his enemies. We mustn't forget a 'superficial' point: if we are going to represent half the Roman plebs with five to seven men and the entire Roman army with something like nine we can't very well use a sixteen-stone Coriolanus.

W. Usually you're for developing characters step by step. Why not this one?

B. It may be because he doesn't have a proper development. His switch from being the most Roman of the Romans to becoming their deadliest enemy is due precisely to the fact that he stays the same.

P. *Coriolanus* has been called the tragedy of pride.

R. Our first examination made us feel the tragedy lay, both for *Coriolanus* and for Rome, in his belief that he was irreplaceable.

P. Isn't that because the play only comes to life for us when interpreted like this, since we find the same kind of thing here and feel the tragedy of the conflicts that result from it?

B. Undoubtedly.

W. A lot will depend on whether we can show Coriolanus, and what happens to and around him, in such a light that he can hold this belief. His usefulness has got to be beyond all doubt.

B. A typical detail: as there's so much question of his pride, let's try to find out where he displays modesty, following Stanislavsky's example, who asked the man playing the miser to show him the point at which he was generous.

W. Are you thinking of when he takes over command?

B. Something like. Let's leave it at that for a start.

P. Well, what does the scene teach us, if we set it out in such a form?

B. That the position of the oppressed classes can be strengthened by the threat of war and weakened by its outbreak.

R. That lack of a solution can unite the oppressed class and arriving at a solution can divide it, and that such a solution may be seen in a war.

P. That differences in income can divide the oppressed class.

R. That soldiers, and war victims even, can romanticize the war they survived and be easy game for new ones.

W. That the finest speeches cannot wipe away realities, but can hide them for a time.

R. That 'proud' gentlemen are not too proud to kowtow to their own sort.

P. That the oppressors' class isn't wholly united either.

B. And so on.

R. Do you think that all this and the rest of it can be read in the play?

B. Read in it and read into it.

P. Is it for the sake of these perceptions that we are going to do the play?

B. Not only. We want to have and to communicate the fun of dealing with a slice of illuminated history. And to have first-hand experience of dialectics.

P. Isn't the second point a considerable refinement, reserved for a handful of connoisseurs?

B. No. Even with popular ballads or the peepshows at fairs the simple people (who are so far from simple) love stories of the rise and fall of great men, of eternal change, of the ingenuity of the oppressed, of the potentialities of mankind. And they hunt for the truth that is 'behind it all'.

['Studium des ersten Auftritts in Shakespeares *Coriolan*', from *Versuche* 15, 1957]

NOTE: This dialogue, dated 1953, forms the main section of 'Dialektik auf dem Theater', a miscellaneous collection of notes arising out of different productions between 1951 and 1955. Some of these have been omitted from the present volume because they refer in detail to unfamiliar plays by other authors or were not written by Brecht himself (see p. 282 for details). The collection was put together in duplicated form before Brecht's death and subsequently published both in the *Versuche* and in *Schriften zum Theater*.

His unfinished adaptation and translation of *Coriolanus* is printed in *Stücke XI* (1959). It was a long drawn-out project, this first scene having already been published in a preliminary version in *Theaterarbeit* in 1952. An unpublished note (Brecht-Archive 23/53) dated 18 July 1955 says 'Toying with one or two examples for "Dialektik auf dem Theater" I again make an analysis of the first act of *Coriolanus*, and wonder if it would be possible to stage it without additions (made by me two years ago) or with very few, just by skilful production.'

The final version of this scene includes many amendments to Shakespeare's text, some of them as foreshadowed in the dialogue. Thus the play opens without the Second Citizen; instead there is a man with a boy, who proposes to emigrate from Rome. Marcius enters with his armed men, 'unnoticed except by Menenius Agrippa', immediately after the latter's 'And leave me but the bran – What say you to 't?' A messenger speaks to Marcius (in a whisper) before he announces the appointment of the Tribunes, which the Citizens applaud, cheering the Tribunes when they appear. One of them tells the Citizens to follow Marcius to the war (without any mention of the 'disabled man' of the dialogue); the Citizens exeunt instead of stealing away, and the final exchange between the Tribunes is cut down to six lines.

In the dialogue P.'s mention of 'famous forebears' refers to a poem by Brecht. Ernst Busch was the only one of Brecht's main pre-1933 actors (other than Helene Weigel, of course), to join him in the Berliner Ensemble, where his parts included Galileo, Azdak in *The Caucasian Chalk Circle* and the cook in *Mother Courage*.

49 · Cultural Policy and Academy of Arts

The Academy of Arts has published some proposals affecting not only the work of artists in the German Democratic Republic but also the character and condition of such institutions as film, radio and the press. Its right to criticize was questioned. Roughly speaking the argument was that in the past it had failed to acquire a Marxist point of view, that of Socialist Realism, or to give effective support to the government's cultural policy.

The Academy of Arts is at once an old and a new institution. It was founded in 1696. In 1950 it was set up anew by the government of the German Democratic Republic. Distinguished artists were selected to be its members. Their qualification for being invited lay in their progressiveness. Their place of domicile didn't matter. In a sense it is a very incomplete Academy, since there are important artists living in Western Germany who could not join it without being liable to persecution by the authorities there.

It is a mark of the dangerous degree of self-deception found among some of our cultural politicians that they demanded things of the Academy of Arts that one can only ask of Marxists. As it stands the Academy cannot be regarded as Marxist, and however reasonable it is to criticize its work from a Marxist standpoint it would be wrong to go to work with it as if it were a Marxist body. The most that can be said is that its Marxist members – and some of the most important are that – have failed to make Marxists of the others.

I myself am naturally of the view that an artist who is merely progressive (in the generally accepted sense) cannot get the best out of his talents. There has for that matter hardly been a single discussion in the Academy in which the Marxist view has not been strongly put forward. (And those discussions that led to the adoption of the proposals referred to provided a heartening demonstration of unity about some of the most fundamental principles of the German Democratic Republic.) Yet it cannot be denied that the attitude of many of our artists towards a major part of our cultural policy is one of rejection and incomprehension; and to me the reason seems to be that the politicians did not take this great store of ideas and make it available to the artists, but forced it on them like so much bad beer. It was the Commissions, with their unfortunate measures, their policy of dictation-cum-argument, their unaesthetic administrative methods, their cheap Marxist jargon, that alienated the artists (Marxists included) and stopped the Academy from taking up a sensible position in the aesthetic question. It was particularly those artists who are realists that felt certain demands of

Commissions and critics to be more like presumptions. No new state can be built up without confidence; it is surplus energy that builds a new society. But superficial optimism can lead it into danger.

Those features of our social life must be stressed that are full of implications for the future. But prettification and improvement are the deadliest enemies not just of beauty but of political good sense. The life of the labouring population, the struggle of the working class for a worthwhile creative life is a grateful theme for the arts. But the mere presence on the canvas of workers and peasants has little to do with this theme. Art must aim at a broad intelligibility. But society must increase the understanding of art by general education. The needs of the population have to be satisfied. But only by fighting at the same time against its need for trash. Often the right thing is asked for but the wrong kind of thing encouraged.

For administrative purposes, and given the officials available, it may well be simpler to work out definite proformas for works of art. Then the artists have merely to fit their thoughts (or possibly those of the administration?) into the given form and all will go smoothly. But the living material so urgently demanded then becomes living material for coffins. Art has its own regulations.

Realism from a socialist standpoint: that is a great and comprehensive principle, and a personal style and an individual viewpoint do not contradict it but help it on. The campaign against formalism must not simply be regarded as a political task, but must be given a political content. It is part of the working class's struggle for authentic solutions to social problems, so that phoney solutions in the arts must be combated as phoney social solutions, not as aesthetic errors. Politicians may be surprised, but most artists find the language of politics easier to understand than a hastily scraped-together aesthetic vocabulary which has nothing to offer but ex-cathedra pronouncements of a nebulous kind.

Looked at from the point of view of the arts, has our artistic policy of the past few years been a realistic one? Our artists are producing for a public recruited from various classes. Its level of education and also its degree of demoralization are very varied. Equally various are the needs that art must satisfy. The state is primarily interested in the workers; our best artists are primarily interested in them too. But at the same time there are other classes' tastes and needs that must be taken account of. All this can only be accomplished by a highly qualified, highly differentiated art. For a truly socialist art the question of quality is politically decisive.

Here again political quality plays a considerable part. It is the job of art criticism to reject what is politically primitive. Our artistic policy too has not been unsuccessful in this regard. We cannot expect to achieve the political level of the Soviet Union in a few years, but its example is a help to us. Following that example however would lead nowhere if we were unable to modify it to suit our own particular conditions. To put it crudely, we have more of the old and less of the new. Large sections of our population still have a completely capitalist way of looking at things. This is even true of parts of the working class. In getting rid of this attitude the arts must do their bit. We have been too quick to turn our backs on the immediate past, anxious to set our face to the future. But the future will depend on our overcoming the past. Where are the works of art that show the vast defeat suffered by the German workers before 1933, from which they are only slowly recovering? At the same time they would have to show heroic examples of a resolute struggle. And they would inspire our present struggle by providing it with knowledge and examples.

Our socialist realism must also be a critical realism.

Our republic has made notable cultural achievements. Favourable conditions have been created. If we can manage to increase the general productivity of the whole people, and not only certain production figures, then art will acquire and transmit an entirely new impetus. Our theatres, exhibitions, concerts and libraries will be visited by larger and larger crowds, more and more well-educated people, people with new and fascinating objectives. Freed from administrative shackles the great conception of socialist realism, of a deeply human, earth-orientated art which will liberate every human capacity, will be greeted by our best artists as the blessed gift of the revolutionary proletariat, which is what it is.

['Kulturpolitik und Akademie der Künste', from
Neues Deutschland, East Berlin, 12 August 1953]

NOTE: Two short poems by Brecht – 'Nicht feststellbare Fehler der Kunstkommission' and 'Das Amt für Literatur' – both published in 1953, show him and the Academy attacking the State Commissions responsible for the administration of the arts in East Germany before the Ministry of Culture was formed. One of these had overruled the jury of the Third German Art Exhibition at Dresden and excluded a number of works; the other had allocated paper for inferior books but not, to Brecht's annoyance, for the republication of the works of the novelist Ludwig Renn.

The (East) German Academy of Arts was set up on the ruins of the old Prussian academy, and was originally designed to be an 'all-German' body. Among its members have been Brecht, Eisler, Feuchtwanger, Heinrich Mann, Arnold Zweig, Renn and Anna Seghers as well as people of more restricted East German reputation like Kurella and Strittmatter. Its review *Sinn und Form*, which is quite the most serious literary periodical in East Germany, was criticized at the Socialist

Unity Party's Cultural Conference of October 1957 for its 'superior reticence' in the question of Socialist Realism. Its editor, Peter Huchel, was removed from his post in the autumn of 1962.

Brecht's own definition of this official aesthetic – or rather his own heterodox adaptation of it – is expressed in a note of September 1954 (Brecht-Archive 12/47–8, quoted by Mittenzwei, p. 393):

1. Socialist Realism means realistically reproducing men's life together by artistic means from a socialist point of view. It is reproduced in such a way as to promote insight into society's mechanisms and stimulate socialist impulses. In the case of Socialist Realism a large part of the pleasure which all art must provoke is pleasure at the possibility of society's mastering man's fate.

2. A Socialist Realist work of art lays bare the dialectical laws of movement of the social mechanism, whose revelation makes the mastering of man's fate easier. It provokes pleasure in their recognition and observation.

3. A Socialist Realist work of art shows characters and events as historical and alterable, and as contradictory. This entails a great change; a serious effort has to be made to find new means of representation.

4. A Socialist Realist work of art is based on a working-class viewpoint and appeals to all men of good will. It shows them the aims and outlook of the working class, which is trying to raise human productivity to an undreamt-of extent by transforming society and abolishing exploitation.

5. The Socialist Realist performance of old classical works is based on the view that mankind has preserved those works which gave artistic expression to advances towards a continually stronger, bolder and more delicate humanity. Such performance accordingly emphasizes those works' progressive ideas.

There are a number of late unpublished notes by Brecht on much the same general theme. One, for instance (Brecht-Archive 49/08), holds that 'no painter can paint with hands that tremble for fear of the verdict of some official who may be well-trained politically and very conscious of his political responsibilities yet be badly trained aesthetically and unconscious of his responsibility to the artist'. Another (23/69) seems like jottings for an article or speech:

It's not the job of the Marxist-Leninist party to organize production of poems as on a poultry farm. If it did the poems would resemble one another like so many eggs.

It has to supply motive force. (You need only look at our poetry to see that's lacking.)

It must concern itself with the development of mankind, not of poetry, if it is to have a *productive* influence on poetry and not just an administrative one.

Accessible to the people or accessible to the official. [*Volkstümlichkeit und Funktionärstümlichkeit.*]

Comprehensibility. Not everything that the Russian working and peasant masses failed to grasp immediately in the Bolsheviks' statements was nonsense.

Yet another (49/05–06) comes close to the *Neues Deutschland* article. 'The principles of a realistic and socialist art,' it says, 'were not examined but simply treated as a style to be imposed on artists of very different sorts, some of them of world-wide reputation. This led to a pernicious levelling and to the discouragement of that individual and independent sense of form without which no art is possible. The campaign against the formalism of decaying bourgeois art was turned into a campaign against the sense of form. . . . Art has no competence to make works of art out of the artistic notions of some official department. *It is only boots that can be made to measure.* In any case many politically well-educated people have mal-educated and therefore unreliable taste.

'Without Marxist knowledge and a socialist outlook it is impossible today to understand reality or to use one's understanding to change it. For art, however, this is not a question of style, least of all today. Style only comes into the matter in so far as the style needs to be as simple as possible, as intelligible as possible; the battle for socialism cannot be won by a handful of highly educated connoisseurs, a few people who know how to understand complicated charades. But I said as simple *as possible*. Certain complex processes which we need to understand cannot be *quite* simply portrayed.'

Such opinions do not apply specifically to the theatre, and it may be wondered why they are reproduced here. But they are relevant to the whole framework within which Brecht chose to work.

50 · Conversation about being Forced into Empathy

B. I have here Horace's *Ars Poetica* in Gottsched's translation. He really expresses a theory that often concerns us, one that Aristotle proposed for the theatre:

> You must enchant and conquer the reader's breast.
> One laughs with those who laugh and lets tears flow
> When others are sad. So, if you want me to weep
> First show me your own eye full of tears.

In this well-known passage Gottsched cites Cicero writing on oratory, describing how the Roman actor Polus played Electra mourning her brother. His own son had just died, and so he brought the urn with his ashes on to the stage and spoke the relevant verses 'focusing them so painfully on himself that his own loss made him weep real tears. Nor could any of those present have refrained from weeping at that point?'

I must say there is only one word for such an operation: barbaric.

W. You could equally well have Othello wounding himself with the dagger in order to give us the pleasure of sympathizing. Though it might be simpler to have somebody hand him one or two favourable notices about a fellow actor before coming on. That would be as good a way as any of putting us in that pet state where it is impossible to refrain from tears.

B. In any case the object is to fob us off with some kind of portable anguish – that's to say anguish that can be detached from its cause, transferred *in toto* and lent to some other cause. The incidents proper to the play disappear like meat in a cunningly mixed sauce with a taste of its own.

P. All right, let's admit that Gottsched's attitude is barbaric, and Cicero's too. But Horace is talking about a genuine feeling stimulated by the actual incident portrayed, not about some borrowed one.

W. Why does he say 'If you want me to weep. . . .' (Si vis me flere)? Is the idea to trample on my soul until tears come and liberate me? Or is it that I should be shown episodes that soften me until I become humanely disposed?

P. What's to stop you, if you see a man suffering and are able to suffer with him?

W. Because I must know why he's suffering. Take Polus for instance; his son may have been a scoundrel. That needn't stop him suffering, but why should I suffer too?

P. You can find that out from the incident that he played and lent his sorrow to.

W. If he lets me. If he doesn't force me to surrender at all costs to his sorrow, which he wants me at all costs to feel.

B. Suppose a sister is mourning her brother's departure for the war; and it is the peasant war: he is a peasant, off to join the peasants. Are we to surrender to her sorrow completely? Or not at all? We must be able to surrender to her sorrow and at the same time not to. Our actual emotion will come from recognizing and feeling the incident's double aspect.

['Gespräch über die Nötigung zur Einfühlung', from *Schriften zum Theater*, 1957]

NOTE: Dated 1953, this short dialogue forms the last section of 'Dialektik auf dem Theater'. Horace was a favourite author of Brecht's; his short poem 'Beim Lesen des Horaz' dates from the same year. The passage quoted is a translation of lines 99–103 of the *Ars Poetica*.

51 · Classical Status as an Inhibiting Factor

There are many obstacles to the lively performance of our classics. The worst are the theatrical hacks with their reluctance to think or feel. There is a traditional style of performance which is automatically counted as part of our cultural heritage, although it only harms the true heritage, the work itself; it is really a tradition of damaging the classics. The old masterpieces become as it were dustier and dustier with neglect, and the copyists more or less conscientiously include the dust in their replica. What gets lost above all is the classics' original freshness, the element of surprise (in terms of their period), of newness, of productive stimulus that is the hallmark of such works. The traditional way of playing them suits the convenience of producers, actors and audience alike. The passionate quality of a great masterpiece is replaced by stage temperament, and where the classics are full of fighting spirit here the lessons taught the audience are tame and cosy and fail to grip. This leads of course to a ghastly boredom which is likewise quite alien to them. Actors and producers, many of them talented, set out to remedy this by thinking up new and hitherto unknown sensational effects, which are however of a purely formalist kind: that is to say, they are forcibly imposed on the work, on its content and on its message, so that even worse damage results than with traditional-style productions, for in this case message and content are not merely dulled or flattened out but absolutely distorted. Formalist 'revival' of the classics is the answer to stuffy tradition, and it is the wrong one. It is as if a piece of meat had gone off and were only made palatable by saucing and spicing it up.

Before undertaking to produce one of the classics we must be aware of all this. We have to see the work afresh; we cannot go on looking at it in the degenerate, routine-bound way common to the theatre of a degenerating bourgeoisie. Nor can we aim at purely formal and superficial 'innovations' which are foreign to the work. We must bring out the ideas originally contained in it; we must grasp its national and at the same time its international significance, and to this end must study the historical situation prevailing when it was written, also the author's attitude and special peculiarities. Such study poses its own problems, which have often been discussed and will be discussed much more. I shall not go into that for the moment, as I want to speak about a further obstacle which I call inhibition by classical status.

Inhibition of this sort is due to a superficial and mistaken conception of a work's classical status. The greatness of the classics lies in their greatness, not in a surface 'greatness' (in quotes). The tradition of performance long 'cultivated' at the court theatres has moved further and further away from this human greatness in the theatres of a declining and degenerate bourgeoisie, and the formalists' experiments have only made things worse. The true pathos of the great bourgeois humanists gave way to the false pathos of the Hohenzollerns; the ideal to idealization; winged sublimity to hamming, ceremony to unctuousness, and so forth. The result was a false greatness that was merely flat. Goethe's marvellous sense of humour in *Urfaust* was out of keeping with the pompous olympian strutting expected of classic authors – as though humour and true dignity were opposites! His brilliantly-conceived actions were treated only as a step to effective declamation; in other words they were entirely neglected. The falsifying and trivializing process went so far that, to take another instance from *Urfaust*, such essential incidents in the play as the great humanist's pact with the Devil – which is after all significant for Gretchen's tragedy, for without it this would take a different form or not occur at all – are simply thrown away, presumably in the conviction that a hero cannot behave unheroically in a classical play. It is true that *Faust* and even *Urfaust* can only be produced with the purified and converted Faust of the end of Part II in mind, the Faust who beats the Devil and moves on from an unproductive enjoyment of life (as provided by the Devil) to productive enjoyment. But what is left of this magnificent transformation if the first stages are skipped? If we allow ourselves to be inhibited by a fake, superficial, decadent, petty bourgeois idea of what constitutes a classic then we shall never achieve lively and human performances of the great works. The genuine respect demanded by these works entails that we expose any respect of a false, hypocritical, lip-serving kind.

['Einschüchterung durch die Klassizität.' From *Schriften zum Theater*, p. 124]

NOTE: Thought to have been written in 1954, this was published as one of 'Zwei Aufsätze zur Theaterpraxis' in *Sinn und Form*, Potsdam, 1954, No. 5/6. For earlier evidence of Brecht's concern with German classical productions see p. 229, and also the fragmentary record (*Schriften zum Theater 1*, pp. 146–56) of what appears to have been a projected discussion between him and Herbert Ihering about the latter's book *Reinhardt, Jessner, Piscator oder Klassikertod* (Rowohlt, Berlin, 1926). This shows Brecht, Piscator and Engel as having all been concerned to single out 'what we called the gestic content' of any classical play. The same approach is very evident in the *Coriolanus* dialogue above.

The occasion for the present essay was evidently the bad official reception of the Berliner Ensemble's production of *Urfaust* (directed by Egon Monk), which *Neues Deutschland* (27 May 1953, quoted by Esslin pp. 160–1) termed a 'denial of the national cultural heritage' and saw as evidence that the Ensemble was 'being led in a wrong direction by the methods and principles applied in the adaptation of the classics by Bertolt Brecht'. Other classical plays adapted by the Ensemble, besides *Der Hofmeister*, were Kleist's *Zerbrochener Krug*, Molière's *Don Juan* and Farquhar's *The Recruiting Officer*.

52 · Can the Present-day World be Reproduced by Means of Theatre?

I was interested to hear that in a discussion about the theatre Friedrich Dürrenmatt raised the question whether it is still at all possible to reproduce the present-day world by means of theatre. In my view this question, once posed, has to be admitted. The time has passed when a reproduction of the world by means of theatre need only be capable of being experienced. To be an experience it needs to be accurate.

Many people have noticed that the theatrical experience is becoming weaker. There are not so many who realize the increasing difficulty of reproducing the present-day world. It was this realization that set some of us playwrights and theatre directors looking for new artistic methods.

As you know, being in the business yourselves, I have made a number of attempts to bring the present-day world, present-day men's life together, within the theatre's range of vision.

As I write, I am sitting only a few hundred yards from a large theatre, equipped with good actors and all the necessary machinery, where I can try out various ideas with a number of mainly youthful collaborators, while around me on the tables lie 'model' books with thousands of photographs of our productions, together with more or less precise descriptions of the most variegated problems and their provisional solutions. So I have every possibility; but I cannot say that the dramatic writing which I call 'non-aristotelian', and the epic style of acting that goes with it, represent the only solution. However, one thing has become quite plain: the present-day world can only be described to present-day people if it is described as capable of transformation.

People of the present-day value questions on account of their answers. They are interested in events and situations in face of which they can do something.

Some years ago in a paper I saw an advertisement showing the destruction of Tokyo by an earthquake. Most of the houses had collapsed, but a few modern buildings had been spared. The caption ran 'Steel stood'.

Compare this description with the classic account of the eruption of Etna by Pliny the Elder, and you will find that his is a kind of description that the twentieth-century playwright must outgrow.

In an age whose science is in a position to change nature to such an extent as to make the world seem almost habitable, man can no longer describe man as a victim, the object of a fixed but unknown environment. It is scarcely possible to conceive of the laws of motion if one looks at them from a tennis ball's point of view.

For it is because we are kept in the dark about the nature of human society – as opposed to nature in general – that we are now faced (so the scientists concerned assure me), by the complete destructibility of this planet that has barely been made fit to live in.

It will hardly surprise you to hear me say that the question of describing the world is a social one. I have maintained this for many years, and now I live in a state where a vast effort is being made to transform society. You may not approve of the means used – I hope, by the way, that you are really acquainted with them, and not just from the papers; you may not accept this particular ideal of a new world – I hope you are acquainted with this too; but you can hardly doubt that in the state where I live the transformation of the world, of men's life together, is being worked at. And you may perhaps agree with me that the present-day world can do with transforming.

For this short essay, which I beg you to treat as a friendly contribution to your discussion, it may be enough if I anyway report my opinion that the present-day world can be reproduced even in the theatre, but only if it is understood as being capable of transformation.

> ['Kann die heutige Welt durch Theater wieder-
> gegeben werden?' From *Schriften zum Theater*, p. 7]

NOTE: Written in 1955, to be read as a contribution to the Fifth 'Darmstädter Gespräch', a discussion on theatrical problems held at Darmstadt (West Germany). Published in *Sonntag* (E. Berlin) 8 May 1955, and in draft form in *Sinn und Form* 1955, No. 2.

The 'large theatre' is the Theater am Schiffbauerdamm in East Berlin, which the Berliner Ensemble took over in March 1954. Previously the company had been a guest of the Deutsches Theater when playing in Berlin. This Theater am Schiffbauerdamm, home of the original *Threepenny Opera*, has since been rechristened 'Theater am Bertolt Brecht-Platz'. It seats around 700.

53 · Appendices to the Short Organum

(The numbers refer to the relevant paragraphs of the work)

3

It is not just a matter of art presenting what needs to be learned in an enjoyable form. The contradiction between learning and enjoyment must be clearly grasped and its significance understood – in a period when knowledge is acquired in order to be resold for the highest possible price, and even a high price does not prevent further exploitation by those who pay it. Only once productivity has been set free can learning be transformed into enjoyment and vice versa.

4

(a) If we now discard the concept of EPIC THEATRE we are not discarding that progress towards conscious experience which it still makes possible. It is just that the concept is too slight and too vague for the kind of theatre intended; it needs exacter definition and must achieve more. Besides, it was too inflexibly opposed to the concept of the dramatic, often just taking it naïvely for granted, roughly in the sense that 'of course' it always embraces incidents that take place directly with all or most of the hall-marks of immediacy. In the same slightly hazardous way we always take it for granted that whatever its novelty it is still theatre, and does not turn into a scientific demonstration.

(b) Nor is the concept THEATRE OF THE SCIENTIFIC AGE quite broad enough. The Short Organum may give an adequate explanation of what is meant by a scientific age, but the bare expression, in the form in which it is normally used, is too discredited.

12

Our enjoyment of old plays becomes greater, the more we can give ourselves up to the new kind of pleasures better suited to our time. To that end we need to develop the historical sense (needed also for the appreciation of new plays) into a real sensual delight. When our theatres perform plays of other periods they like to annihilate distance, fill in the gap, gloss over the differences. But what comes then of our delight in comparisons, in distance, in dissimilarity – which is at the same time a delight in what is close and proper to ourselves?

19

In times of upheaval, fearful and fruitful, the evenings of the doomed classes coincide with the dawns of those that are rising. It is in these twilight periods that Minerva's owl sets out on her flights.

(43)

True, profound, active application of alienation effects takes it for granted that society considers its condition to be historic and capable of improvement. True A-effects are of a combative character.

45

The theatre of the scientific age is in a position to make dialectics into a source of enjoyment. The unexpectedness of logically progressive or zigzag development, the instability of every circumstance, the joke of contradiction and so forth: all these are ways of enjoying the liveliness of men, things and processes, and they heighten both our capacity for life and our pleasure in it.

Every art contributes to the greatest art of all, the art of living.

(46)

The bourgeois theatre's performances always aim at smoothing over contradictions, at creating false harmony, at idealization. Conditions are reported as if they could not be otherwise; characters as individuals, incapable by definition of being divided, cast in one block, manifesting themselves in the most various situations, likewise for that matter existing without any situation at all. If there is any development it is always steady, never by jerks; the developments always take place within a definite framework which cannot be broken through.

None of this is like reality, so a realistic theatre must give it up.

53

(a) However dogmatic it may seem to insist that self-identification with the character should be avoided in the performance, our generation can listen to this warning with advantage. However determinedly they obey it they can hardly carry it out to the letter, so the most likely result is that truly rending contradiction between experience and portrayal, empathy and demonstration, justification and criticism, which is what is aimed at.

(b) The contradiction between acting (demonstration) and experience (empathy) often leads the uninstructed to suppose that only one or the other can be manifest in the work of the actor (as if the Short Organum concentrated entirely on acting and the old tradition entirely on experience). In reality it is a matter of two mutually hostile processes which fuse in the actor's work; his performance is not just composed of a bit of the one and a bit of the other. His particular effectiveness comes from the tussle and tension of the two opposites, and also from their depth. The style in which the S.O. is written is partly to blame for this. It is misleading often thanks to a possibly over-impatient and over-exclusive concern with the 'principal side of the contradiction'.[1]

55

And yet art addresses all alike, and would confront the tiger with its song. What is more, he has been known to join in. New ideas whose fruitfulness is evident irrespective who may reap the fruits are liable to rise to the 'top' from classes on their way up, and to get a grip on people who ought by rights to be combating them in an effort to preserve their own privileges. For members of a given class are not immune to ideas from which their class cannnot benefit. Just as the oppressed can succumb to the ideas of their oppressors, so members of the oppressor class can fall victim to those of the oppressed. In certain periods when the classes are fighting for the leadership of mankind any man who is not hopelessly corrupt may feel a strong urge to be counted among its pioneers and to press ahead.

(64)

The story does not just correspond to an incident from men's life together as it might actually have taken place, but is composed of episodes rearranged so as to allow the story-teller's ideas about men's life to find expression. In the same way the characters are not simply portraits of living people, but are rearranged and formed in accordance with ideas.

These rearrangements often in various ways contradict the knowledge which the actors have gained from experience and from books: a contradiction that the actors must seize and maintain in their performance. The source of their creation must lie at the same time in reality and in the imagination, for both in their work and in that of the playwright reality must appear vivid and rich in order to bring out the specific or general features of the play.

(65)

For a genuine story to emerge it is most important that the scenes should

[1] Mao Tse-tung: 'On Contradiction.' One of the two sides of a contradiction is bound to be the principal one.

to start with be played quite simply one after another, using the experience of real life, without taking account of what follows or even of the play's overall sense. The story then unreels in a contradictory manner; the individual scenes retain their own meaning; they yield (and stimulate) a wealth of ideas; and their sum, the story, unfolds authentically without any cheap all-pervading idealization (one word leading to another) or directing of subordinate, purely functional component parts to an ending in which everything is resolved.

(73)

A quotation from Lenin: 'It is impossible to recognize the various happenings in the world in their independence of movement, their spontaneity of development, their vitality of being, without recognizing them as a unity of opposites.'[1]

It is a matter of indifference whether the theatre's main object is to provide knowledge of the world. The fact remains that the theatre has to represent the world and that its representations must not mislead. If Lenin's view is right, then they cannot work out satisfactorily without knowledge of dialectics – and without making dialectics known.

Objection: What about the kind of art which gets its effects from dark, distorted, fragmentary representations? What about the art of primitive peoples, madmen and children?

If one knows a great deal and can retain what one knows, it may be possible perhaps to get something out of such representations; but we suspect that unduly subjective representations of the world have anti-social effects.

(A Separate Note)

Studying a part means at the same time studying the story; or rather, it ought at first to consist mainly in that. (What happens to the character? How does he take it? What opinions does he come in contact with? etc.) To this end the actor needs to muster his knowledge of men and the world, and he must also ask his questions dialectically. (Certain questions are only asked by dialecticians.)

For instance; an actor is due to play Faust. Faust's love for Gretchen runs a fateful course. The question arises whether just the same thing wouldn't happen if they got married. This is a question that is not usually asked. It seems too low, vulgar, commonplace. Faust is a genius, a great

[1] Lenin: 'On the Question of Dialectics'.

soul striving after the infinite; how can anyone dream of asking a question like 'Why doesn't he get married?' But simple people do ask it. That in itself must lead the actor to ask it too. And once he has thought about the matter he will realize that this question is not only necessary but extremely fruitful.

We have first of all to decide under what conditions this love affair takes place, what is its relation to the story as a whole, what it signifies for the principal theme. Faust has given up his 'lofty', abstract, 'purely spiritual' attempts to find satisfaction in life, and now turns to 'purely sensual' earthly experiences. His relationship with Gretchen thereby becomes a fateful one. That is to say he comes into conflict with Gretchen; his sense of union becomes a division in two: his satisfaction turns into pain. The conflict leads to Gretchen's utter destruction, and Faust is hard hit by this. At the same time this conflict can only be portrayed correctly by means of another much wider conflict which dominates the entire work, Parts I and II.

Faust manages to emerge from the painful contradiction between his 'purely spiritual' escapades and his unsatisfied and insatiable 'purely sensual' appetites, and this thanks to the Devil. In the 'purely sensual' sphere (of the love affair) Faust comes up against his environment, represented by Gretchen, and has to destroy it in order to escape. The main contradiction is resolved at the end of the whole play; it is this that explains the lesser contradictions and puts them in their place. Faust can no longer behave like a mere consumer, a parasite. Spiritual and sensual activity are united in productive work for mankind; the production of life leads to satisfaction in life.

Turning back to our love affair we see that marriage, though utterly 'respectable', out of the question for a genius and in contradiction with his whole career, would in a relative sense have been better and more productive as being the conjuncture which would have let the woman he loved develop instead of being destroyed. Faust would of course scarcely in that case have been Faust; he would have been bogged down in pettinesses (as suddenly becomes clear) and so forth.

The actor who sympathetically asks the question that bothers simple people will be able to make Faust's non-marriage into a clearly-defined stage of his development, where otherwise, by following the usual approach, he merely helps to show that whoever wishes to rise higher on earth must inevitably create pain, that the need to pay for development and satisfaction is the unavoidable tragedy of life – i.e. the cruellest and most commonplace principle: that you can't make omelettes without breaking eggs.

NOTE: After Brecht's death some twenty sheets of notes were found among his papers, headed 'Appendix to the Short Organum' ('Nachtrag zum kleinen Organon'. Brecht Archive 23/30–52). Those here numbered 3, 12, (43), 45, (46), 53(a), (65) and (73), and also the final unnumbered section, were printed in an edition of the *Kleines Organon für das Theater* in the series 'Suhrkamp Texte' (Frankfurt, 1960). All are due to appear in *Schriften zum Theater 7*. We have rearranged them to correspond with the order of reference to the 'Short Organum' itself. Often the manuscript specifies the paragraph referred to; where it does not the translator has inserted what seems the relevant number in brackets. The last and longest section refers to the production of *Urfaust* rather than to anything in the 'Short Organum'; it is included here because it was classed with the remainder both in manuscript and in the published selection.

The dates of the various notes is not certain, but clearly they bear on Brecht's final preoccupation with 'dialectics in the theatre'. The penultimate paragraph of the published selection runs thus:

> An effort is now being made to move on from the epic theatre to the dialectical theatre. In our view and according to our intention the epic theatre's practice – and the whole idea – were by no means undialectical. Nor would a dialectical theatre succeed without the epic element. All the same we envisage a sizeable transformation.

Almost as interesting as the change of terminology proposed here (and also in appendix 4 above) is the fact that none of these notes was published in Brecht's lifetime. He was not yet ready to go quite so far as they suggested.

54 · 'Dialectics in the Theatre': an editorial note

Certainly in the last year of his life Brecht seemed to be overhauling his entire theory yet again with a view to presenting it under the new label of 'dialectical theatre'. Like so many of Brecht's concepts, this was one which had already existed in embryo before 1933, in the project labelled 'On a dialectical drama' which was announced at the back of *Versuche 1* and apparently later renamed 'non-aristotelian' (see p. 46 above). Now, however, 'epic theatre' itself is to be discarded in its favour. For that term so closely associated with Brecht 'has fulfilled its task if the narrative element that is part of the theatre in general has been strengthened and enriched', says a preliminary note (Brecht Archive 23/14; the same point is also made in 23/19). It has become 'almost a formal concept, which could equally well be applied to Claudel or even Wilder' (23/20). In other words it has come to cause as much trouble as it is worth.

In 1956 he made a last collection of theoretical writings under the title 'Dialectics in the Theatre' (*Versuche 15*, in which it appeared, was published posthumously, but he had passed the volume for the press). This opens with the following short introduction:

> The works which follow relate to paragraph 45 of the 'Short Organum' and suggest that 'epic theatre' is too formal a term for the kind of theatre aimed at (and to some extent practised). Epic theatre is a prerequisite for these contributions, but it does not of itself imply that productivity and mutability of society from which they derive their main element of pleasure. The term must therefore be reckoned inadequate, although no new one can be put forward.

In other words the actual phrase 'dialectical theatre' was still to be held in reserve. Moreover the collection itself is a miscellaneous one which is far from presenting a coherent argument: so much so, in fact, that it has been thought more important in the present volume to print its main elements chronologically than to keep it as a whole. Three of its items are seemingly not even by Brecht. ('Another case of Applied Dialectics' and two notes on the production of the modern Chinese play *Hirse für die Achte*.) The others, besides the two dialogues printed above, are 'Relative Haste' (short note on the production of Ostrovsky's *Ziehtochter* in December 1955), 'A Diversion' (about a proposed cut in *The Caucasian Chalk Circle*), 'Letter to the Actor playing young Hörder in *Winterschlacht*' (an indifferent play by Johannes R. Becher, which Brecht produced himself on 12 January 1955), and 'Two ways of acting *Mother Courage*' (a note dated 1951). The *Coriolanus* dialogue is the backbone of the whole affair, occupying two-thirds of the space.

'Dialectics in the Theatre' was as near as Brecht got to launching the idea outlined in the appendices to the 'Short Organum'. Despite its length, which makes it look at first sight like a counterpart to the 'Short Organum' itself, it is something of a makeshift, an interim report. But Manfred Wekwerth, describing a visit to Brecht's country house at Buckow in August 1956 (*Sinn und Form*, Potsdam, 1957, No. 1–3), suggests that the next step was already assumed. 'Brecht had often of late been talking of dialectics in the theatre. He now normally referred to his theatre as "dialectical theatre".' And again: 'Narrating a story on the stage was really at the same time a "dialecticizing" of the events.' The word *dialektisieren* is here being used just as *episieren* had been used earlier.

According to Wekwerth it was on the same occasion and at his collaborators' request that Brecht typed out the notice that follows.

55 · Our London Season

For our London season we need to bear two things in mind. First: we shall be offering most of the audience a pure pantomime, a kind of silent film on the stage for they know no German. (In Paris we had a festival audience, an international audience – and we ran for a few days only.) Second: there is in England a long-standing fear that German art (literature, painting, music) must be terribly heavy, slow, laborious and pedestrian.

So our playing needs to be quick, light, strong. This is not a question of hurry, but of speed, not simply of quick playing, but of quick thinking. We must keep the tempo of a run-through and infect it with quiet strength, with our own fun. In the dialogue the exchanges must not be offered reluctantly, as when offering somebody one's last pair of boots, but must be tossed like so many balls. The audience has to see that here are a number of artists working together as a collective (ensemble) in order to convey stories, ideas, virtuoso feats to the spectator by a common effort.

(*Sgd.*)   BERTOLT BRECHT

[From the original notice]

NOTE: Dated 5 August 1956, this was the last of Brecht's messages for the Berliner Ensemble's notice board at the Theater am Schiffbauerdamm. He died on 14 August. The Ensemble's first (and so far only) London season opened on the 27th, with Helene Weigel playing the title part in his production of *Mother Courage*.

Other Translations

(listed under the corresponding sections of this book.
Translators' names in brackets.)

1. FRANK WEDEKIND
An Expression of Faith in Wedekind. (Erich A. Albrecht.) *The Tulane Drama Review*, New Orleans, VI, 1, September 1961, p. 3.

4. THREE CHEERS FOR SHAW
Ovation for Shaw. (Gerhard H. W. Zuther.) *Modern Drama*, II, 2, September 1959, p. 184.

14. THE LITERARIZATION OF THE THEATRE
Notes to the Threepenny Opera. (a) (Eric Bentley.) In Bentley (ed.): *From the Modern Repertoire I*. University of Denver Press, 1949. (b) (Desmond Vesey.) In Brecht: *Plays I*. Methuen, London, 1960.

19. THEATRE FOR PLEASURE OR THEATRE FOR INSTRUCTION
Theatre for Learning. (Edith Anderson.) (i) *Meanjin*, Melbourne, XVII, Spring 1958, p. 300. (ii) *Mainstream*, New York. XI, 6 June 1958, p. 1. (iii) Revised version in Haskel M. Block and Herman Salinger (ed.): *The Creative Vision*, Grove Press, New York; Evergreen Books, London, 1960, p. 149. (iv) *The Tulane Drama Review*, VI, 1, September 1961, p. 18.

23. ALIENATION EFFECTS IN CHINESE ACTING
(a) The Fourth Wall of China. (Eric Walter White.) (i) *Life and Letters Today*, London, XXIV, No. 254, 1956, p. 19. (ii) *Adam*, London, XXIV, No. 254 (Joint number with *Encore*), 1956, p. 19.
(b) Chinese Acting. (Eric Bentley.) (i) *Furioso*, Northfield, IV, 4, Fall 1949, p. 68. (ii) *The Tulane Drama Review*, VI, 1, September 1961, p. 130.

29. ON RHYMELESS VERSE WITH IRREGULAR RHYTHMS
On Unrhymed Lyrics in Irregular Rhythms. (Beatrice Gottlieb.) *The Tulane Drama Review*, II, 1, November 1957, p. 33.

30. ON EXPERIMENTAL THEATRE
On the Experimental Theatre. (Carl Richard Mueller.) *The Tulane Drama Review*, VI, 1, p. 3.

31. THE STREET SCENE
A Model for Epic Theater. (Eric Bentley.) *The Sewanee Review*, Sewanee, LVII, 3, Summer 1949, p. 425.

32. NEW TECHNIQUE OF ACTING
(a) A New Technique of Acting. (Eric Bentley.) Omitting the appendix. (i) *Theatre Arts*, New York, XXXIII, 1, January 1949, p. 38. (ii) *New Theatre*, London, V, 9 March 1949, p. 20. (iii) In Toby Cole (ed.): *Actors on Acting*, Crown Publishers, New York 1949. (iv) In Barnet, Berman and Burto (ed.): *Aspects of Drama*, Little, Brown & Co., Boston, 1962.

(b) A Short Description of a New Technique of the Art of Acting which Produces an Effect of Estrangement. (Anon.) *World Theatre*, Brussels, IV, 1, 1955, p. 15. (This includes the appendix *in toto*.)
(c) The E-Effect. (Anon.) *Gemini*, II, 8, Autumn 1959, p. 35.

35. ALIENATION EFFECTS IN THE NARRATIVE PICTURES OF THE
     ELDER BRUEGHEL
Twelve Pictures of Brueghel: Some Jottings. (Eric Bentley.) *Accent*, Urbana, XVI, 2, Spring 1956, p. 137.

39. A SHORT ORGANUM FOR THE THEATRE
A Little Organum for the Theater. (Beatrice Gottlieb.) *Accent*, XI, 1, Winter 1951, p. 13.

NOT INCLUDED

Prospectus of the Diderot Society. (Mordecai Gorelik.) *The Quarterly Journal of Speech*, XLVII, 2, April 1961, p. 114.
Brecht on Theater 1920 (James L. Rosenberg.) *The Tulane Drama Review*, VII, 1, Fall 1962.

Index

In this index, besides proper names, etc., will be found headings corresponding to Brecht's main concepts or areas of interest. They may help to show the evolution of Brecht's thought; at the same time they identify the basic German terms used. The fact that the book is arranged chronologically allows the reader to see approximately when particular ideas arose or were discarded. The more important references to a given entry are printed in bold type.